THE NEW PEOPLE OF GOD
A Short History of the Church

THE NEW
PEOPLE OF GOD

A Short History of the Church

by Jean-Marie Leroux

translated by Jex Martin

FIDES PUBLISHERS, INC.
Notre Dame, Indiana

And I saw the holy city, the New Jerusalem,
coming down out of heaven from God,
made ready as a bride adorned for her husband.

And I heard a loud voice from the throne saying,
"Behold the dwelling of God with men,
and he will dwell with them.
And they will be his people,
and God himself will be with them as their God.
And God will wipe away every tear from their eyes,
And death shall be no more;
neither shall there be mourning,
nor crying,
nor pain any more,
for the former things have passed away."

Apocalypse, 21:2-5

INTRODUCTION

The Church, God's People

It used to be that ecclesiastical historians described the life of the Church within a framework of a philosophy (or theology) of history in which the Incarnation of the Word represented the principle and climax.

More recently, the combined demands of doctrine and science have required a differentiation of approaches: On the one hand, theologians have applied themselves to expressing the inner nature of the Church and have been concentrating more and more intensely on the "Mystery" of this Church, especially in its sociological dimensions. On the other hand, historians have confined their research to the temporal aspect of the Church, giving meticulous, precise descriptions of events. The result has been a surer knowledge of teachings on the Church and of the historical evolution of Catholicism.

However, at a time when Christians are inquiring, often with much distress, into the authenticity of doctrine and the present institutions of the Church, and when others, suffering from a guilt complex, are imagining that medieval Christendom or the early Church were the most authentic expressions of the Mystical Body of Christ, the shortcomings of these parallel studies, which separate the profound reality of the Church from its historic expression, are more clearly sensed. Consequently, some are tempted to contrast the existing Church with the theoretical ideal of a mystical Church.

What seemed to be needed, therefore, was to bring together doctrine and history and to compare them as aspects of one reality.

This book, then, is not a history manual; it does not aim at being exhaustive or at presenting a complete summary of Church history. Neither does it seek to be a theological treatise, for I claim neither the right nor the competence to enter into this domain. My aim is exclusively to make Christians aware of the profound vitality of the Church in its earthly reality and, through this approach, to bring them to understand it better and to love it more.

The mystery of the Church—Christ's continuing presence on earth—is that it is at once divine and human. ✓ Its mission, defined by its founder, imposes on it strict duties of unity, teaching, and sanctity. The limits of my study are therefore clearly defined: it will pursue the fulfillment of each of these requirements in the Church's historic evolution. Repetitions have inevitably resulted, for the same event often fulfills each requirement. Far from rejecting the repetitions, it seemed to me that it was necessary to maintain them and sometimes to emphasize them; they constitute a way of making tangible the decisive elements in the history of the Church.

Some will regret that current problems have not been approached, but the work's limits and its stated purpose did not permit me to bring up such questions, which might be made the subject of another volume.

Such as it is, then, and in spite of its deficiencies, this work may prove a useful contribution for Catholics who wish to deepen their knowledge of the Church. This is the wish I express as I acknowledge my gratitude to all the authors of theological and historical works whom I unfortunately cannot list and who have supplied me with the elements needed for the composition of this work.

TABLE OF CONTENTS

9

Part I

You Shall Renew
The Face of The Earth

Christians constantly have to transform their lives, to make them more consistent with the Gospels. In this sense, the Church's mission of leading all mankind to salvation is never finished. Until the end of time, it must guide men toward God and transmit to them the divine life. Though unchanging, it remains the leaven of humanity, and through her each generation takes its place in God's plan of salvation. It may thus be said that the Church escapes history: its nature and its mission are immutable.

On the other hand, as a society composed of men, it knows the vicissitudes of human societies. Yet this corporeal aspect is not definitive. The historical evolution of the Church shows glorious periods of progress alternating with moments of stability, and indeed of retrogression. Thus is written here on earth the absorbing story of the evangelization of the world, a gigantic struggle in men's hearts and in their institutions between Christ and the Evil One.

We can distinguish three stages on the road of salvation that extends from Golgotha to our own time. At the end of each of these periods a certain balance was attained between the Church and the City of Man, justifying, in a sense, the missionary effort of the people of God. But, each time, this dangerous state of balance threatened to link the Church too closely with the temporal order—a situation, by its very nature, precarious. Besides, such a balance induces in Christians a feeling of euphoria which usually results in a state of affairs prejudicial to the redemptive mission of the Church.

The first period runs from the end of Christ's earthly mission to the beginning of the fifth century. At this time the Gospel message had been proclaimed throughout the Roman empire, whose limits coincided with the limits of the known world. Many of the faithful thought that the word of Christ had been fulfilled and that at last the "Good News" had been proclaimed unto the ends of the earth. The barbarian invasions put an end to all this and required of the Church a new effort which, after harrowing experiences, was to be expressed in new progress.

The second period comprises the entire Middle Ages, with the high point coming in the thirteenth century. Having converted the barbarians and Christianized their institutions, the Church played a dominant role in temporal affairs, and it could be justly said that Europe was then Christendom. But the coming of the modern world was to shake the Church both inwardly and outwardly.

In the course of this third period, which extends almost to the twentieth century, the Church's role is less decisive on the temporal level. It tries to maintain positions reached during the Middle Ages but must compromise, and gradually loses its material power. On the other hand, an impressive missionary effort now extends the Gospel to the ends of the earth.

However, upheavals of constantly increasing proportions are teaching Christians that evangelization cannot be judged on the basis of geography alone. Social and political evolution demand that Christians attempt to reflect on the function and essential nature of the Church, whose children they are. This better understanding of the Church is not taking place without profound reactions, but it is awakening in Christian communities everywhere a renewal and enthusiasm which, in more than one respect, recall the zeal and ardor of the apostolic age.

1. From Pentecost to the Fall of the Roman Empire

Fire Upon the Earth

Having brought the Apostles together in a last farewell, Jesus said to them: "All power has been given me in heaven and on earth. Go therefore, make disciples of all peoples, baptizing them in the name of the Father and of the Son and of the Holy Spirit, and teach them to observe all that I have commanded you. And I am with you always until the end of the world" (Matt. 28:19-20). At these words He was taken up to heaven before them, and a cloud came and hid Him from their sight.

The moment had come when the Apostles, on their own responsibility, were to spread the Gospel and establish the Church in the world. Now they withdrew to the Cenacle, partly from a desire to meditate, partly out of fear of their countrymen, and thus, in the first known act of the Church, they combined generosity with human weakness. Ten days later, the Holy Spirit descended upon the disciples and, strengthening their courage, established the authenticity of their mission in the sight of all.

With the passing of the feverish period that followed this Pentecost, and in which the most extraordinary events transpired, the Apostles ardently undertook the preaching of the Good News, first at Jerusalem, then throughout Palestine.

While He respected the Apostles' liberty, the Lord Jesus, as He had promised, was guiding the first footsteps of the Church. And the Acts of the Apostles brings us this story in which we see sanctity and sin, generosity and weakness going side by side. On every page we feel the presence of Christ and the Spirit, ensuring that this irregular pace will never deter the Church from the goal assigned it by God.

The Spirit led the Apostles to understand that the Kingdom preached by Christ was not a state characterized by new economic and social structures. However, they were divided on a serious question. Some, drawn to the old revealed religion, were trying to preserve certain elements of Judaism and preferred preaching only to the Jews. Others, aware of the universality of salvation, were deliberately turning to the pagans, the "Gentiles," according to the New Testament term. The conversion of the Centurion Cornelius, followed by that of Paul, provided dramatic episodes in this harrowing debate, which had its outcome in the Council of Jerusalem (about A.D. 50). Paul, Peter, and James, united in the same love of Christ, reconciled the antagonistic groups and sealed the unity of the Church.

From that day on, Christianity spread throughout the Roman Empire. Paul in particular redoubled his expeditions, the story of which has come down to us in the Acts of the Apostles. He traveled through most of the known world and created communities everywhere, with no concern for the difficulties of every kind that beset his path. While less well known, the zeal of the other Apostles was nonetheless equal to Paul's. Peter at Antioch and Rome, John throughout the East, James in Jerusalem, Andrew in Greece preached the Gospel. The others shared the rest of the world, preaching, according to tradition, in Armenia, Persia, Ethiopia, and even as far as India.

When the Apostles died, communities had formed in all the large cities of the Empire: Jerusalem, Corinth, Rome, Thessalonica, Ephesus, Antioch, Alexandria. The communities were, as yet, not very important, but they existed, and there were some who were already thinking that, according to Christ's word, the Gospel was known everywhere. In these circumstances the first persecutions led to belief in the imminent coming of the Antichrist, and at the end of their days the Apostles had to put the faithful on guard against a premature expectation of the judgment.

The Blood of the Christians

The world could not long remain indifferent to a Gospel that ran counter to accepted notions. Indeed, Jesus had warned the Apostles of this on many occasions. The martyrdom of Stephen and then that of James confirmed the warning. All through his ministry, Paul was persecuted, by the Jews and sometimes by the pagans. But these attacks remained isolated incidents, and the civil power rarely intervened.

Suddenly, about the year 64, under the Emperor Nero, persecution became bloody and widespread. Nero had a large number of Christians put to death, among them Peter and Paul. He thus opened an era of legal persecution that was to continue for 250 years.

It should be noted, however, that massacre of the Christians was not constant. Quite often the faithful benefited from a de facto tolerance that applied to a whole region and indeed, at certain times, to the entire empire. However, for almost three centuries, Christians were not protected by the laws, and adherence to Christ's teaching constituted a misdemeanor that might be suppressed at any time, depending on the province, the strictness of officials, or the good pleasure of an emperor. At times, the Christians were persecuted on the basis of denunciations; at other times popular uprisings decimated communities. Sometimes, more cunningly, the governors attacked only bishops and more active laymen. Although persecution did not generally assume the spectacular aspect given it in legend, there was never a year went by that, in one place or another in the Empire, the faithful did not shed their blood for Christ. Several times persecution struck all of the communities with a savagery that defies description. This was the case in the persecutions of Decius, Valerian, and Diocletian. In these three dark eras the prisons and deportation camps were filled with the faithful, with "confessors" as they were called, who had declared their faith in spite of refined torture and who sealed their testimony with an atrocious death—drowning, the stake, crucifixion, or the wild beasts in the amphitheater. Sometimes, less spectacularly, it was a slow death in the Empire's terrible copper mines.

The First Communities

The Apostles' missionary effort is related in the Book of Acts and the various Epistles of the New Testament. But preoccupied with their task of teaching, the Apostles did not judge it opportune to write their memoirs. The Book of Acts itself, much of which can be regarded as a journal of Paul's travels, is confined to essentials, for it is more concerned with spreading the teaching of Christ than with showing us the life of the first communities. Still, in general, the documents reflect certain characteristic features of these communities and enable us to discern their spirit.

These apostolic texts emphasize the importance of unity in faith and love. Brought together through their common faith in Christ and marked with the seal of baptism, the Christians were henceforth to have one heart and soul (one body, St. Paul was to say), of which the head is Christ. Their community was manifested in prayer and the Eucharistic celebration.

The Apostles showed a lively concern for spreading in the community doctrine that was strictly faithful to the teaching of the Lord Jesus. They strove to set up, according to Christ's wish, not mere spiritual brotherhoods, but concrete communities; the structure of these is not always clear to us, but they were real, nonetheless.

All these communities or "Churches" maintained close relations, which went beyond mere spiritual harmony and were based on strict supervision by the Apostles and their representatives, as St.. Paul shows on several occasions. Thus, from the time of its founding, the Church exhibited its essential features, which were to be perpetuated through the ages, undergoing modifications as circumstances required but without ever profoundly altering, just as the small child already prefigures the adult.

The Church of Silence

The death of the Apostles neither reduced the fervor of the Church nor the missionary efforts of its members. Unfortunately, a series of complex circumstances prevent us from knowing in detail the life of the Church in this era. The Christians do not seem to have written much at this time. Their faith was nourished directly through the testimony of the Apostles, explained by their immediate disciples. Because of the relative proximity of events, an account of the Churches' teaching and history seemed unnecessary. Besides, a certain prudence was required in view of the persecutions. Only a few episodic documents now remind the historian of the Church's existence in this period.

The communities founded by the Apostles and provided with bishops through their care, still flourished. While missionary expansion did not exhibit the spectacular character of the apostolic journeys, local communities regularly developed and organized themselves. As early as the reign of Trajan (c. 110), Asia Minor already included a large number of Christians, and toward the middle of the century renewed persecution brought to light important Churches in North Africa, Lyons, and Egypt. Rome had long possessed a Church, which as early as the year 100 was in correspondence with the other communities. And Tertullian could write, about the year 250: "We came into being only yesterday and are already invading the structures of society."

By this date the Church is appearing routinely in the documents that have come down to us and is taking a larger and larger place in Roman society. Religious life is beginning to be expressed openly. And while in certain tragic periods, the Christians sometimes have to go into hiding, they are established in the cities and own places of worship known to all. The bishops are becoming important figures whom emperors pursue or bargain with, according to their policies. Freed from their fears, Christians are beginning to publish books explaining their conduct or demanding of the public authority the right to exercise their religion freely. Neither sarcasm, nor calumny, nor persecutions will be able to check this impetus.

The advances of the Church were continued regularly throughout the third century. A constantly increasing number of works proposed not only to justify Christianity in the eyes of the pagans, but to define the teachings of the Church, to develop instruction, to organize Christian communities. Having become more numerous, the faithful appear more demanding. They are no longer satisfied with elementary instruction, and doctrinal works become necessary. This requires the ecclesiastical authority to intervene in order to orientate this research and to fix gradually what will eventually be called "orthodoxy" of thought. Likewise, bishops are establishing the Church's line of conduct with regard to organization of public worship as well as the regulation of Christians' conduct.

In quality, in numerical importance, the Church is increasing. And leadership is developing in all domains. A final persecution, the most frightful of all, decimated the

Church for ten years and strengthened Christians still more. Then there came the event that had been so long awaited, which some thought impossible: the Emperor recognized Christianity and presented it with freedom of the city. This was in 313. Ten years later this recognition was effective throughout the Empire.

The Emperor Who Brought Peace to the Church

For the historian, in spite of its extraordinary context, the attitude of the Emperor Constantine appears to be almost a normal outcome of the profound revolution in the Roman world. Many regions had become Christian, dating sometimes from several generations. In certain cities, such as Carthage, Alexandria, and Antioch, the majority of the population was Christian. Henceforth, Christianity was a force with which the civil power had to reckon. The failure of the persecution of Diocletian established that force and logically imposed on the political power a change of outlook.

This is why the gesture of Constantine has sometimes been interpreted as the expression, not of profound conviction, but of political realism. It seems more likely that the two elements were closely linked. The faith of Constantine is undoubted, but quite probably the sagacious emperor was able to make the most of political expediencies and his personal religious convictions.

In any case, the edict of Constantine was an event with very considerable consequences. For the first time in history the existence of the Church was officially recognized by the state. Henceforth the Church as an institution is regarded as an integral part of Greco-Roman society, and is recognized as a power which will influence the evolution of the state. The consequences of such an act were incalculable. In particular, the words of Christ, declaring the opposition of the Church to the world were going to be considered from a new point of view. Until now, the problem had been simple, since the "world" rejected Christianity and remained alien to it if not hostile. Now the "world," concerned about the power of the Church, was seeking to become its ally, and, not having been able to destroy it, was trying to incorporate it. Henceforth, fidelity to Christ would no longer be measured by the heroic but relatively simple option of martyrdom, but would require a permanent effort at inner renewal in order to avoid any collusion with this dangerous ally.

The Burdens of Peace

Full of the enthusiasm of victory, the Christians of the fourth century did not at once perceive the difficulties raised by the edict of toleration. As they saw it, Constantine remained a providential instrument, and they awaited the time when he would become the symbol of the temporal power of the Church, a symbol which, in this era, was never a reality. The Church, in short, sought to preserve its autonomy. And in circumstances that were occasionally dramatic, standing up to the immediate successors of Constantine, the most eminent representatives of the Church declared the Church's independence of the civil power.

By freeing the Church, the edict of toleration favored an expansion of Christianity. In less than a century, the Gospel impregnated the structures of the Roman Empire and rallied its masses of undecided men. Then were established in the Church the temporal structures which persecutions had rendered impossible up to that time.

However, the peace was disturbed with reactions, burdened with rancor. During the persecution of Diocletian the heroism of martyrs had been paralleled by weaknesses and multiple apostasies. Moreover, the imperial police had systematically increased the confusion by encouraging informers and by declaring that pastors had succumbed even though they had remained faithful. When it was finally possible to speak openly, certain Churches, such as those of Egypt or Africa, were cruelly torn by inner rivalries. The bishops worked to overcome bitterness, but plotters who sometimes gave themselves the title "confessors," men who were all the more disturbed because they were hoping to have their own weaknesses forgotten, produced real splits: the Melitian schism, the Donatist schism. A hundred years later, Augustine was to be struggling again against the descendants of these dissidents, strongly established throughout North Africa.

The massive conversions likewise constituted a heavy burden for the Church. How was it possible to be sure that this host of new converts possessed the necessary generosity, the indispensable inner accord with the Gospel? And soon many bishops were showing themselves more concerned with the comforts of life than with the requirements of their vocation. Religious literature of this period abounds in bitter criticism of the conduct of Christians. However, there is no need to overemphasize these diatribes by vigilant pastors. While the vices of a few leaders and the mediocrity of many might henceforth be exposed to the public, most of the Church remained fervent and the sanctity of many Christians compensated fully for the sins of their brothers. The end of the fourth century saw the emergence of a generation of shepherds who combined learning and sanctity, and through their virtues earned a place in the memory of Christians—the first place after that of the Apostles. Their teaching and example produced an outpouring of faith that enabled the historians to call this era, in all justice, the golden age of the Church.

When the Seed Becomes a Tree

A genuine enthusiasm possessed theologians and intellectuals at this time, and kept the Church stirred up for a period of fifty years. As the persecutions ended, it seemed necessary to compare the positions of various Christian thinkers, for theological writings were multiplying. In the course of the third century, in the Church of Alexandria in particular, there was intense study and research, encouraged by the presence there of two noted scholars, Clement and Origen. But the speculations which ensued, in spite of their interest, threatened to distort revealed doctrine and the traditional faith of the Church, to the extent of challenging even the divinity of Christ. Toward the year 320, a priest of Alexandria named Arius began to hold forth publicly on questionable subjects. The bishops met in plenary session at Nicea in 325 to settle the matter. Unfortunately, the dispute was disturbed by personal rivalries and the Arian crisis ravaged the Church for half a century. The faith was safeguarded, thanks to the indomitable tenacity of Athanasius, Patriarch of Alexandria.

This painful struggle was followed by a short period of glory, illuminated by Basil of Caesarea; Gregory, Bishop of Nyssa; Gregory, Bishop of Nazianzus (these three in Asia Minor); Ambrose at Milan; Augustine in North Africa; and John Chrysostom in Constantinople. These great bishops wrote remarkable works which became fundamental documents of Christian thought. Joining sanctity to wisdom, they inspired a deep religious life in their Churches. Under their direction a Christian elite strove to lead an exemplary life and played a decisive role in the development of public morals.

The emergence of monastic life likewise testifies to the vitality of Christianity in this period. Of course, religious life had always been honored by the Church. St. Paul had concerned himself with the temporal and spiritual position of virgins, those women who devoted themselves to the service of the Lord and the Church while remaining in their homes. As soon as the persecutions ended, men felt the need of living as hermits and withdrawing into the desert. In a few years, monks had spread throughout the deserts of Egypt and Syria. While encouraging this attempt at perfection, the bishops were disturbed by it, because the untimely zeal of certain monks repeatedly led to disorder and anarchy.

From out of their solitude, such men as Pachomius, Basil (a future bishop of Caesarea), and sometime later, Benedict, channeled this fervor and gave it an institutional character. Thanks to them, monastic life was able to be developed for the good of all, and in our day still, thousands of monks bear witness to their spirit and their rule. The bishops were inspired by the principles of religious life to raise the spiritual standards of the clergy and faithful. They encouraged their priests to establish centers of community life in their own homes, and among contemplative monks they developed groups of religious whose duties were to aid the bishops and to work in hospitals and hospices.

After the official acknowledgment of its existence, one of the first tasks of the Church was to carry out the mission of charity that Christ had assigned it. There was plenty of occasion for this, because Greco-Roman society was hard on the poor. First the Church tried to improve the slave's de facto position, and then his juridical situation. She also worked to improve the position of women, endlessly proclaiming the equality of the sexes and the reciprocity of rights and duties in family life.

Having become, thanks to the gifts of the faithful, a real material power, the Church organized a series of charitable works which are still continuing today. Basil of Caesarea created the first hospital, the direction of which he entrusted to monk-nurses. Chrysostom, promoted to the see of Constantinople, followed his example, and soon each church had its hospital for the sick and its hostel for travelers and strangers. Soup kitchens were set up to help the poor. An immense network of charity and brotherhood was developed across the entire Empire.

But the relief of material distress was not the essential concern of the bishops. They knew that the Kingdom of God is a work of faith and salvation. Therefore, they had to give themselves up first to developing faith and Christian values in the world. They tirelessly repeated to their flocks that official adherence to Christianity and religious practice are not enough to merit salvation. In the sight of the Lord, far from being a guarantee, nominal membership in the Church will count against unworthy Christians. The reception of Baptism implies an obligation which must be expressed through a perpetual conversion. Hence the important place devoted in the works of the Fathers to the moral reform of Christians. This moral preaching, however, was regularly associated with an urgent doctrinal instruction to which the faithful did not remain indifferent. The violence of religious crises is evidence of the active participation and profound convictions of the Christians. On several occasions, particularly at Antioch, laymen made up for the weakness of the clergy and maintained the orthodoxy of the community.

Some, it is true, carried away by the victory that had been won under Constantine and confirmed by Theodosius, confused the material success of Christianity with the coming of the Kingdom of God and believed this alliance of the civil power and the Church was eternal. For these, evangelization of the world had been completed. Was not the name of Christ revered from one end of the Roman Empire to the other? Beyond its frontiers there were nothing but barbarians, whose only salvation consisted in adhering to the Christian faith and Roman civilization. However, in spite of certain panegyrics whose importance should not be over-emphasized, the Church as a whole did not share this opinion. At no time did the pastors relax their effort for the deepening and extension of Christian life. Concern for the evangelization of the barbarians obsessed the bishops. The Church of Antioch, especially, sent out numerous missions, which made the name of Christ known beyond the banks of the Danube and even in the depths of Asia.

But the ties between Church and state were daily growing closer, especially in the East, and this union was tending more and more towards a theocracy. The Church seemed to be becoming constantly more subjected to the civil power when, suddenly, the Roman Empire, which had been faltering for a century, collapsed under the onrush of the barbarians.

A new era was opening.

2. Christianity of the Middle Ages

The Barbarians

When the barbarian tribes spread out across the West, many a Roman thought of the coming of the Antichrist. However, they might well have foreseen this development. For a long time Rome had been maintaining its power only through the assistance of mercenaries, who were recruited from these very tribes who were now attacking the Empire. But such was the belief in the grandeur of Roman civilization, that the Christians themselves could not conceive of a different state of things. The awakening was all the ruder when, in less than a century, the Germans overwhelmed the remains of Caesar's empire.

The situation of the Church appeared critical. Was Christianity going to founder with the Empire? Among the barbarian tribes, certain clans had been converted to Christianity, but they had joined the Arian sect, which separated them still farther from the Catholic Church. Men as eminent as Augustine and Leo the Great understandably shared the dismay of their fellow Christians.

However, the Church rapidly recovered and faced the danger. Bishops who, in the eyes of posterity, did not measure up to their predecessors, nonetheless maintained the faith of the people in these difficult times. Some, such as Bishop Cesarius of Arles, while appearing as belated witnesses of Roman civilization, managed to make the

German princes respect their religious authority. Others worked directly for the conversion of the conquering tribes, such as St. Réml, the bishop of Rheims, who baptized King Clovis in his cathedral on Christmas day in 506. This event, moreover, was to become the symbol of the conversion of the barbarians to the Catholic religion. At this time it affected only a small fraction of the barbarian world, but the Baptism of Clovis and his Franks was the starting point for a vast movement of evangelization which, in the course of more than two centuries, gradually brought western Europe to Christianity. It was the work of the monks that brought all Europe under the vigilant supervision of the popes and bishops, especially during the pontificate of St. Gregory the Great. In the sixth century, the Visigoths rallied to Christianity. At the request of St. Gregory the Great, the monk St. Augustine, namesake of the illustrious Father of the Church, undertook the re-conversion of England and became the first archbishop of Canterbury. From Ireland, which had been converted by St. Patrick and had kept the faith, legions of monks under the leadership of St. Columban and St. Boniface went off to preach Christ to the tribes that had settled in Switzerland and Germany. As early as the beginning of the seventh century, the Catholic Church was again extending its influence across the territory of the old Roman Empire and was bearing witness in a completely new world. It was even to become the vital element of the civilization that was to arise there.

The Agony of the Eastern Church

While the Western Church, at the expense of long and arduous labor, was trying to hold back the pagan flood, the Church of the East, battening on a false prosperity, was squandering the patrimony of its ancestors. For a few years more, several great bishops, such as St. Cyril, the

Patriarch of Alexandria, Theodoret, Bishop of Cyr, continued the tradition of their predecessors, but they could not offset the lethargy that was gradually overcoming the Greek-language Churches. Unable to restore themselves in the intellectual domain, these Churches were destroyed in endless quarrels and disputes that consumed the vital energies of Eastern Christianity. Furthermore, the autocratic emperors often interfered in the life of the Church itself. Disabled by heresy and schism, tied ever more closely to a despotic civil power, the magnificent Christian communities of the East found themselves deprived of their substance, ready to crumble at the slightest shock.

The Crescent and the Cross

At the beginning of the seventh century, in Arabia, Mohammed began preaching a new religion. In a few months the followers of the "prophet" multiplied, and at his death, in 632, they were numerous enough to undertake conquests. The Mussulman forces proved much more dangerous for the Church than the barbarians. The latter sought simply to supplant the Roman power. Islam, on the other hand, based its warlike efforts on a genuine religious motive and took as its mission the annihilation or at least the subjugation of all other religions.

Drowsing in luxury, blinded by its palace rivalries, the Byzantine Empire presented an easy prey. The Arabs invaded Syria, crushed the army of the emperor, and took possession of Jerusalem in 658. Continuing their victorious advance, they conquered Asia Minor and threw out advance posts as far as the Indies. In the West, they took possession of Egypt and of the Mediterranean coast as far as Tangiers. Ruined as much by its own mediocrity as by the power of the conquerors, the magnificent empire of the Basileus was sinking. However, in a surge of heroism, the Greeks resisted victoriously in the siege of Constantinople in 673, and checked the Arab expansion in that direction. They maintained an embryo state, secluded, incapable of developing.

The Eastern Church, bled white by internal dissention, sterilized by the "Byzantium" disputes, was unable to act. It made peace with the conqueror and, except for a few great saints such as John Damascene, lived on in a pathetic situation in the midst of the Arab world.

Drunk with victory, the Arab troops crossed the Strait of Gibraltar and threw themselves into the conquest of the West. But after a few spectacular successes, they were crushed by Charles Martel at Poitiers and withdrew into Spain. Rescued, the Western Church had nothing to regret except the destruction of the newly-converted Church of Spain. Even on the peninsula, the Christians did not capitulate altogether. In large numbers, they retreated into the mountains of the Central West, ready to reconquer their country at the first opportunity.

Charlemagne

After three centuries of upheavals, the Church was able to continue its advance in peace. The seed was already bearing fruit everywhere, with a promise of greater progress. In the same way as civil society, the Church had been deeply affected by the disappearance of the Roman civilization in which Christian thought had taken shape. The monks of the early Middle Ages succeeded in preserving the intellectual and spiritual heritage of the preceding centuries, but they proved incapable of any really creative effort. In this time the Church lived on its past, fortunately rich enough to permit it to wait, secure from danger, for the new generations which would bring fresh efforts.

The first sign of this renaissance came from Spain. The conversion of the Visigoths, during the sixth century, had given rise to a flourishing Church, eager for development. Scholars appeared again, the most famous of whom was St. Isidore of Seville (d. 636). Unfortunately, the Arab conquest halted this effort at renewal.

The coming of Charlemagne restored political stability in the West and brought the Church the means of renewal. The monks could work in peace, thanks to the Emperor, who gave the full support of his authority to the renaissance of profane and ecclesiastical studies, thus favoring a program of humanization which he did not always practice himself.

Although Charlemagne set himself up as the most trustworthy and devout champion of the Church, his support, while often helpful, was not without danger. He strove to protect the missionaries without meddling in their work, but when they had difficulty he did not scruple to obtain the Saxons' conversion by force. In those days, when the sword was king, the event did not seem particularly scandalous. But the state of mind that had produced such a decision was subsequently to result in immense ravages in the Western Church. This collusion of the spiritual and temporal powers to insure evangelization, by force if necessary, was often to recur, in spite of the unchristian character of these obligatory conversions.

Continuing the work of his predecessors, Charlemagne completely freed the Roman pontiff from Byzantine dependency by confirming the pope in the temporal sovereignty of his states. Henceforth, the pope had a task which was to be justified, perhaps, in its historical context—the political situation at this time was precarious—but which was to hinder the direction of the Church seriously until 1929, when the Lateran Treaty was signed. The spiritual mission of the head of the Church was ill-suited to the administration of a domain which could provoke envy and at times seriously affect the concerns of the Vicar of Christ. It was to take almost a thousand years to find a solution that was suitable with regard to the spiritual mission of the sovereign pontiff and the independence needed for the exercise of his duties.

In any case, the reign of Charlemagne enabled the Church to find a formula which was going to govern it for many centuries. But difficult trials were awaiting before it could know again the doctrinal and spiritual splendor of the fourth century.

The East Breaks Away

Painful as they had been, events up to this date had not affected the nature of the Church. From the fourth to the ninth century, it had undergone external attacks, but Christ had predicted this. Freedom of action was reduced, but the faith remained unchanged, at least in the West. Was there not new reason for belief when one observed how the Church had survived cataclysm and chaos? The storm had passed and the Church remained and had become the ruling principle of the new civilization. Unfortunately, the upheaval had been too severe, and this time profound reactions were going to shake the very foundations of the Church. The most dramatic of these was the separation of the Churches of the East. Though they were still flourishing at the time of the barbarian invasions, the Eastern communities had become aloof, indifferent to the events in the West, following a path strewn with petty disputes. The untimely interference of the Byzantine emperors as the Church's representatives only aggravated the already difficult relations with the Roman pontiff.

When the Mohammedan invasion, after having destroyed the unity of the Eastern Churches, left only fragments of communities remaining, the Greek Church, confined to the narrow territory of the Empire of Constantinople, and soon suffering the infirmities of age, lived in the memory of its former glory. From this time on, the break became inevitable. Henceforth everything separated the two divisions of Christianity. Begun under the Patriarch Photius in 890, the separation was completed by the Patriarch Michael Cerularius in 1054.

Apart from a severe break, which produced bitterness not yet forgotten today, the schism was to have painful consequences for the evolution of the Catholic Church itself.

For centuries thereafter, the limits of the Catholic Church were to coincide with those of the Latin West. Certainly, it was easier to set up homogeneous structures in a Christianity in which the majority of the faithful lived under the same culture, obeyed identical laws, sometimes under the protection of the same civil power. But in this way the Church was to become inevitably oriented toward an exclusively Latin way of thinking, and the resultant uniformity of structures in medieval Christianity was not without dangers. Indeed, while by right and by vocation the Church remained universal, for centuries it was actually reduced to living "occidentally." As long as Europe was identified with the known world and as long as it kept its mastery of the world, this anomaly did not seem disturbing. But reconversion seemed difficult at times when this order was upset. The confusion between the Catholic Church and Western civilization had lasted too long. There is no doubt that the maintenance of unity between Churches of differing culture and vocation would have better prepared the bark of Peter for the difficulties that awaited it.

The Iron Age

The break between the East and West came at a time when the Church was experiencing the darkest hours in its history. Certainly, the Carolingian renaissance, followed by a new period of religious progress exemplified by the Abbey of Cluny, gave a promise of happier days. Unfortunately, the material riches which had accumulated through the centuries for the help of the poor, were a source of covetousness in every diocese. Quite often, too, the bishop had to provide for the physical protection of his people and thus added to his temporal power and religious responsibilities. The papacy itself possessed territories, and implacable rivalries for the see of Peter arose. For 200 years the Church was prey to the worst corruption, and the clergy of Rome provided a sad example of degradation. Extortion, treachery, assassination, prostitution, fornication, avarice—Rome was subjected to everything, and the Chair of Peter became the subject of rivalry between ecclesiastical clans, the prey of secular princes. Twenty popes, most of whom died a violent death, succeeded each other in less than a century. A woman, Marozia, managed to have her lover and his bastards raised to the supreme power. In a horrible climax, the body of Pope Formosus was torn from his tomb, judged by his rivals in the Vatican Basilica, condemned to the stake, and thrown into the Tiber.

Never had the Church's situation appeared more desperate. The see of the Apostles was being sold to the highest bidder, surrendered to the most brutal.

However, the corruption of numerous ecclesiastical dignitaries did not besmirch the faith of the Church. In the midst of their filth, these predators did not touch doctrine, and at times displayed evidence of faith that astonishes the historians. In the final accounting, in spite of the spectacular character of this depravity, the vital forces of the Western Church remained intact. This debasement was less dangerous than the torpor of the East.

Salvation came through the monks.

In this painful era, Cluny was in a period of full expansion. In many monasteries the holy abbots Odo and Odillo maintained fervor and austere behavior. It is true that the

monks of Cluny subsequently succumbed to the evils of
the age, but the spiritual fervor stirred up by the abbots
could not be erased. A wind of reform began blowing
through the Church, and soon Rome took the leadership
of the renewal, just as it had been in the forefront of the
decline.

Pope St. Leo IX restored the pontifical court to health,
and his successors undertook to return the Church's lost
splendor. Led by St. Bernard, the monks eagerly collabor-
ated in this work, and in less than a century the Church
was again obeying the call of the Lord Jesus. As in the
fourth century, a period of glory was beginning, bringing
forth a host of saints, scholars, mystics, and missionaries.

Christendom

The ephemeral Carolingian renaissance was to give the
first impetus to a doctrinal development that reached its
peak in the thirteenth century. Little by little, the West
resumed interest in studies. Intellectual centers were developed around the bishoprics or in the monasteries. St.
Anselm and St. Bernard restored ecclesiastical learning to
a place of honor and were soon followed by the school of
Chartres and the Abbey of St. Victor of Paris.

Rome knew how to exploit the aspirations of young men
eager for knowledge and reorganized instruction which
was then, actually and legally, a monopoly of the Church.
The pope gladly encouraged the wishes of the student
body and offered the new-born universities a privileged
position which guaranteed the quality of instruction while
keeping a check on the doctrine that was dispensed.

Soon, new religious orders rivaled each other in this
field: the Dominicans achieved distinction with St. Albert
the Great and St. Thomas Aquinas, the followers of St.
Francis with Duns Scotus and St. Bonaventure.

Thus was born what is commonly called Scholasticism,
the doctrinal achievement of this age, characterized by its

magistral aspect, scholarly in the best sense of the word, and by its attempt at synthesis. The writings of St. Thomas Aquinas, the prince of scholastics, possess the austerity and purity of line of the Gothic cathedrals that were their contemporaries. It was necessary to bring order into the treasures of thought and learning that had been heaped up in the preceding ages, somewhat haphazardly. A methodical procedure adopted, however, had the danger of creating an excessively rigid structure. This technique, incomparable when used by a master of the stature of St. Thomas Aquinas, subsequently, in less expert hands, was to stifle the intellectual enthusiasm of the Church, and cripple it with formulas. This decadence of scholasticism was to result in serious disorder in the fifteenth and sixteenth centuries.

The intellectual vitality of the Church was accompanied by an unprecedented spiritual revival. An increase in religious vocations attested to this revival. The call to a more perfect life awakened interest everywhere. After engendering the Cluniac reform, the vigor of the Benedictines resulted in the birth of the Cistercians, prompted by St. Bernard of Clairvaux.

New institutions appeared in answer to human needs. St. Dominic founded the Order of Preachers to combat heresy. His disciples soon devoted themselves to teaching and preaching. About the same period, St. Francis Assisi founded the Order of Friars Minor in response to the desire of an increasing number of Christians for poverty and simplicity. Thus these two great saints provided channels for the generous impulses that were manifest in the Church, sometimes with a certain propensity for anarchy. After them came a host of saints.

These two families, which soon became popular, nevertheless, had no monopoly on sanctity. The desire for perfection of many Christians led to the birth of contemplative orders such as the Carmelites, Augustinians, of Hospitaliers, and even military orders.

The influence of the monks on the Church was remark-able, transforming morality and bringing peace to a society that was subject to factional rivalry and power struggles.

Increasingly concerned with the expansion of the King-dom of God, the Christians became preoccupied with dis-tant missions. This unrest was first seen in the desire for recovering the Holy Places, a desire that gave rise to the Crusades and which always remained one of their objec-tives, even when political or economic aims introduced less innocent incentives. Nevertheless, while the conquest of the Holy Places demanded a display of strength, the Church was not forgetful that evangelization was above all a work of peace. Consequently, this task fell not to the military orders, but to the religious ones. Thus, St. Francis of Assisi set up within his order a province of the East and went in person to preach to the sultan of Egypt. Follow-ing this famous example, Franciscans and Dominicans preached the message of Christ in the Near East and in Morocco. Certain Franciscans even ventured into the cen-ter of Mongolia and appeared before the great Khan. Several Dominicans evangelized Persia and Turkestan. A Franciscan, John of Montecorvino, embarking in 1290, dared to journey to the limits of the known world and established a flourishing mission in China. All these pion-eers, in spite of the relative defeat of their efforts, attested the Christian vigor of their age.

Thus, at the highpoint in its history, the medieval Church showed that it was Catholic in the strongest sense of the word, since certain of its members, encouraged by the pope, went to spread the Gospel message even to the ends of the earth. This universal calling of the Church was unquestionable even at this period but was not conspic-uous because of the unusual strength of the Western Church, commonly called Christendom.

At this time the life of the Church was marked by har-mony between the civil power and religious authority.

This agreement, the nature and effects of which we shall see subsequently, closely united the Church with the society of which it was a guiding element. Everything was influenced by religious motives, even military expeditions —crusades in the Holy Land, crusades against the Albigensians and other heretics. Moreover, the Church exercised a strict control over the private life of the citizen, as is evidenced by the various ecclesiastical regulations and especially by the establishment in 1198 of the Tribunal of the Inquisition, which was supposed to judge "crimes" of faith. This entry of the Church into the temporal domain did not take place without some disadvantages. Thus, the Crusades and the Inquisition were the result of legitimate religious concern but rapidly degenerated. The civil power used them for its own purposes and was assisted in doing this by certain clerics who were more anxious about their material success than the real calling of the Church.

An inevitable accompaniment of easy success, these abuses, nevertheless, could not outweigh the extraordinary achievements of this medieval Christendom, a nursery of saints, which established Christianity so deeply that after a thousand years the world still senses this beneficent influence.

However, the danger of this success was not so much these abuses as its very perfection, placing its indelible imprint in every domain—morality, law, thought, technique, science, and art. From this time on, the very structures of Western society were in some ways inhibited by Christianity. Henceforth, faith is dependent upon institutions. Also, the Church was relaxing its vigilance. Relieved of personal decision, Christians surrendered to the ease which often leads to mediocrity. Fascinated by the Golden Age of the thirteenth century, they could not see the coming of a new world. A kind of spiritual and intellectual stagnation left the Church bogged down at the very instant that society was experiencing a new impulse in every domain. This crisis did not have the brutality of the barbarian invasion. The medieval world slowly crumbled away while the Church remained cramped by its structures and unaware of the mortal danger until an almost fatal crisis brought a rude awakening.

It is the history of this third period that must now be told.

3. From The Middle Ages To Our Time

Christendom Collapses

The high point of medieval Christendom was reached during the pontificate of Innocent III (1198–1215), and the luster of this brilliant period extended throughout the thirteenth century. Even during this century, however, the first signs of decline appeared; heresies were to be seen here and there, and above all, Christendom seemed crushed under the weight of its wealth and power.

The theocratic doctrine, defined by Innocent III with an implacable rigor and maintained by his successors, conflicted more and more with the aspirations of sovereigns who wanted to escape the restriction of Rome's yoke. Numerous incidents arose between the two powers, often favoring, as it happened, the momentary success of the papacy. But the princes were encouraging certain autonomous tendencies of their clergy—more or less openly, according to the circumstances. This state of mind, commonly called "Gallicanism," became increasingly evident for several centuries, and resulted in severe damage to the Church.

The first important result of Gallicanism was the move of the popes to Avignon. Succeeding Boniface VIII, a noted adversary of Philip the Fair of France, Pope Clement V, who had been elected through the influence of

French diplomacy, settled on the banks of the Rhône, in the midst of a court remarkable for its brilliance and intrigues. This deplorable situation lasted for seventy years, until under strong pressure from two women, St. Gertrude and St. Catherine of Siena, Pope Gregory XI agreed to return to Rome in 1377.

This return should have restored pontifical authority but resulted in new tribulation. Factionalism developing after the pontificate of Gregory XI produced a schism in the Western Church. For forty years the Church was ruled by two, and sometimes by three, rival popes, each supported by ardent partisans.

And the end of the Great Schism did not mark the end of the Church's Calvary. A century of intrigues had destroyed the fervor of the pontifical court, which had become more concerned with the charms of the Renaissance than with the austere morality of Christ. A series of popes of evil memory—Innocent VIII, Alexander VI, Julius II— brought back to the see of Peter a type of morality that had not been seen since the tenth century.

Among the thinkers, the Renaissance was advancing, and humanists were plunging with delight into the rediscovered treasures of antiquity. As compared with this vitality of profane culture, the universities offered only a Scholasticism of formulas, a feeble caricature of the works of the thirteenth-century masters. Christian teaching seemed stricken with sterility.

Such a decline seemed doomed to end in catastrophe. This catastrophe took place in 1517, when Martin Luther attacked the traffic in indulgences.

Reform or Surrender?

The condition of the Church obviously called for a reform. The sterility of theologians, the discrediting of papal authority, the limitless luxury and even debauchery of a large part of the clergy were affecting the vitality of the Church. It was necessary to act quickly and decisively. The successful effort of Cardinal Ximenes in Spain showed a possible solution, thanks to the still lively faith there. Unfortunately, the reform measures proposed for the Church as a whole were too timid. Their sponsors—Pope Julius II, too concerned with his own temporal interests, and Leo IX, too involved with humanism—were unable to devote themselves to this task seriously. The indispensable renewal came under the worst circumstances and inevitably resulted in serious reactions.

The revolt of Luther and, some years later, that of Calvin were proposed as attempts at purification. These efforts were assured of success, the more so since they could count on the selfish support of princes tempted to confiscate the Church's possessions.

In itself, the Reformation might have been a great benefit—if it had been motivated by the spirit of St. Bernard, Gregory VII, or the great reformers of the twelfth century. Unfortunately, Luther and Calvin were not satisfied with chastising abuses or with applying needed modifications to certain historical (and thus contingent) aspects of the Church; they attacked its basic structure. Acting as doctrinaires, they soon challenged doctrine itself. The reformers were becoming innovators. The Catholic Church, whose origin and foundations they challenged, could not permit this. The armed assistance of the German princes emphasized the military nature of the new movement and brought the protagonists of the Reformation into the venture. After a century of bloody struggle in which religious conflicts were closely tied in with political interests, a third of Europe left the Catholic Church. Only Italy and Spain escaped war. England, through somewhat different processes, became definitely associated with the Protestant cause in 1559. In France, a fratricidal war decimated the country from 1562 to 1598 and ended with victory by the Catholics.

When the Church emerged from the conflict it was bled white. Now indeed—too late—it was going to carry out its own reformation. But for a long time it was unable to muster sufficient strength to face the tasks that were waiting. Besides, the cruel wars between Catholics and Protestants had produced distrust and rancor that were hard to forget. For over 300 years, under the cloud of the Protestant threat, Christian thought was to prove incapable of any creative undertaking, while ecclesiastical disciplines were dominated exclusively by concern with anti-heretical apologetics.

The Council of Trent

The importance of the Protestant movements precluded any half-measures on the part of the Church. It was quite obvious that there had to be speedy and strict suppression of all abuses and a straightforward reform of certain institutional practices. At the same time, however, the Church had to state clearly the bases of its internal structure and the various external aspects that had been challenged by the Protestants. A program of this kind required close collaboration of the entire Church with its leader. This is why, in spite of the unpleasant memory of the Council of Basel in 1449, the pope agreed to summon an ecumenical council.

Meeting in the city of Trent, in northern Italy, the council held three sessions: December 13, 1545, to March 11, 1547; 1551 to 1554; and January 18, 1561, to December 4, 1563. Various circumstances interrupted the work of the participants. Drawing its inspiration mainly from scholastic philosophy, the council defined the principal dogmatic points challenged by the Protestants: the teaching mission of the Church supported by Scripture and Tradition; justification through faith and works; sacramental theology; the mystery of the Mass. In addition, many disciplinary measures were taken, one of the most important of which was the decree creating seminaries for the education of the clergy.

The next popes, especially Pius V, were deeply concerned with carrying out the acts and decrees of the council. St. Pius V published the Missal and Breviary that were to be used by the entire Church, and the Catechism of the Council of Trent, a summary of the Church's teaching as an outcome of the Christian tradition defined by the council. This catechism became the model of those still used today. Gregory reformed the calendar on a more scientific basis, and Sixtus V, creator of the modern organization of the Church, brought out an official edition of the Vulgate (the Latin text of the Bible). Thanks to their efforts, recovery was rapid and, at the end of the century, the Church had found once more, if not its glory, at least the fervor of former times.

A Catholic Reformation

The program of rehabilitation undertaken by the Council of Trent, as a response to the Protestant crisis, was soon to bear fruit. The Franciscans, Benedictines, and Carmelites carried out their own reforms. New orders appeared, growing out of a concern for the apostolate, which led to their adopting a kind of life as close as possible to that of secular priests. The most famous of these institutions, the Society of Jesus (Jesuits), founded by St. Ignatius of Loyola, received papal approbation in 1540. Organized along completely military lines, the Society rendered immense service to the Church. With its vitality and discipline, it was destined to have a stormy history, which was not without its grandeur. Other orders shared in the sanctification of the clergy, popular preaching, the care of the sick, and education. With all their power, the bishops worked for the renewal of the secular clergy, and the Church was given such men as St. Charles Borromeo and St. Philip Neri.

This immense effort continued in the seventeenth century and was especially noticeable in France, due to St. Francis de Sales, St. Vincent de Paul, Cardinal de Berulle, St. John Eudes, and Father Olier, who were themselves assisted by a large number of collaborators of intense faith. Their main objective was the education of the clergy, and for this purpose they founded religious societies; the Lazarists, Eudists, Sulpicians.

In a reaction against earlier abuses, the faith of the period assumed a character that was imbued with rigorism, if not puritanism—a character that was apparent in all the spiritual writing of the time and which developed to an exaggerated degree in Jansenist circles.

The Catholic reformation also brought a rebirth of ecclesiastical studies and a desire for penetrating more deeply into the fundamental facts of faith. However, this could hardly be called a doctrinal revival. While pastors and theologians devoted themselves to inculcating in the people the teaching of the Council of Trent, they left no work comparable to that of the Fathers or the great Scholastics.

Religious interests centered more around spirituality and mysticism. These two aspects of Christian thought, always revered by the Church, had enjoyed some favor in the thirteenth century and were cultivated in the following century by the Dutch school of spirituality, whence came the *Imitation of Christ*. But at the time of the Council of Trent, spiritual literature had entered a golden age, as exemplified by St. Teresa of Avila, St. John of the Cross, St. Francis de Sales, and the authors of the French school. Continuing the tradition of the sixteenth century humanists, bands of scholars grouped mainly around the Port-Royal movement and the Benedictine Abbey of St. Maur, carried out learned projects and edited the texts of the Fathers of the Church with a competence and concern for exactitude that are still recognized by modern scholars.

The art of preaching also flourished, with Bossuet, Massillon, Fléchier, Bourdaloue, and many other less famous orators. The sermon became an institution, and crowds flocked to them as they did to the theater. These preachers often managed to steer clear of the dangers of success and united great talent with unquestionable faith. But they were not creators, and as a whole their works are remarkable chiefly for their mastery of earlier thinking.

The Missions

On the other hand, the work of recovery that followed the Council of Trent had a decisive influence on the mission situation. The discovery of America awakened intense enthusiasm, and numbers of missionaries sailed for the New World. Under the direction of the Dominicans and Jesuits, missions developed rapidly in Central and South America. St. Francis Xavier, one of the first companions of St. Ignatius, traveled through Japan and the Indies, and died off the coast of China. Some time later, one of his colleagues, Father Ricci, was to lay the foundations of the Church in China. These early missionary teams understood that evangelization necessarily implies honoring the legitimate traditions of native peoples as well as accepting and working within civilizations still ignorant of the Word. In this respect, of course, they were merely following the example of the Apostles and Christian tradition. Unfortunately, it seems that the theological knowledge of the missionaries was not as strong as their zeal, and their projects sometimes resulted in certain abuses. Moreover, Catholic thinking, concentrated as it was on the Protestant initiative, was not prepared to grasp the importance of the missionary problem. The arrival of Franciscans and Dominicans in the same territories brought on regrettable competition, which was not lessened by the establishment of the Society of Priests of the Foreign Missions. And Pope Benedict XIV prohibited "Chinese rites." The failure of this attempt at adaptation to the yellow world, together with quarrels between religious congregations, led to the destruction of these splendid Christian communities that had been so promising. Elsewhere, however, missionaries continued their efforts with varying success, bearing witness to the vitality of Catholicism.

Still, the distinctive feature of the Church in the seventeenth century was the development of home missions for teaching the people, particularly in the country. Most influential in this work was the popular St. Vincent de Paul, founder of the Congregation of Priests of the Mission, or Lazarists. Many priests went into this field and were followed in the next century by St. Grignion de Montfort and his Company of Mary.

Not satisfied with providing the people with Christian instruction, these apostles devoted a great deal of their efforts to charitable works. The Sisters of Charity of St. Vincent de Paul and the Daughters of Wisdom, founded by St. Grignion de Montfort, attest to this.

The Century of Mediocrity

The religious expansion of the seventeenth century should have led to a new high point in Church history. But the reactions had been too severe. Thinking was practically paralyzed by post-scholastic logic-chopping and polemics against Protestants. Tormented by Gallican tendencies and the sequels of the Reformation—occasionally dangerous ones, as in the case of Jansenism—the Church exhausted its strength in foolish arguments, while the rationalism of Voltaire and the philosophy of Rousseau were engendering a movement of unheard-of violence against religion in general, especially against Catholicism. Although it managed to correct the most flagrant abuses, the Church was unable to end the venal exploitation of monasteries and benefices which literally tied the churchmen involved to the civil power and put many appointments at the disposal of princes.

Little by little, the Church became buried in mediocrity. It is true that scandals were confined to isolated cases and did not reach the catastrophic proportions of Renaissance times; but fervor was disappearing. The popes of the eighteenth century were honest men and without distinction. Many bishops were preoccupied with peaceful enjoyment of the revenues of their dioceses, and fiercely defended the wealth of the Church. Though numerous, the clergy lacked distinction. The generation of great scholars and preachers had not been replaced; the religious literature of the period was soulless and insipid. The abbeys, invaded by lukewarmness, were soon empty, except for a few which rallied against the decline of discipline and readily found recruits—a response indicative of the Christian generosity of the people.

In the French Revolution, which it could not foresee or prevent, the Church was helpless.

The struggle began August 11, 1789, with the suppression of tithing and the nationalization of the possessions of the clergy, followed by the ban on religious orders and, in 1791, by the Civil Constitution of the Clergy. The hesitancy of Pope Pius VI, influenced by religious motives, but also by a fear of losing Avignon, sowed confusion among Catholics, and the belated decision to reject the constitutional oath led to a division of the clergy into two factions. Under the Legislative Assembly, events moved quickly and open and often bloody persecution occurred. This continued for four years, with alternating periods of terror and peace. On the whole, the clergy proved themselves worthy and through their courage erased the unhappy memory of their mediocrity. While most of the bishops went abroad, many priests continued their ministrations under dramatic circumstances and ensured the transmission of the faith.

The Revolution having failed to enslave or destroy the Church, Bonaparte strove to restore peace. He succeeded, but not without difficulty, because of his attempts to meddle with the internal affairs of the Church, which did not make his relations with the pontifical power any easier. At the same time the influence of the French Revolution was spreading throughout Europe, and throughout the nineteenth century the Church had to contend with ideological and social upheavals. The consequences of this conflict were incalculable, for it prevented the Church from giving sufficient attention to developments which, even then, were preparing for the rise of the worker.

The Nineteenth Century

The Christian can only wonder, in sadness, at the history of the Church in the nineteenth century. The Catholic Church had successfully survived the experience of the Revolution. Henceforth, scandals were avoided and were restricted to a few isolated cases that did not besmirch the entire community. The prestige of the papacy was increasing daily. Catholic leaders were becoming more numerous and were vigorously making themselves heard. Yet so much effort and good will were wasted in attempts to defend a past that was irrevocably ended and, besides, often chimerical, or to protect legitimate but secondary interests! No voice was raised to draw the attention of Christians to those seething forces that were at work, preparing for the twentieth century.

Thus the powerful personality of Pius IX was entirely absorbed in the defense of the temporal power of the Holy See. This question—an untimely one for both the Church and the civil power—was to be a serious handicap to the Church's development until the day when animosities were ended and the Lateran Treaty, signed in 1929, reestablished a one-square mile pontifical state, a symbolic guarantee of the independence of the Church. The ambiguity of the problem in those days was evident in the choice of Cardinal Antonelli as counsellor of the pope. This sly, clever, and disreputable individual—he was not even a priest—would have been better fitted to appear beside a Julius II than with this great pontiff.

About 1830 appeared Liberal Catholicism, which was to split French Catholic leaders and lead to the apostasy of the younger Lamennais—this while the publicist Louis Veuillot influenced the Christian masses in the direction of narrow and rigoristic conservatism.

Thus, in the nineteenth century, Christians remained more or less unaware of the social problems born of the industrial revolution. The leaders of social Catholicism never had the ear of the hierarchy. Tolerated until 1851, this movement was officially repudiated at the time of the unconditional rally of the episcopacy in the Second Empire and then stifled by a paternalistic, conservative trend which severely hampered Christian influence among the mass of the people.

Nevertheless, the threats which overshadowed the papacy together with the harassment of the bishops and clergy by liberal governments, strengthened the prestige of the pope and destroyed the remnants of Gallicanism, which were still found here and there. Then came the idea of a council which would continue the task of the Council of

Trent and officially ratify papal supremacy by proclaiming the dogma of infallibility. Some questioned the timeliness of this gathering. The authority of the sovereign pontiff was unquestionable, and there was no need to strengthen it by dogmatic definition. After much uncomfortable shifting about, the council finally met on December 8, 1869. As it happened, once the extent of pontifical power had been clearly defined, the council was cut short by the turn of events and adjourned *sine die*. Its work was not without value, however. It asserted the Church's loyalty to its leader at a time when liberalism was doing its utmost to weaken the prestige of the See of Peter, and it put an end to the interminable arguments, not about the principle, but about the exercise of pontifical power.

This activity only poorly concealed the doctrinal poverty of Christians in the nineteenth century. The honorable character of the clergy did not compensate for its ignorance in an era in which rationalist and positivist thinkers were studying various religious disciplines—metaphysics, Scripture, Church history—in an effort to demolish the very principle of religion. It is shocking to see how little scientific or religious value there was in the books then in use for the education of the clergy. They were nothing but hasty compilations, lacking any critical spirit and unable to awaken the priests' curiosity either about the events of their age or the doctrinal riches of the Church. The masterpieces of Christian thought in the fourth and thirteenth centuries were unknown or were published in truncated or faulty editions, which adulterated the meaning of the originals. Books on spirituality were feeble things which drew their inspiration from the naturalism of Rousseau and the Romantic spirit rather than from the great mystics of the sixteenth century. Thus the atheistic thinkers had a clear field for expounding their theories and were assured a hearing among the intellectuals and the leaders of Europe's middle-classes.

Thus while the Church apparently remained secure in Western Europe, its heritage was disappearing; the ruling classes were drawing away from it and the world of the worker was being built without it.

Recovery

The end of this nineteenth century brought a wonderful reawakening of the Church, signs of which had been apparent for some time—first in the Protestant Churches, rather paradoxically.

Intellectual recovery began in Germany about 1830. Ecclesiastical scholars in Tubingen and Munich were busy refuting the works of liberal Protestants and rationalist philosophers. Their efforts were limited to controversies, but they realized that the best service they could render the Church was to bring back the scientific spirit to the studies on which controversy centered—especially in theology, history, and Scripture.

In England the renewal began in the Anglican Church, with the Oxford Movement, started by a number of young professors. Led to a deeper study of the origin of the Church and to reading the texts of the fourth-century Fathers, they felt drawn to the Catholic Church. There followed a series of dramatic conversions, notably those of the future cardinals Newman and Manning, which contributed greatly to the restoration of the Catholic Church in England.

Held captive by the spirit of eloquence, the French Church felt no need for any such recovery. The numerous preachers sometimes stirred their audiences but almost never convinced them. Their long-winded instruction was always superficial. A few laymen, such as Auguste Nicolas and Frederick Ozaman, were alone, or almost alone, in defending the scientific value of religious thought. There was to be no reaction until the publication of the *Life of*

Jesus by Renan, in 1863. Then such scholars as Father Lagrange, Monsignors Hulst and Duchesne restored Catholic thought to a place of honor in scientific circles.

On the other hand, France held first place in the missionary movement which, in the nineteenth century, bore witness to the eternal vitality of the Church. On the eve of the First World War there was no region on the globe where the message of Christ had not been preached. We are ill informed about the extraordinary devotion that was the motive power of this expansion. While at times it may have been mingled with a certain feeling of superiority on the part of the white missionaries, this deep faith offset in most cases the predominant colonial spirit and permitted the development of native Christian communities, independent of the protective powers.

Growth or Decline of the Church

The struggle by Catholics against liberalism during the pontificate of Pius IX seemed to have ended in defeat. One by one, the laws that still afforded the Church a privileged position were abolished. The possessions of the Church were seized. In a critical development, the anticlerical advance led in 1906 to the separation of Church and state in France. Paradoxically, the power of the Church increased, even on the political level. Freed from temporal concerns, it became established as an unparalleled spiritual force, with which the political power would have to contend. In addition, the work of Leo XIII and his successors proved particularly helpful. For better than some of their predecessors, these popes knew how to serve as the representatives of a universal Church, a Church free from politics, whose interests did not coincide with those of any state.

For more than a hundred years now, the Church has had the good fortune to have at its head pontiffs whose personal talents and sanctity have contributed to the

Church's renown and led to an intellectual, spiritual, and apostolic revival worthy of the most glorious ages of the past.

It would be untimely here to attempt even a rough sketch of the complexity of the life of the Church today. Nevertheless, two dominant features must be mentioned: a keen awareness of the Church's catholicity—which has led Christians to study the theology of the Church—and, as a direct consequence, the evangelization of the world.

The intellectual and spiritual education of the clergy became the principal concern of the sovereign pontiffs, who reformed seminaries and supplied detailed programs for developing instruction. Speedily checked at the beginning of the century, the modernist crisis forced the hierarchy to heed the importance of educating the clergy. And the rise of lay leaders with certain responsibilities in the very heart of the Church led to legitimate demands from this element. Their desire for a deeper religious education called for priests who were more cultured and in closer touch with modern life.

Various reforms likewise led to a revival of spiritual life, with new growth in the religious congregations and a gradual escape from the artificialities of the preceding century. Some very timely liturgical reforms reinforced the universal expression of the Church.

Finally, the apostolate once more enjoyed the vigor of the early centuries. In the light of events of the preceding era, Christians acquired a new awareness of their responsibilities, and there was fruitful consideration of the Church's theology, its incarnation, and the resultant missionary obligation. Aware of its universal vocation, the Church realized that missionary work had to be freed from national tendencies and even from the domination of the West. Pius XI, who installed a native clergy, was the founder of this great work, which was continued by his successor, Pius XII. Calling for communities deeply rooted in Catholic tradition but conforming to the legitimate aspects of native civilizations, the Church found again its original missionary tradition and once more became Catholic, not only by right but in fact.

In spite of violent opposition from a class that had little fervor but was interested in tying up Catholicism with its own destiny, social Catholicism received encouragement from Pope Leo XIII. In *Rerum Novarum*, an encyclical regarded at the time of its appearance as a revolutionary document, the sovereign pontiff gave his essential directives. Then came Catholic Action, which received its official consecration from Pope Pius XI. Completing the instruction of Leo XIII and adapting it to post-war conditions, Pius XI published the encyclical *Quadragesimo Anno*, which attracted world-wide interest.

The upheavals following two world wars led Christians to fruitful reflection on the incarnation of the Church and its historic destiny. This often impassioned quest—which continues today—was reflected in a keen awareness of the apostolic vocation of the Church. The Christian today can rejoice: We know now that evangelization is not merely a simple geographical expansion, subject to the vicissitudes of history. The painful discovery of the neopaganism that has infiltrated so-called Christian cultures has reminded Catholics that there must never be any relaxation in the preaching of the Gospel. Christ's command is ever present. Evangelization does not consist of a simple territorial conquest but of the education of minds and hearts. It requires a continuing effort to develop and maintain Christ's presence in the world.

At the conclusion of this rapid survey a question naturally comes to mind: Will the Church grow or decline? Let us hear from a more authoritative source:

> . . . never perhaps has the action of the popes been felt in such a universal way as during the last fifty years. The Church has not forgotten her essential mission of teaching: "Go and teach all nations." "By the will of God and the

mandate of Christ . . . guardian of the natural and super-natural order" the Church has not failed "to proclaim to her sons and to the whole world, the unchanging basic laws" which should inspire human life (Pius XII, Christmas message, 1942). This desire to make herself heard by a modern world, preoccupied above all with its temporal organization, does not make her lose sight of the fact that the Kingdom of God ought to be proclaimed above all else. Recent history shows that among the faithful, those who have best known how to answer the call of their time are the very ones who showed themselves most anxious to hear the voice of the Vicar of Jesus Christ. The voice of the popes has been heard far beyond the circle of the baptized. Leo XIII opened to the Church a new path for a social teaching in conformity with the Gospels. Pius XI proclaimed his uncompromising refusal to closed nationalisms or the procedures of totalitarian states. Pius XII [urged] all mankind to join the efforts of the Church to liberate the human person threatened in its very being and in the family, which is its normal extension.

After pointing out the condition of the Church in France, Cardinal Suhard added:

In conclusion, who could make us believe, after this . . . enumeration, that the Church is dying? Is one justified in speaking of agony in the presence of this vitality? These great forces which traverse the Church, these undercurrents which uplift it are not signs of death. They portend the sap rising in the vine, the coming of Spring (*Growth or Decline*, pp. 49-50, 58).

Part II

One Lord, One Faith, One Baptism

The Catholic Church is the continuing, permanent, immediate action of God and of Christ in humanity. Conscious of its responsibility, the Church has always jealously safeguarded the unity of its members. Thus, first of all, St. Paul, on several occasions in his Epistles to the Corinthians, Galatians, and Ephesians, defended this unity, according to the command several times expressed by Christ and developed by Him in His discourse after the Last Supper. The principle of unity, clearly defined in the New Testament, has never occasioned any serious disputes in the Church.

On the other hand, the conditions of this unity are closely linked with the history of the Church—a history of painful schisms—and with the Church's internal organization, which has established bonds of varying strength between diverse communities.

1. The Heresies

Focusing on the Church's temporal evolution, the historian has no need to enter into theological speculation about membership in the body or in soul of the Church. From his point of view, which sees only the visible aspects of the Church, it appears that when doctrinal or disciplinary disputes arose, the Church had to define matters of faith in order to insure its own unity, to guarantee its members a unity that went deeper than a simple moral or affective tie, and in order not to betray the divine message of which it is the guardian. The necessity of determining requisites for membership in the Church have led inevitably to divisions. Some of these resulted from doctrinal differences, and these are heresies; others arose from misunderstandings which do not directly concern dogma, and these are schisms. But always the result was a painful rupture.

The limitations and the purpose of this study certainly do not permit the preparation of even a sketchy list of the heresies that have marred the Church's progress. Besides, many of them have merely incidental interest and most often were individual errors on a particular point, without serious bearing on the life of the Church. Every generation has seen small, more or less anarchical groups that develop on the margin of the main community, subsist briefly, then fade into oblivion.

Quite different are what might be called heresies of growth. Here we are dealing not with deviations from the

norm but with permanent problems. And periods of doctrinal agitation—an obvious token of the Church's vitality
—require the sort of surgical operations described below.
Theoretically, we could have doctrinal evolution in peace
and harmony, but to desire such a utopian development
would be to misunderstand the human aspect of the
Church and the passions that necessarily animate its
members.

Thus, heresies, or, in a broader sense, heterodox tendencies, while they have seriously affected the unity of the
Church, constitute, most often, the inevitable counter-
part of doctrinal progress. Punctuating the history of the
Church, they stress the various aspects of religious thought
on which Christians have successively concentrated.

Certain heresies have had a more special bearing on the
practical consequences of Christian doctrine—marriage,
virginity, etc. I shall deal with these later.

Gnosticism and Judeo-Christianity

Basic doctrinal problems had already appeared during
the lifetime of the Apostles. We are not too well informed
about the details of these problems, which are referred to
incidentally in the New Testament and in writings just
subsequent to it; besides, recent discoveries are obliging
scholars to be more prudent in interpretation of familiar
texts.

The two problems that were faced by the Apostles and
their immediate successors concerned the connection to
be kept with the old Jewish religion and the matter of
Gnostic ideas entering into the explanation of Revelation.

The first of these concerns gave rise to the Judeo-
Christian tradition. The Christians could rightfully claim
to be the heirs of the old revealed religion, and the Church
was founded to receive not only the inspired writings—the
Bible—but also certain Jewish customs, without abandon-

ing the spirit of its Founder. The Epistle of St. James, for example, attests an Orthodox Judeo-Christian trend, and many Christian practices have their origin in the usages of the religion of Israel. On the other hand, some Christians contended that they should retain certain rites essential to Judaism, such as circumcision, as well as certain ritual prohibitions. Unconsciously, they were making Christianity a Judaizing sect, a mere reform of the old religion, whereas Christ had expressly declared His desire for a renewal. The Church had to reject these particularist sects, of which certain survivals can be discerned four centuries later. Again, the Church had to deal severely with those who completely rejected the heritage of Israel, including the Bible. The most noted representative of these heretics was Marcion.

As for Gnosticism, this was a very complex way of thinking which impregnated an entire sector of the civilization of the time, especially Jewish intellectual circles. The Church did not reject the support of Gnostic thought a priori, no more than it had indiscriminately refused Jewish customs. Its incarnation in the world required it to accept everything in human thinking that was proper for it. Thus there was a Gnostic orthodoxy that continued on during the first centuries. But it is customary to reserve the term "Gnostic" for those sects which tended to distort the Christian ideal by emphasizing certain themes incompatible with the teachings of the Gospels. For a long time the Church had to struggle against this tendency and to suppress it severely.

Montanus

Gnosticism and Judeo-Christianity were the price of Christian penetration into the pagan and Jewish worlds. As the second century ended, Christians began to reflect upon the consequences of their faith. One of the problems,

latent since the beginning, was how to know whether the
Church instituted by Christ represented the final stage of
Revelation or whether it was necessary to await a more
perfect era, which would produce the outpouring of the
Holy Spirit. The anarchical temptation of a spiritual
Church in which every member claims to be divinely
inspired was to come frequently in the history of the
Church and was to be accompanied each time by exces-
sive strictness and strange, usually debased practices. In
this era the idea of a spiritual Church was propagated by
Montanus and spread rapidly, particularly in Asia and in
Africa, where it captivated Tertullian. The Church managed to check the spread of this error. However, Montanist
communities existed in the Empire until the fifth century.

Arianism

The religious peace that came about with Constantine
brought on a veritable flowering of religious thought.
Christians were no longer satisfied to merely live their
faith, they wanted to illuminate it with all the resources
of their knowledge, profane as well as religious. The
Church was hard pressed to keep this intellectual enthusiasm within the bounds of tradition. It was a delicate job,
because enthusiasm for research inevitably engendered intense passions. Violent controversies, and resounding condemnations were the outcome of this vitality. Far from
denoting decadence, they indicated, on the contrary, the
resources and strength of Christian faith at this time.

For some time, Christians had been concerned about the
problem of the Trinity. Two thousand years of Christianity
have accustomed us to this mystery of a single God in
three Persons. The modern Christian considers this proposition as almost obvious. But long reflection was necessary
for the Church to incorporate this mystery which, today,
fails to arouse any discussion among believers.

The gigantic struggle that developed around this question is known in history as the Arian controversy. Begun at the opening of the fourth century, it did not end until 381, at the Council of Constantinople.

Logically, the equality of the Father and the Son in the Trinity of Persons leads to admitting the divinity of the Son of God and thus of the Word Incarnate. Arius rejected this. If the problem had been put in these terms, it would have been solved easily, since Christians in general were agreed on the divinity of Christ. In fact, total Arianism, utterly contrary to the traditional faith of Christians, was always rejected by the real representatives of the Church. But unfortunately, at its very beginning the controversy set two great minds in opposition, Eusebius of Caesarea and St. Athanasius, Patriarch of Alexandria, both of whom suspected each other of collusion with the heretics. St. Athanasius denounced—and rightly—a certain penchant of Eusebius for the arguments of Arius. And Eusebius could not fail to be alarmed at seeing the friendship of Athanasius for a certain Marcellus of Ancyra, who professed ideas abhorrent to the Church and who had been condemned himself. The fickleness of Eusebius, lover of compromise, together with Athanasius' brutal rejection of compromise and, paradoxically, his loyalty to his friends, provided an opening for intrigues by another Eusebius, Eusebius of Nicomedia, an unscrupulous bishop and a great friend of Arius.

The intervention of the civil power, personal rivalries, the reawakened ill feelings caused by the persecution of Diocletian, enkindled passions and the conflict tore Christendom asunder. The tenacity of Athanasius saved the Church from an irreparable catastrophe, and finally, the greatest disturbance the Bark of Peter had suffered ended with a general reconciliation and restored unity. However, the conversion of the Goths, in the fourth century, by an Arian bishop was to enable this heresy to continue until the sixth century among the barbarian tribes that invaded the Empire of the West.

The Christological Heresies

The Arian crisis was followed (after 381) by a short peaceful period—scarcely thirty years—during which the Greco-Roman Church attained its peak. Then, violent controversies regarding the person of Christ brought on disturbances in the East that were fatal to the magnificent Christian communities there, which broke up into rival sects.

It is true that for some time the Christians had been asking questions about the mystery of the Incarnation. At the same time, however, the question was usually considered with regard to its "economy," that is to say, its effects upon mankind. The Trinitarian discussions centered upon the person of Christ. How are the divine and human natures united in the person of Christ? This was the question Christians asked themselves. At the end of the Arian crisis, the errors of Apollinaris on the nature of the Word Incarnate had been condemned at the same time as Arianism.

But the problem was to come up again some years later, when Nestorius, Patriarch of Constantinople and a great champion of heretics, used some rash statements in his sermons. Whereas orthodox Christian theology regards Christ as God become man, Nestorius—and eventually his supporters—considered Christ as a man become God. The difference was important. While, in the first case, the unity of the persons was formally stated, Nestorius's formula of a divinized man did not necessarily imply this unity. With Nestorius, you could no longer see any essential difference between Christ and any inspired man. It took only a few weeks for the East to break into flame again. Unfortunately, orthodoxy's champion, St. Cyril of Alexandria, had neither the wisdom nor the experience of his predecessor,

Athanasius. While he succeeded in rousing unanimous opposition to the heresy of Nestorius, he tried to do too much and included in the condemnation various personal explanations of his own that were hardly reliable, at least as they were presented. At this, the dispute flared up again. Cyril's successor drew from his statements consequences that were at odds with the Church's teachings and brought on a new heresy, Monophysism, which was condemned by the Council of Chalcedon in 451. Unsettled by these shocks, the Eastern Church broke up. One section remained faithful. But the great majority of Christians in Egypt and in the Churches of Armenia and Abyssinia adhered to Monophysism. Elsewhere, the Christians of Persia rallied to the doctrine of Nestorius. These dissident groups have survived, until our own day. Monophysism lives on in the Coptic Churches of Egypt and Abyssinia and in the Armenian Church; the Nestorian tendency is found in the Persian Church.

Pelagius

The breaking away of the Monophysite and Nestorian sects did not take place without shocks and recantations. Various attempts at conciliation only brought in a new error—Monothelitism, condemned in 680. It may be conceded, however, that the major questions and arguments about the Trinity and about Christ were definitely settled by the Council of Chalcedon in 451.

These discussions, which also went on in the West, produced no serious disturbance there. At this time, at the beginning of the fifth century, another conflict was dividing Western Christians. While St. Augustine, in a condensed summary of the true doctrine, was stressing the eminent place of divine grace in man's advance toward sanctity, a Breton monk, Pelagius—a very virtuous man, as it happens—was insisting on our personal role in salvation and minimizing to the utmost the action of God

and the Redemption. He thereby reduced Christianity to
a kind of moralism—of great value, undoubtedly, but
stripped of religious significance. His teaching, Pelagianism, did not outlive its originator; but for more than a
century north Africa and southern Gaul were to be divided into two tendencies, and ascetic communities gladly
welcomed a sort of mitigated Pelagianism. This influence,
which especially disturbed cultural circles and produced
an abundant literature, never seriously upset the structures
of the Church. However, it obliged the Church to define
its teachings on sanctity and the spiritual life.

The Catharist Heresy

Doctrinal clarifications on faith in the Trinity and in
Christ did not exhaust the contents of Revelation. Many
questions had not yet occasioned any intervention by the
responsible teaching authority, either because Christian
thinking was not sufficiently alerted on them or because
the teaching on those questions had not provoked controversy. The lack of a rich intellectual life during the high
Middle Ages favored a sort of peace, and the revival in
the twelfth and thirteenth centuries did not produce any
serious controversies. There were, it is true, some academic
discussions regarding the real presence in the Eucharist.
These disputes had no consequences among the faithful,
and merely served to define the Eucharistic teaching.

On the other hand, an anarchistic and reform trend
caused great damage. The depravity of the Roman court
and of part of the clergy necessarily resulted in attempts
at reform either independent of the hierarchy or in opposition to it. This agitation crystallized in the Catharist
heresy, a revival of the old Manichean tendency, which
was rampant in a large part of the Church and especially
in the south of France.

Manicheism, like certain diseases, has always existed in

the Church in an endemic stage. Its essential principle, a
perfectly simple one, consists in the absolute opposition of
good and evil. From the good come the mind and the
soul. From evil, personified by Satan and the Demiurge,
come the created world and the flesh. It follows that the
purpose of religion is the utmost possible liberation of the
soul from everything carnal. Whence, the rejection of
marriage and procreation and opposition to any civil or
religious society. This completely spiritual cult led to a
mystical and often hysterical adoration of Mind. In this
respect it could satisfy lunatics of every sort as well as
all social misfits. After exerting dangerous pressure on the
Church—St. Augustine himself, before his conversion, succumbed to the attraction of Mani's teaching—Manicheism
was soon submerged in a number of minor groups. But at
the end of the eleventh century, due to a reaction against
decadent Christian morals and the depravity of part of
the clergy, Manicheism again became virulent and spread
through the south of France with epidemic violence.

The Church opposed it with preaching and persuasion;
the princes, concerned about this revolutionary movement,
employed force. Then came popular uprisings that ended
in massacres. Overwhelmed, and distraught by the death
of several preachers, including the Pope's legate, the
Church accepted the support of the secular arm and organized the Albigensian Crusade. The heretics were fero-
ciously suppressed. In a laudable attempt to moderate this
repression and to give it a juridical status, the Church
created the tribunals of the Inquisition. But, unfortunately, these courts often exceeded the limits of their
mission and were guilty of abuses which gave the Church
a bad name.

Mention must also be made of the nominalist teaching
of William of Occam—about 1340—which was to play an
important part in the unrest that preceded the Reformation.

The Protestant Crisis

The masterly work of the Scholastics consisted of a systematization of existing knowledge rather than original research. New objectives appeared, unfortunately, after the disappearance of the great Scholastic scholars. The sixteenth century possessed neither a St. Thomas, nor a St. Athanasius, nor even a St. Cyril to overcome the difficulty.

In spite of some fundamental differences, the various movements of the Reformers all centered on the doctrine of individual salvation. They were concerned with promoting the idea of justification by faith alone, to the detriment of works, and consequently they rejected the Church's role as dispenser of divine grace. The question was thus posed, somewhat awkwardly, as to the Church's part in the plan of redemption. Until then, in fact, Christians had lived in and through the Church without concerning themselves seriously with thinking about its mystery or defining its significance. The Protestant crisis oriented Christian theology in this direction. While the Church had succeeded in establishing the doctrine of justification, the relation of Scripture and Tradition, and the nature of the sacraments, it left undefined important points which did not seem to be at issue, such as the nature of the Christian community itself. The violence and seriousness of the discussions with the Protestants—they even shook the foundations of the Church by questioning the meaning and nature of the clergy and the hierarchy—led the Fathers of the Council of Trent and the theologians to conclusions that were juridical and authoritarian in form. Their abstract formulas and peremptory decisions obscured the spirituality of the mystery of the Church. Particularly emphasizing the distinction between the Church-that-teaches and the Church-that-is-taught, this tendency led lay people to adopt a passive attitude which was extremely prejudicial to the life of the Church. Likewise, regulations with regard to Bible reading and the liturgy for a long time checked progress in these areas.

The work of the Council of Trent remains great, nevertheless. It saved the Church from ruin. Subsequent events have proved this. While the framework of Christianity was crumbling under the repeated blows of the Reformers, the Council averted the catastrophe and rebuilt the structure. Through it the Church regained its energy and its faith. And even the Protestant Churches are indebted to it for not having succumbed to anarchy.

The Protestant crisis was the last serious disturbance involving questions of doctrine. Jansenism in the seventeenth century and liberalism in the nineteenth century produced momentary tensions which were accompanied by some impressive divisions, but they did not affect the unity of the Church.

The Modernist crisis, at the beginning of the twentieth century, should be mentioned. But can one really apply the word "heresy" to a movement whose teachings actually led to denial of Christ and the divinity of the Church? Its supporters could not create a rival sect but could only leave the Church. Besides, this difficulty was soon overcome, for the turn of events soon rendered the position of the Modernists untenable.

Today, doctrinal development resulting from scientific discoveries, the great intellectual activity of the clergy, political and social upheavals, the militant fervor of the laity, and the apostolic concern of everyone are creating in the Church a tension which may have occasioned severe but necessary cautions and some painful conflicts but which seems, at the moment, beneficial. Christians can hope and pray that as it develops this revival will avoid disaster and will lead to a period of progress comparable to the age of the Fathers and of the Scholastic era.

2. The Schisms

Not all of the divisions in the Church were caused by controversies about doctrine. Conflicts of individuals or of special interests or wounded pride were also factors when there was no disagreement affecting the faith. Schism, the technical name for this attack on unity, thus consists in a break with legitimate hierarchy (especially with the pope) on the part of a portion of the faithful whose faith remains practically identical with that of the Catholic Church.

Even more resistant to historical analysis than heresies, were the many minor schisms that arose from personal issues and which lacked any real connection with the profound life of the Church. From Apollo, responsible (perhaps unintentionally) for a schism in the first community at Corinth, down to the Old Catholics who rebelled against the decision on papal infallibility by the Vatican Council in 1870, there were a great number of men who created schisms, and human passions will continue to produce these divisions until the end of time. Sometimes there was an unexpected solution of a dilemma, as when Pope Pontianus and his rival, Hippolytus, were reconciled in a martyrdom borne courageously by both.

Only one of these schisms resulting from sheer personal animosity had serious consequences. This was in 1378. The disputed election of Pope Urban VI, coming after the residence of the popes in Avignon, set off the Great Schism which, for forty years, severely damaged pontifical power.

74

The other great schism had more complex causes than mere personal rivalry.

The Sequels of Persecution

Thus many schisms sprang from persecution. With the expansion of the Church, there was a notable increase in the number of Christians who apostasized out of weakness or cowardice during persecution. By the middle of the third century this question was important enough to be a serious concern of the bishops. The persecution of Decius, about the year 250, caused one of the first conflicts. St. Cyprian and the Church of Rome, while displaying a proper severity toward the *lapsi* who had faltered during the persecution, recommended clemency. The rigorists formed their ranks around Novatian.

Important in another sense were the two schisms following the persecution of Diocletian. They resulted in a deep split between the African and Egyptian Churches. Here again, rigorists opposed the clemency shown by the legitimate hierarchy. But the schismatic faction was reinforced by those who had originated the disturbance and by last-minute confessors, who were all the more eager to condemn apostates since they themselves had waited for the first signs of religious peace before pledging their tardy allegiance to the faith. Thus the Donatist schism ravaged the Church in Africa for a century. In Egypt the Meletian schism increased tension at the time of the Arian crisis and was, in part, responsible for its expansion.

The Orthodox Church

The history of the separated Eastern Churches deserves a special place, for the causes of the break were very complex. This schism was consummated in 1054 by the patriarch Michael Cerularius, and has been explained according to a well-established tradition as the result of a matter of precedence. In reality, the history of the Eastern Church shows that the separation was the consequence of a chronic misunderstanding between East and West. This conflict was evident from the beginning of the fifth century and never stopped producing more or less lengthy breaks. In all, there were two hundred years of secessions.

Apparently, no doctrinal conflict ever divided these two factions of the Church, both of which ratified the work of the first seven ecumenical councils. However, it must be noted that the task of these councils consisted in solving problems that had arisen among the Eastern Churches, which, one after another, were called to the witness stand to defend themselves. Reconciliations never quite ended the rivalry that had led the West to intervene. The almost complete misunderstanding of Eastern ways often shown by Rome on these occasions could only increase the ill will. This was particularly obvious at the time of the Arian crisis. The West irrevocably alienated the Church of Antioch, at that time the most important of these Greek-rite Churches. To the credit of the pope and the Western bishops, it should be admitted that the doctrinal questions argued by the Greeks were extraordinarily hazy and that it was difficult to discern the truth in this impossible clutter of formulas.

The growing allegiance of the Patriarch of Constantinople to the Byzantine emperor did not improve matters. The Emperor was endlessly meddling in ecclesiastical affairs and, occasionally, playing on the ambitions of the Patriarch. In the West, the instability of civil power (except during the reign of Charlemagne) saved the Church from Caesaro-papism. But this situation led the Patriarchs of Constantinople to work perseveringly to increase the supremacy of their episcopal see. Neither law nor tradition justified such a pretension. Created during the third century, the see of Constantinople could not claim an apos-

tolic origin, as could the great metropolitan sees of Jerusalem, Antioch, and Alexandria. To justify their claim, in
the Middle Ages the patriarchs of Constantinople developed a theory that led to lumping together the ecclesiastical and civil organizations. We can see at once the
danger of a Church tied in this way to the vicissitudes
of the civil power. The primacy of the pope rests on the
pre-eminence of Peter and upon the fact that the Bishop
of Rome is the legitimate successor of Peter, the first head
of the Church. But the Church has avoided tying this
primacy to the physical presence of the pope in the city
of Rome. While Rome can have no other bishop than the
pope, the latter is not obliged actually to reside in this city.

The Orthodox Church later learned through sad experience the consequences of their theory. Broken up into
national autocephalous Churches (practically independent
of each other), it lost all missionary zeal and was at the
mercy of the civil power.

Nonetheless, this conflict of jurisdiction and the interference of political powers would not have sufficed in
themselves to bring on an irrevocable break. Other factors
subtly undermined the unity of the Church. The conduct
and way of life of the two factions of the Church were a
constant source of misunderstanding between Greeks and
Latins. As soon as the trend to conversion reached the cultured classes, the Greeks began to show their disdain for
the Latins, and the doctrinal quarrels of the fourth century
once more demonstrated the Greeks' feelings of superiority. While the Empire lasted, East and West were linked
by a certain community of interests. The passing of the
Church to the barbarians and the decline in the West of
the old culture ended this precarious balance. While the
East was succumbing to Caesaro-papism, the papacy was
daily increasing its influence and was becoming less and
less tolerant of the outbursts of the Byzantine patriarchs.
The year 1054 saw the completion of the break and subse-

quent attempts at reunion proved ineffective. The petti-
ness of the arguments on both sides seems odd. That there
could have been quibbling about the use of unleavened
bread in the Eucharist and about wearing of beards by
ecclesiastics seems really scandalous. However, recent
events, such as the reluctance met in the Catholic Church
at the time of the modification of the Eucharistic fast and
the introduction of evening Mass, show how certain details
that are apparently quite insignificant may express a whole
code of behavior. Because of their symbolic character they
are not to be scorned. Behind these arguments are two
conceptions of the Church, identical on the essentials of
doctrine but too different to permit a complete reunion
immediately.

The Anglican Church

The history of the breaking away of the Anglican
Church shows that the frontiers between schism and
heresy become indistinct when the split affects a large
part of the Church.

Founded at the request of the Holy See itself in the
sixth century, through the mission of St. Augustine, the
first archbishop of Canterbury, the Church of England
was indeed the "daughter" of the Church of Rome. This
relationship showed itself not only in identical doctrine
but also in the liturgy and arts. However, from the thirteenth century, a certain English individualism led to almost constant tension between this kingdom and Rome.
Still, there was nothing to suggest that there was to be a
schism in the future; the problems were no greater than
elsewhere.

An accident, the divorce of Henry VIII in 1537, brought
on the break in relations. Twice before, a similar incident
had led French kings to oppose the pope. However, the
difficulties of Robert the Pious and Philip Augustus had

not had such regrettable consequences. But in this case, as ill luck would have it, the accident coincided with the first stirrings of the Reformation. A short time later, "every Englishman of fifty years had been successively Catholic, Lutheran, Calvinist, and once more Catholic." The Church of England was finally established in 1552. Midway between Catholicism and Protestantism came the Anglican Church, which from then on pursued its way independently. Here again, the mutual ill will and persecutions of "Bloody" Mary, the Catholic, and Elizabeth increased the hostility between Catholics and Anglicans. Since 1850, thanks especially to the Oxford Movement, a considerable rapprochement has been manifested, reflecting a sincere desire on both sides for unity.

*   *

Here then, in its main lines, is the painful story of the divisions the Church has suffered. All Christians are aware of these wounds today, and a movement toward unity is becoming more prominent every year. We should not believe, however, that unity will come suddenly and that soon, as at Antioch in 404, the Bishop of Alexandria will come in a procession to welcome the sheep returning to the fold. Between the official end of the schism and the return of a number of dissenters, more than ten years elapsed. This recollection may help to remind the impatient that unity is to be attained by prayer and by an attempt at understanding, based above all on a deep faith.

When and how will unity be realized? Let us not doubt for an instant that Christ will bring His own together into one body at the right moment if we persevere relentlessly in our effort.

3. The Roman Primacy

The history of the schisms that have torn the Church could almost lead us—if we were less cautious—into an error on the profound significance of the unity Christ wanted. The position of the separated sects and Churches has become established in relation to an unchangeable orthodoxy. The hierarchy's authority has often been manifested in this domain under its coercive aspect. Does the Church conceive of unity only under a strongly centralized government exercising its power in quasi-dictatorial style? The reality is much more complicated. The Church has always protected itself against any doctrinal or disciplinary interpretation that more or less directly threatened its deepest nature. On the other hand, its desire of incarnation leads it to adapt to peoples' aspirations and customs to the extent that they are compatible with its own vocation. There has resuled from this, over the ages, an evolution of the Church's internal organization. While the power of the pope and bishops constitutes an untouchable condition in the life of the Church, this power is exercised under a great diversity of aspects. The authority conferred on Peter and his successors seems to be the most obvious expression of the Church's unity. But the system of the relations of the Holy See and the bishops, distributed throughout the world in the various Christian communities, must, through its flexibility, insure this very bond between the unchanging nature of dogma and the contingency of history.

In the Time of the Fathers

We have little information on the organization of the Church in the first two centuries. However, the occasional texts at the beginning of the second century are enough to show the perfect continuity between the thought of their authors and the teaching contained in the Epistles of St. Paul.

Each local community, each Church as they said in those days, had an organization made up of leaders and the faithful and according to which each was to remain in his place in order to insure harmony. This idea, already strongly expressed by St. Paul in his Epistles—particularly in those that he addressed to the Corinthians—was to be constantly reasserted. Moreover, the leader of the community, who was soon to be given the title of bishop, held his power directly from the Apostles, and the various writings of this period show us the communities' concern about establishing a line of succession between their bishop and one or another of the Apostles. Starting with this outline, the internal organization of the Church was to have no further essential modification. Only certain secondary points were to vary, for example, the extension of episcopal jurisdiction or the administrative organization of dioceses, but throughout the centuries there would never be any question of the nature and origin of episcopal power.

Each local Church, then, felt it was organically united with the universal Church. In the beginning, this bond was naturally maintained by the Apostles themselves. Thus we see St. Paul insuring a permanent and direct jurisdiction over all the Churches he had founded and at the same time maintaining close relations with Peter and the other members of the Apostolic College.

With the disappearance of the Apostles, the Church had to concern itself with its internal organization. The relations which multiplied at the time between the Churches demonstrate the Christian concern for unity. These bonds moreover, were not merely affective and spiritual: they contained the seed of the Church's future organization. Thus, the Church that was at Rome did not hesitate to intervene energetically when there was an internal crisis in the Church at Corinth. But because of the weakness and dispersion of the first communities, these external manifestations of the Church's unity could be only sporadic and tentative. It would be years before there was any reason for frequent exchanges between the communities and longer still before they would need a well-defined juridical and administrative organization. This phenomenon is undoubtedly surprising to the modern Christian, who is used to living in a solidly implanted Church. We should remember, that even in our own time it takes several decades before it is possible to endow a mission territory with normal ecclesiastical jurisdiction. During the long period between the appearance of the first community and the naming of a residential bishop, many problems are settled as they arise. A special organization, the Congregation of Propaganda, has even been created to solve special difficulties in these missionary communities.

At the end of the second century a situation arose between the Churches of Asia and the Churches of the West that demonstrated the development of organic bonds reflecting the predominance of the see of Rome. From this time on, increasingly numerous documents enable us to follow the development of ecclesiastical organization. Rights and customs common to the communities of a particular region justify speaking of a Church of Rome, a Church of Africa, a Church of Egypt, and a Church of Asia. But these convenient expressions do not mean that autonomus communities actually existed, nor could we even speak of a federal type of organization. In fact, all these communities had a keen sense of unity, resulting from a single faith and identical basic organization. Among them, Rome held an eminent place, although it is not possible for us today to indicate precisely the details of its activity because of the empirical character of its intervention. But the principle of this supremacy was unchallenged. An incident that took place at Antioch illustrates this remarkably well. Two bishops were disputing certain ecclesiastical properties in this city and appealed for the emperor to arbitrate. And this pagan recognized as the legitimate bishop the one who declared himself to be in communion with the bishop of Rome.

The Church at Peace

The peace of Constantine enabled the Church to acquire its definitive organization. Various decisions developed previous usages and established conditions for the validity of episcopal ordinations. In spite of their violent doctrinal disputes, all Christians supported the unity of the Church, and the Roman pontiff played a decisive part in safeguarding it. Meanwhile, great councils, arising from the importance of the doctrinal discussions and from various historical circumstances, promulgated decisions indispensable for the progress of the Church on both the doctrinal level and in the domain of discipline.

Apart from the supremacy of the pope, which was more and more clearly illustrated by events, the Church in this period was seeking for practical forms of organization. At first it seemed to be tending toward the establishment of vast patriarchates in which the metropolitan became the head of the Church of an entire region. This was merely a tendency, and no one challenged equality of power among the bishops, who were all successors of the Apostles. One might rather speak of an administrative organization aimed at giving more solidarity among the bishops of the same region. This was never fully realized, however, except in Egypt, where the power of the Bishop of Alexandria maintained centralization. The only results of this attempt—a deplorable effort—was to awaken rivalry among the patriarchs of Constantinople, Alexandria, and Antioch. The first of these claimed precedence and gave himself a very doubtful title. Strongly supported by the imperial power, he reinforced this precedence with more and more prerogatives. But it is noteworthy that, until the ninth century, he never questioned the supremacy of the pope. Only the final years before the schism saw the Patriarch of Constantinople issuing claims contrary to pontifical authority. This patriarchical organization never became general in the Church. This was fortunate, for such organization opened the way to domination by civil power and weakened the apostolic and missionary sense of Christians.

At this time the Church adapted with great flexibility to the conditions it met with in the world. Each community, faithfully bound to tradition, maintained the greatest liberty in expressing its faith. The Fathers liked to recall the universality of the Church, the obvious token of which seemed to them to be precisely this adaptibility to all forms of civilization. Each prayed in his own tongue and according to his traditional customs. But this diversity did not preclude a genuine concern for unity, shown in continual exchanges between the communities and in constant recourse to the universal tradition of the Church. Also, this variety of uses cannot be invoked as a precedent for a quasi-federalist form of the Church. Such an idea was inconceivable at that time. If we recall the violence of the doctrinal or disciplinary crises that shook the Church in those days, we will understand that unity was indeed the principal concern of Christians. The very passion that animated these discussions could not be explained except as arising from the desire of defining a common doctrine for the whole Church. The rival factions expended every effort to obtain the support of their colleagues, by force if necessary. This characteristic is worth noting, particularly with regard to the Bishop of Rome.

The Middle Ages

The territorial reduction of the Church during the Middle Ages had serious consequences for its organization. The political break between East and West, the Mohammedan advance, and finally the schism of the Eastern Churches, made the geographical limits of the Church co-extensive with those of the Latin West. Latin and Western customs then became the dominant if not the exclusive characteristic of the Church's life. Never, it is true, did the Church repudiate the legitimate uses of the Eastern communities, which have continued down to our time with its approbation and encouragement. But most Christians are actually ignorant of the existence of these authentic Catholic communities which kept their ties with Rome, often at the cost of heroic efforts. Theologians themselves easily overlook the existence of these deserving minorities and often consider the Latin Church as the only legitimate heir of the great Catholic tradition. This attitude has left a profound mark upon Latin Catholics, who find difficulty in understanding a unity in which they would not have the advantage of a privileged position.

The schisms of the Eastern Churches, which set themselves up as independent national Churches, stressed the danger of divergent customs when this diversity was not balanced by a keen sense of unity. Justly concerned, the hierarchy subsequently was very reluctant to authorize customs differing from those of the Latin Church—a reluctance which is easily explained by the danger of schism when the desire for adaptation weakens the sense of catholicity.

Rome was the only Western Church of apostolic origin. Beyond its universal primacy it had a much stricter supervisory and administrative right over this part of the Church. Guarantor of faith and tradition, it directed usages and discipline. Various historical circumstances reinforced this hegemony of the pope over the Latin dioceses.

Under the absolute authority of the pope, the Church's unity was reflected even in its discipline. The benefits of this situation appeared at the time of the great depravity of the eleventh century. Thanks to their universally acknowledged power, two energetic popes—St. Gregory VII and Innocent III—succeeded in reforming the Church without any serious incidents and in freeing it from the dominance of the temporal. Pontifical authority did not confine itself to spiritual supremacy, but the claims of the metropolitans who, during the tenth century, attempted a certain decentralization to their advantage, were soon cut short. Henceforth, the pope was to be recognized as the sole and universal head of the Church, and his action could extend to all domains.

Innocent III went too far, perhaps, in asserting his authority. He thought of the world as organized theocratically, and he attempted to apply the formula of St. Bernard according to which "the spiritual sword and the material sword both belong to the Church." Due to a lack of any shades of distinction, this doctrine was to be, subsequently, a source of conflict between the Church and the civil power. On the other hand, the internal reorganization of the Church undertaken by St. Gregory VII and Innocent III had the most fortunate results. They cleaned up the circumstances of episcopal elections and reduced to the utmost the intervention of the civil power in this sort of affair. And finally, they placed the great religious orders under direct obedience to the Holy See. This stroke of genius considerably strengthened the authority of the pope, who henceforth had at his disposal completely reliable executive agents, able to act at once and in the best interests of the Church wherever it needed to make its action felt—in preaching, teaching, missionary activity, etc.

The death of Innocent III marked a decisive turning point. Then at its height, but attacked from without and within, Christendom slowly declined until the day when, due to the pressure of events, the Church succeeded in freeing itself from the myth of this same Christendom. In the course of time, the faithful had come to consider Christendom as the ideal form of the Church, whereas it had merely been a limited expression of it. This dangerous success of the thirteenth century was to weigh heavily upon the future of the Church. The battle strategies of the reforming pontiffs became transformed into principles. A certain confusion became fixed in peoples' minds between the historical reality of Christendom and true Catholicity. A serious consequence was that, thereafter, missionary effort was envisaged as a mere extension of Christendom, and the Church's message was uselessly burdened with contingent customs which were often revealed as obstacles to true evangelization. The Protestant Reformation, by further restricting the territorial limits of Christendom, was to stress this dangerous tendency again. Catholics in countries that had remained traditionally faithful to the Church acquired a superiority complex which, in the long run, was to undermine deep religious convictions and, for many, was to reduce Christianity to a mere façade, useful in preserving a temporal order in decline.

The consequences of these developments mainly affected the faithful, and the danger did not appear until much later. But, besides this, the attitude of the popes of the thirteenth century and the abuses of authority by the successors of Innocent III, who multiplied ecclesiastical sanctions until they rendered them inoperative, brought about a violent reaction of the clergy. A so-called "conciliar" tendency, supported by the princes and encouraged by the decadence of the Roman court, spread among the theologians and bishops. This asserted the pre-eminence over the pope of bishops meeting in a universal council. This theory would have opened the door to an organization of the federal type, in which national churches would have enjoyed a great autonomy. After some difficulty, the pope finally won out in 1449 and the conciliar theory was abandoned. Thereafter nobody challenged the absolute primacy of the Sovereign Pontiff. But the conciliar theory continued under another form until the middle of the nineteenth century. It was then called Gallicanism, for it was in France, in the middle of the seventeenth century, that the most striking examples occurred, thanks to the support of Bossuet. While its purpose was no longer the establishment of a Church of the federal type—an attempt completely abandoned—it sought a broad decentralization to the advantage of national Churches. Certainly, this position was not contrary to the doctrine of unity, but it remained dangerous, nevertheless. Such a decentralization would have enabled governments to take control over the bishops of their nation and thus weaken the unity of the Church. The obvious interest of kings in the Gallican movement shows that this danger was not an illusion. In the meantime, moreover, the Council of Trent was working on the final organization of the Church, as it exists today, and the Gallican tendency was definitely disposed of at the Vatican Council in 1870 with the proclamation of papal infallibility. The pope's primacy and his universal authority, with the possibility of control over the bishops and all ecclesiastical administration, was also restated and defined. Some theologians questioned, not the doctrine, but the timeliness of solemnly defining this doctrine. However, the effects of the council were fortunate. Freed from the bond of Gallicanism, the Church was able to face modern problems with greater independence.

The pope's authority, henceforth unquestioned in law as well as in fact, permitted the Church to search boldly for the solutions needed for the evangelization of the working masses and of peoples on the road to emancipation. The positions taken by Pope Pius XI and by his successor Pius XII with regard to the Churches of Africa and Asia show that, in spite of its thousand-year-old organization, the Church can still present to the world the eternally youthful features of the Lord Jesus.

Part III

Go, Teach All Nations

After having related the vicissitudes of the growing Church, after having explained the limits and methods of its unity, I have now to speak of its essential purpose: teaching. Certainly, the Church has the task of maintaining the continuing presence of Christ on earth, of making us children of God, and ensuring the salvation of all humanity. But it can attain its vocation only through teaching. That is why, from the beginning to our day, answering Christ's express command, the Church has always vigilantly carried out that mission.

The mission of teaching, as Christ wished it should, falls to all Christians and not, as some might think, to the clergy or the hierarchy alone. Through Baptism each of us contracts the obligation of enlightening himself and others to the full extent of his capacity. However, to remain compatible with loyalty to the Church, the teaching duty must be accomplished in an orderly way, each person fulfilling his mission at the level assigned him. Thus, elementary instruction is one thing, and is taken care of by the clergy and their assistants. It is their role to dispense the Church's teaching and to make it penetrate the morality of the city. And no one can escape this obligation.

Study of doctrine presumes more extensive knowledge and a more tested competence. In this sense, the teaching function properly belongs to the Apostles and their successors as the exclusive custodians of Catholic doctrine. Consequently, the task of defining, controlling, and directing this kind of study remains a specific function of the ecclesiastical hierarchy. I will consider here only these two latter aspects of the teaching mission. My first section will give the history of doctrinal studies, the second will recount the history of the supervision of thought by the magisterium.

1. Catholic Thinkers

From the time of Jesus to our day, the stages of the history of Christian thought correspond to the various phases of the growth of the Church, with alternating periods of gloom and glory.

The first period, the patristic era, was the age in the development of Catholic thought that was concerned with discussing and exploring the essential problems of Christianity.

The second period coincided with the medieval Church and was dominated by an immense systematizing effort, culminating in the great Scholastic syntheses.

The third period opened with the Protestant Reformation. It produced fewer great minds. Catholic thought confined itself to the defensive and—we might as well admit it—went to sleep.

Fortunately, this period seems to have ended and for some years has been succeeded by an extremely fruitful research effort.

THE PATRISTIC ERA

The Writings of the Apostles

The Church of the first century received its instruction directly from the Apostles who, thanks to the assistance of the Holy Spirit, fulfilled their roles as teachers with great distinction. Because of this inspiration, their writings, which make up most of the New Testament, have an unquestionable authority, like the other books of the Bible, since they are the source of the Church's teaching, the inexhaustible object of Christians' study and reflection. The Church must keep a careful watch over this sacred deposit. Numerous counterfeiters attempted to attribute to the Apostles writings that often contained fanciful or suspect ideas. The Church, however, soon established the Canon, that is, the official list of inspired books which the Church itself regards as authentic. These books are found collected in the Old and New Testaments.

The Apostolic Fathers

The following generation wrote little. The communities were giving circulation to the letters of Christ's disciples, which were sufficient to maintain the Christians' spiritual life. Nevertheless, the bishops occasionally wrote letters that reflect in their inspiration the proximity of the preaching of St. Paul and St. John. The most noted of these venerable authors are Clement, the third successor of Peter, and Ignatius, Bishop of Antioch.

Two other writings, of anonymous authorship, also have inestimable value because of their age. The works in question are a letter attributed (wrongly) to the Apostle Barnabas and a brief manual of religious instruction, known by the name of the *Didache*.

Does this mean that this was the extent of intellectual life? Undoubtedly not. Undoubtedly, the first communities were made up mainly of poor people, and literate persons were rare. However, the legend of the lack of culture among the early Christians, supported for contrary reasons by both Catholics and their adversaries, must not be accepted without reservation. The pagans ridiculed those Christians who attacked the culture of antiquity, and taunted them for their ignorance. On the other hand, preachers often gloried in this supposed ignorance, which proved, they said, the manifest superiority of Christ's teaching over pagan wisdom. The examples of Paul, John, and Ignatius are the real proof that the Christians of the early centuries were not all ignorant. The cultural level must have varied greatly from one community to another. Thus, quite soon, Alexandria probably had an active Christian intellectual center. But the Gnostic tendency rendered the literature there suspect in the eyes of the Church, which refused to acknowledge it. Consequently, a Christian inspired literature whose importance is difficult to evaluate today was either lost by accident or systematically destroyed.

The Apologists

The teaching of the first century was almost exclusively oral. The critical point was passed about the year 150, at the moment when the Church was important enough to constitute a basic problem for the Roman world. It was then becoming impossible to ignore its existence or to disregard its development, for Christianity was starting to win converts in cultivated circles. The presence of these cultured people, moreover, was to bring a great change in the Church's behavior.

Up to this time, in cities like Alexandria, writings had not gone outside a circle of initiates. But the second-century authors fully displayed Christian teaching. They addressed the pagans directly in defense of their faith, whence the name *apologists* that is applied to them, *apology* meaning in Greek the speech of an accused person in his defense. In fact, their discourses far exceeded mere legal pleas. In the ardor of their youthful faith, answering Christ's request, the apologists turned their pleading into preaching. The apologies were therefore genuine works of instruction that tended to demonstrate the unquestionable

superiority of Christianity over pagan philosophy and religion and, if the question arose, over Judaism.

This literary activity was carried on mainly by laymen.
Justin and Tertullian, the two best-known apologists, were
respectively a philosopher and, probably, a lawyer; neither
ever had any definite ecclesiastical position. This point,
which is often overlooked, allows a better understanding
of the nature and defects of apologetical literature. Because they were involved only as individuals, the apologists benefitted from great freedom of expression, and they
explained to the pagans only certain aspects of their faith—
aspects which, as they saw it, had the most significance. On
the other hand, they frequently used intemperate language
and were not always too precise about doctrine. Perfectly
adapted to their tasks of preaching to the pagans, they
were less fortunate in their theological speculations. They
had less sense of tradition than the bishops. The most
famous apologist, Tertullian, was unable to avoid the
perils of a brilliant, paradoxical mind, and prided himself
on his skill in remonstrating with his teachers in the faith.
After serving as an incomparable defender of the Catholic
faith, at the end of his life he turned toward the Montanist
heresy, and allowed himself to be beguiled by the sect's
austerity and its illuminism, which suited his own character.

The work of St. Irenaeus, Bishop of Lyons, toward the
end of the second century, was quite different. His aim was
not only to explain the Christian faith to the pagans—a
type of preaching which had its limits and deficiencies—
but to strengthen the thinking of the faithful who might be
influenced by the philosophers, and especially to denounce
the Gnostic deviations. More than anyone else, Irenaeus
can be called the Father of Christian theology. He was the
first to attempt a synthesis explaining the true faith, basing
his argument solidly on Scripture and Tradition.

Some years later, about the middle of the third century, St. Cyprian, Bishop of Carthage, completed through his work the doctrinal instruction of Irenaeus. A schism that ravaged the Church at Rome and had repercussions in Africa gave him the opportunity of writing a book, *The Unity of the Catholic Church*, the first theological work on this important question.

Apart from its historical interest, the doctrinal work of the Fathers of the second and third century gave the thought of the Church a lasting orientation. Their writings, especially those of Irenaeus and Cyprian, were long an inspiration for later writers and can still nourish our faith.

Rome and Alexandria

At Rome and Alexandria appeared the first teaching centers maintained by theologians who were concerned with extending the study of Christian doctrine quite apart from any polemical purpose. True, these men did not fail to defend the faith, but this was no longer the principal (if not exclusive) aim of their literary production. Apologetics was giving way to actual instruction. The development of Christian communities in the two cities made possible this important advance in the intellectual life of the Church. Oral catechesis was becoming inadequate, and many educated Christians were demanding more advanced instruction. Thus were born those intellectual centers that dispensed their teaching by word and writing.

On his own responsibility, Justin the Apologist had already founded a school at Rome. A half-century later, St. Hippolytus likewise was to spread his teachings in the city. Unfortunately, his extensive work, partly destroyed, presents difficult problems to the scholars who are trying to establish its authenticity.

Long since, too, the Christian community at Alexandria had proved its cultural worth. Gnostic centers were thriving in the Egyptian metropolis. As early as the beginning of the third century, Clement distinguished himself with a course on religion that marks an epoch in the history of Christian thought. His *Protreptich, The Pedagogue,* and the *Stromates,* through their wealth of doctrine and vast erudition, have won Clement of Alexandria the well-deserved gratitude of theologians.

Origen

Origen is one of the three or four greatest names in Christian literature. With him begins the era of the great theologians who combine a deep faith, burning zeal, intelligence, and culture.

Whereas all his predecessors were converts, Origen was a Christian by birth. He had not received his faith as the result of a clearly defined choice. The Church represented in some sense a normal dimension of his intellectual universe. Contrary to what a superficial mind might suppose, this characteristic firmly establishes faith and strengthens convictions. This point is worth stressing: exactly like Origen, the most famous Fathers of the Church—Irenaeus, Athanasius, Basil, Gregory Nazianzen, Gregory of Nyssa, Augustine, and John Chrysostom—had fervent and militant Christian parents.

After the death of his father, Leonidas, during the persecution of Decius, Origen, in spite of his youth, had to provide for the support of his mother and his young brothers. At eighteen he was noticed by the Bishop of Alexandria, who gave him the responsibility of giving catechetical instruction. From then on, Origen devoted himself entirely to teaching. It is impossible to summarize adequately the immense work of this scholar. Nothing that concerned Christianity was unknown to him. Philosopher, theologian, apologist, catechist, preacher, and exegete, he remains an inexhaustible mine of theological knowledge. Among other works, he produced the first scientific edition of the Bible, which was subsequently used by the entire Greek Church. His writings attest a deep faith, exceptional intelligence, and a surprising erudition. However, this vast mind was not free from error. Some of his ideas, obviously erroneous, were never accepted by the Church. Besides, the general direction of his thought and his exegesis unfortunately invited dangerous, if not heterodox, interpretations. Also, in spite of its affectionate gratitude to this teacher, the Church has not found it possible to include him among the saints. Origen thus suffered the fate of pioneers. His work, which constituted a first attempt at a synthesis of Christian thought, could not possibly be perfect. Many of those who utilized it took pleasure in pointing out the imperfections of its theological structure, too readily forgetting the amount of detachment, faith, and apostolic ardor this enormous work represented. This unfortunate scholar even missed the chance of his own martyrdom. Put in prison, he suffered frightful tortures; but he did not die until a few months later from the brutality he had undergone. His right to the glorious title of witness to the faith has been challenged by some, but, happily, Christ knows how to reward His loyal servants.

An Age of Giants

Origen had opened the way, and the Church at last was going to receive the recompense for three hundred years of persecutions. Her triumph was complete. From the throngs who now joined Catholicism the Spirit brought forth a Pleiad of saints and scholars who were to assure the Church unchallengeable glory. We have no intention of relating here the history of Christian thought in the fourth century. It is necessary to make a selection—always a difficult task—and to retain only the greatest—the ones who, after the Apostles, remain as the pillars and support of the Church.

These men who left their indelible mark on the Church were all—or nearly all—in pastoral positions. They did not seek to create a coherent theological system, still less to write scholarly books, but only to instruct the faithful, to enliven their faith, to develop their generosity. Never did they write out of sheer intellectual pleasure; they answered the needs of Christians and the call of the Church. When they sensed a need for defense of traditional teaching, they did not hesitate to enter the struggle with a savage energy, reckless of obstacles and suffering. And only victory or death put an end to their combats. The passion that bound them to Christ held them fast, revealing their virtues and defects in a glaring light. Endowed with exceptional intelligence and a burning compassion, these bishops brought the Church to its high point. The study of their life and work is never monotonous. Through the majesty and vigor of their faith, their writings suggest the great Gothic cathedrals. The similarity of their flood of achievements conceals treasures on which each has placed his personal imprint and style.

To the Bishop of Alexandria, Athanasius the Great, fell the honor of defending the Church against the attacks of Arianism throughout half a century. This champion of Christian thought carried on the fight with tenacity and intelligence and sometimes found himself alone or almost alone in defending the faith in critical times and maintaining the honor of the successors of the Apostles. Consider his achievements. Bishop of Alexandria, the second city of the empire, when he was not yet thirty years old, he soon encountered the Arians. Exiled five times by the emperors Constantine, Constantius, Julian, and Valens; excommunicated and deposed on various occasions by gatherings of bishops out of loyalty to the emperor; insulted, calumniated, ridiculed, and at last proscribed, with a price on his head, Athanasius still remained at his post. He escaped from his enemies, disappeared into the desert, and took refuge among his friends the monks; but, protected by the people of Alexandria, who revered him, he always returned at the right moment to restore courage and to sow disorder among his enemies. We readily forgive this fighter for a certain lack of finesse and for his rigorous judgments of opportunists. Christ rewarded this hero, whose faith and hope never failed. After fifty years of dramatic adventures, the triumphant Athanasius died in peace, and the grateful Church venerated him as it did the martyrs. This was in 378. Athanasius was the first "confessor" to be given public veneration.

His early adversary, Eusebius of Caesarea, has not been numbered among the saints by the Church. Prudent as the serpent, this great scholar, a disciple of Origen, administered his diocese with perfect moderation. He flattered the emperor without too much obsequiousness, and kept the support of the great men without drawing personal profit from it. As a humanist, he appreciated the arguments of the Arian clan but did not himself succumb to the formal heresy. This peaceable soul did not esteem the unyielding attitude of Athanasius and regarded him as a troublemaker. He had a penchant for compromise, and he sought vainly for a doctrinal formula that would satisfy everyone; and, in the end, it was he who brought discord to the Church. Athanasius was justly severe toward him. In this era, the endangered faith needed fighters, not diplomats; athletes, not aesthetes. But Eusebius—we must give him his due—was a great scholar and a holy bishop. In more peaceful times his glory would have been left unspotted. But he lacked the stature the age required.

At the other end of the Empire, Hilary, Bishop of Poitiers, played the modest role of lieutenant to Athanasius. A gentler spirit but quite as firmly attached to the orthodox faith, he gave himself to maintaining a single doctrine in the West. Eloquent, sentimental, and a bit of a poet, he had to write polemic works. But he also composed theological books of great value and zealously applied himself to various pastoral tasks. Assisted by the great St. Martin, who was a member of his entourage, he strove to raise the spiritual level of his people.

At the same time, in Jerusalem, Cyril left posterity the memory of a zealous bishop, a witness to the traditional faith, and a simple and popular message—the *Catecheses.*

Basil, Bishop of Caesarea in Cappadocia, was, in the fullest sense of the word, a prince of the Church. A talented orator, this son of a family of saints became bishop at a time when Arianism was entering into its critical phase. He had every advantage: sanctity, wide culture, eloquence, knowledge, a shrewd mind. He had an indomitable spirit and commanded the attention of the Emperor Valens, who was afraid to contend with him. His works spread dismay among the heretics. With a keen sense of administration, he reorganized the Church of Asia Minor and put at the head of the bishoprics adjoining his own, trusted friends, men of unquestionable orthodoxy. He gave equal attention to the spiritual and material needs of the faithful. Basil founded hospitals, multiplied charitable works, awakened religious vocations, organized monastic life, watched over the piety of his flock. His universal and indefatigable zeal won him the title of "the Great."

Quite different was his brother Gregory, whom Basil put at the head of the Church of Nyssa. A contemplative and mystic, Gregory administered his little diocese coolly and thoughtfully, and when necessary helped out his brother in doctrinal disputes. But the cumbersome personality of his older brother frightened him a little, and he preferred to exercise his talents in speculative study. His works, which exhibit deep intelligence and a somewhat ingenious

spirit, still have authority in theological circles and are
an inexhaustible source of piety for all Christians.

Gregory, Bishop of Nazianzen, completed the team of
Cappadocians. His talent was the gift of speech. An orator
and poet, he was brought into the struggle in self-defense,
by his friend Basil. Afraid of incurring Basil's wrath, Gregory bowed to his wishes. Then the spirit of solitude seized
him again, and he withdrew from the fight to write his discourses and some poems. Successively, he was Bishop of
Sasimes, Nazianzen, and Constantinople. In fact, though,
he never set foot in his first diocese, concerned himself
little with the second, and resigned the see of Constantinople after a few weeks, disgusted with the rivalries that
had made antagonists of his colleagues gathered in council.
In language of great purity, his works explain in simple
terms the traditional teaching of the Church. His thought,
lacking the subtle depths of that of his friend Gregory of
Nyssa, more peaceful than that of Athanasius or Basil, was
authoritative in the early Church, whence he was called
"the Theologian."

In Milan, Ambrose was reigning. "Reigning" is the right
word, for this one-time imperial prefect who had been
called to the episcopacy by the voice of the people while
he was still a catechumen, retained in his priesthood the
strictness and the sense of duty of a high Roman official.
The former government official was able to make the imperial power respect the Church's independence. But this
great administrator was also a pastor attentive to the
proper progress of his flock. At his death, he left a large
number of books, carefully composed for the evangelization of the faithful and for the advancement of their religious culture. Ambrose, who took no pride in originality,
drew heavily upon his predecessors. With a lucid and
somewhat juridical mind, he displayed a sure judgment
in the sources he used, and his writings expound a solid

doctrine. The writings of Ambrose, who was Augustine's guide on the road to Baptism, have always been in favor with the clergy because of their seriousness and clarity.

Jerome, the *enfant terrible* of the Church, was something else again. Unusual in everything, he was not a bishop, but merely a monk. This scholar had not the encyclopedic intelligence of an Origen or Augustine, but he had a taste for accuracy and a love of truth. He worked patiently at his Latin translation of the Bible, and in our own day his text is still the official version of the Catholic Church. He also wrote excellent commentaries on some of the books of Holy Scripture. But Jerome did not stop here. A caustic and irascible man, violent and a little arrogant, he had a genius for satire, and as he had a remarkably lively pen, he excelled in the art of the pamphlet. He fought all his life long, making himself enemies when circumstances failed to provide them. He irritated practically all his contemporaries, and his judgments do not err on the side of objectivity. Nevertheless, his austere faith and the eminent services he rendered the Church brought him forgiveness for his slips of speech and his maliciousness.

This age of giants that began with Athanasius was to end with Augustine in Africa and John Chrysostom in Asia.

The stature of Augustine challenges description. Posterity has always been fascinated by the image of this flighty young rhetorician who was converted to Christianity after a painful quest, dismissed his concubine, bound himself to Christ with all the strength of his heart, and became in thirty years of priesthood and episcopacy the unchallenged master of Christian thought. His colossal output—a new edition now underway will comprise more than eighty volumes—extends to every domain of Christian thought. While he was, perhaps, less learned than Origen, the precision of his thought and his innate sense of tradition gave his teaching as a whole a coherence and a veracity that were never at fault in essentials. Regardless of the subject of his interest, the Christian scholar is inevitably led to study the works of Augustine, whose presence has invaded the teaching and life of the Latin Church. For sixteen centuries, philosophers, theologians, exegetes, and religious have turned to him. His death, in 430, a few days before the capture of Hippo by the barbarians, is symbolic. The old Church had fulfilled its mission. Its treasures of culture and faith were condensed and stored away in the works of the old dying bishop. The barbarians could come now; the Church would continue.

At the other end of the Empire, John Chrysostom—Augustine's twin, we might say, for they were probably born the same year—was to complete the message of the Bishop of Hippo and bring a new dimension to the thought of the Fathers. Indeed, the works of the Fathers reveal the special gift of each of them: philosopher, theologian, polemicist, orator—Augustine was all of these, and he was the "ecclesiastical man" par excellence. John Chrysostom was the prophet, the man who disturbs our peace and makes us hear clearly the voice of God. His ministry was not notable for any important event. He refuted no heresies, made no journeys; he was neither theologian nor philosopher in the technical sense of the word. He did not strive to find faith, for from a very pious mother he had an unshakable trust in Providence. Of a contemplative turn of mind, John spent long years in prayer and contemplation and was always the pastor who brings the good word to his flock. Over a thousand homelies commemorate this teaching distilled from day to day. His story would have been monotonous if he had been satisfied with presenting a neatly compounded and balanced instruction. But indifferent to the things of this world, John was the man of God who dreams of getting from Christians the literal application of the Gospel ideal.

This prophet, a worthy successor of John the Baptist, had talent. His preaching, for all its apparent simplicity, reached men in the depth of their hearts and forced them to reflect.

As long as he was only a preacher, all went smoothly, for no one was obliged to follow him. But one day the emperor arranged to have him given charge of the imperial church. This was a catastrophe. John inscribed his name in letters of fire on the see of Constantinople. A holy prophet could not be put at the head of the most important diocese of the Empire without consequences. John applied his teaching literally and devoted all his efforts to reforming the Church. In less than two years the herald of God became undesirable at court, where he reviled luxury and demanded of the clergy an exemplary and unselfish life. Excommunicated and deposed by the colleagues whom he had recalled to a more proper notion of their duties, condemned by the emperor, Chrysostom was deported. He died of exhaustion on the way, in a ditch, between two soldiers. He was not sixty years old, and through his martyrdom he ensured the triumph of the Catholic ideal over all material powers.

These were the men who developed and drafted the Church's theology. Their sublime faith and powerful intelligence guarantee the worth of their teaching, and the Church has officially sanctioned it by giving a special value to their opinion, regarded as the authentic expression of Catholic Tradition. The Church was never again to have, at the same time, such a large number of eminent saints.

Two more great bishops are glories of the Eastern Church: St. Cyril, Patriarch of Alexandria, and Theodoret, Bishop of Cyrus. Like Athanasius, his predecessor, Cyril made himself a great defender of orthodoxy. Unfortunately, things that were mere shadows in the case of Athanasius became dangerous defects in his successor.

In lieu of perfectly clear theological thinking, Cyril possessed the art of composing striking formulas. He overwhelmed his colleagues with these to the extent of com-
promising the orthodoxy of his teaching. Moreover, while
his private life was irreproachable, his rigid authoritarian-
ism led him to adopt procedures which did not fit in with
the Gospel ideal. While aware of his rather conspicuous
deficiencies, the Church showed her gratitude to him for
having been a valiant defender of orthodoxy.

Posterity was more unjust toward Theodoret of Cyrus.
Humility and detachment have never been a success formula among men, even in the case of ecclesiastics. Promoted to the head of a small diocese, Theodoret zealously
devoted himself to his flock and refused the honors his
talent brought, so that he could go on working with the
poor. He was a friend of Nestorius and did not believe
that a theological quarrel was sufficient ground for breaking the bonds of friendship. His conciliatory spirit led him
to work for reconciliation of the rival groups. He had reason to regret this, for he made enemies of everyone. In
spite of the assurance of Pope St. Leo, he always continued to be suspect of heresy. Another handicap was that
he was too modest. He admitted quite simply that in his
writings he had made use of earlier works. And people
took him at his word, forgetting his vast culture and his
extraordinary erudition. Unknown by his contemporaries,
this interesting personality is still neglected by many, and
this is a pity.

In the same period, St. Leo, a pope, was another representative of Christian thinking. Except for Clement, at
the beginning of the Christian era, he was the first pope
to figure among the shapers of Christian thought. While
some of his predecessors were remarkable pontiffs, and
influenced the history of the Church, none of them had
the gift of speculative thought. From one point of view,
this was better, for it made it easier for them to perform

their role as arbiters in the great movement of doctrinal expansion. The work of St. Leo fits into this perspective. The long pontificate of this administrator saw a practical strengthening of pontifical authority and illustrated the doctrinal foundations of this prerogative.

His work was splendidly completed, a half-century later, by his successor Gregory the Great, likewise a great administrator and a great theologian, who was a happy combination of the apostle and the man of politics. He was the last representative of the patristic era in the West.

The sap was to dry up less quickly in the East, but the intellectual vigor of the fourth-century masters would be gone.

THE MIDDLE AGES

The barbarian invasion and the breaking up of the Eastern Church did not extinguish all doctrinal effort, but the Church was living on its capital.

The East found itself turning out "selected works" and *catenae*, or "chains," a type of work in which Scripture verses are followed by a series of maxims taken from the Fathers of the Church, without any logical connection. In the West, patristic texts were transmitted haphazardly in anthologies. From time to time, however, a more cultivated mind made a mark and ensured continuity between the Fathers and the thirteenth-century awakening. The best known of these worthy intermediaries are St. Isidore of Seville in the West and St. John Damascene in the East.

The Carolingian Renaissance

An attempt at an intellectual revival took place under Charlemagne. But political and social circumstances ultimately hampered this movement, which was particularly promising in its beginning and in which Paschasius Radbert, Hrabanus Maurus, Archbishop Hincmar of Rheims, and especially Duns Scotus Erigena won distinction. This attempt at renewal was completely obliterated during the terrible "iron age," which brought on a recession in all the intellectual disciplines. All was not lost, however; monastic or episcopal schools existed which were preparing for the coming of a new Christian civilization. Two very different men marked the revival at the beginning of the eleventh century: St. Anselm and St. Bernard.

Anselm

St. Anselm was the man of the future. In many ways, undoubtedly, he pursued an earlier tradition and especially the Benedictine tradition, the pristine purity of which he attempted to recover. At the Abbey of Bec in Normandy, of which he was prior, and later at the Archbishopric of Canterbury, he also appeared as the great defender of the papacy. But the speculative character of his work was a presage of the great masters of the thirteenth century.

Bernard

St. Bernard, on the contrary, in his character, his range of activity, and his way of thinking, was in the line of the Fathers of the fourth century. He overwhelmed the twelfth century with his powerful personality. Ecclesiastical reform, moral reform, monastic reform, intellectual reform—he had a role in all of these. Burning with love of God, Bernard drove himself from one end of Europe to the other. He founded abbeys by the hundred, preached the Crusade here, stopped there to refute a heretic, awakened the enthusiasm and admiration of crowds of people, and spread the word of God in season and out. To recount his life would be to tell the entire history of the twelfth

century. Rarely has a man been able to make such a mark
on his age. Counsellor of kings and emperors, reformer of
the Church, Bernard was the artisan of the advance of
Christendom. But he always remained a humble Cistercian monk, ambitious only to dwell in the love of Christ
and His Mother. The work resembles its author. A remarkable theologian, Bernard triumphed over Abelard
and energetically defended the Roman primacy. But he
was above all a man of the spirit and the theologian of the
love of God and of charity.

The intellectual vitality of the Church was again being
manifested in all domains. Due to the drive of its bishops,
Fulbert and Yves, the episcopal school of Chartres became
justly famous. Rheims, Laon, Paris, Auxerres, Bourges,
Canterbury, Toledo, Bologna, Montpellier, Salerno—all
became important centers, not only for the teaching of
theology but also of medicine and law. But the most celebrated school of theology was that of St. Victor at Paris,
where, under the successive direction of Hugh, Richard,
Walter, and Godfrey, teaching inspired by Augustinian
doctrine was dispensed for a century.

Nevertheless, the man who was to exert the greatest influence on the theological revival did not belong to St.
Victor's. Peter Lombard taught theology at the School of
Notre Dame of Paris from 1135 to 1150. The Master of
the Sentences, as he was called, did not attempt to innovate. He simply aimed at giving a systematic, complete,
and reasoned account of the principal Christian truths.
Concerned with fidelity to Tradition, he held preferably
to the opinions of St. Augustine. Thus understood, his work
constituted a remarkable tool, for it brought together in
a logical grouping ideas scattered through the works of
the Fathers of the Church. For an entire century the theology teachers were going to dispense their teachings in
the form of commentaries on the writings of the Master
of the Sentences.

The clerics of the twelfth century likewise showed an interest in juridical problems. From the beginning, in order to protect its operation, the Church had to decree rules of law. Many were the councils that thus promulgated laws. But these interventions were always episodic, and for a millenium the Church was ruled by a law of usage. Collections of texts began to circulate as early as the ninth century. But it was necessary to wait until the eleventh century to find the first attempt at a system of canon law, one edited by Burchard, Bishop of Worms. His work was resumed by Yves, Bishop of Chartres, but the master work was produced by Gratian, a law professor at the University of Bologna, whose *Decretals*, edited about 1140, was long to remain the canonical charter of the Church. Though without any official character, this work was the basis of the teaching of law. To an increasing extent, it was required of future bishops that they be doctors *in utriusque juris*, in Roman law and canon law, thus giving the administrator an advantage over the pastor.

The Scholastics of the Thirteenth Century

The intellectual advance that began about the beginning of the eleventh century reached its height in the thirteenth. New events influenced the intellectual progress of the Church and at the same time upset teaching methods. More frequent relations with the Arab world and the creation of the Latin Empire of the East introduced into Europe an important Greek and Arab literature. Also, inspired by the social movement that was stirring the West at this time, students organized into corporations and thus gave birth to the great medieval universities, with the University of Paris becoming the leader. Finally, the need for moral and religious reform created new religious orders, which soon took up scholarship and strengthened the role of the popes, who encouraged the universities and brought into them religious who were immediately dependent upon papal authority. All these circumstances transformed the character of teaching itself. The importance of this fact has not always been sufficiently stressed.

Doctrinal research became the prerogative of technicians, of theologians, and generally got out of the hands of the bishops, who preferred to confine themselves to the administration of their dioceses. This is a simple matter of fact, and there was no rule that sanctioned this development. On the contrary, the bishop remains by law the dispenser of doctrine, and the theologian exercises his ministry only through delegation from the bishop or the pope. However, the establishment of authoritative, autonomous teaching and the preference given jurists in admission to the episcopacy led bishops to regard themselves as guardians of faith and not as inspirers of doctrine. Contrary to what took place in the fourth century, scholars were only rarely invested with episcopal power.

The teaching in the universities was that of the schools, that is, theological and abstract. It thus had advantages of clarity and precision, but was farther from reality and life. In the time of the Fathers doctrine was given to the people directly, and during the great controversies ordinary Christians were deeply interested in the theological arguments even though they did not always understand their implications. From the thirteenth century on, the university set up a screen between the teachers and the people. The professors used a technical jargon which soon dissociated itself from theology. For several centuries speculative research was distinct from the pastoral function and the people no longer took part in doctrinal discussions. The importance of this situation has not yet been fully shown. We might see in this one of the remote causes of the lowering of standards for many Christians, who got into the habit of reducing Catholicism to the practice of a certain number of rites and passively accepting the teaching of their clergy.

At the same time, Scholastic teaching, considered in itself, was a decisive step in the intellectual life of the Church. The Fathers of the fourth century had built up Christian thought, but, taken up with their pastoral tasks, they had presented the conclusions of their thinking without any established plan and without indicating the main lines. Their thought had been carried down for five hundred years more or less successfully. The intellectual patrimony of the Church was disintegrating, and it was necessary to infuse some new blood. This was the work of the Scholastics—of two great ones particularly: St. Bonaventure and St. Thomas Aquinas. Brethern and rivals, like their two teachers, Francis and Dominic, they remain united in the same glory, after earthly lives that were notably similar.

Bonaventure was born in Italy in 1221. A Franciscan from about 1243, he became a teacher in 1253 after completing a commentary on the *Book of Sentences* of Peter Lombard. He taught in his order, but the opposition of the seculars did not permit him to become a teacher in the University of Paris until 1257, upon an order from the pope, as was the case with his colleague, Thomas. As minister-general of the Franciscans, he took an active part in the Council of Lyons in 1274, in the course of which he died on July 14.

Thomas Aquinas was also born in Italy, in 1225, and entered the Dominicans about 1245. After completing his commentary on the *Book of Sentences* he became a teacher in 1255. The opposition of the seculars likewise banned him from teaching at the University of Paris until 1257. He taught there until 1259, then left Paris for ten years, spent himself teaching in Italy, and finally, in 1268, resumed his courses at the University. In 1272 he founded a new school at Naples, and then set out for the Council of

Lyons. He died on his way there, on March 7, four months before St. Bonaventure.

People have often contrasted the two teachers. But this contrast did not prevent the two scholars from coming together in their deep faith and knowledge, based on the Scriptures and the Fathers and renovated in profound reflection on the philosophy of Aristotle. Less drawn to philosophic research, St. Bonaventure did not produce a perfectly co-ordinated work, for he took on with his teaching the weighty charge of the general direction of the Franciscan order. However, the Seraphic Doctor played an important role in the evolution of Christian thought, if only in being the first to define the proper work of the theologian as a systematic elaboration of faith.

The work of St. Thomas, in its breadth and importance, is related to that of Origen, St. Augustine, and John Chrysostom. He possessed the charism of teaching in the highest degree. Endowed with a prodigious memory and an extraordinary capacity for work, he also had the two supreme qualities of the teacher—lucidity and a sense of synthesis. He composed, besides about a hundred miscellaneous works, the *Summa Theologica*, which remains one of the most amazing productions of the human mind. His rather severe rationalism has sometimes been opposed to the method used by the Fathers. But this opposition should not be pushed too far. It applies to method rather than to content. Certainly, St. Thomas had the philosophical mind and was able to draw from his knowledge of the Greek philosopher Aristotle a means of renewing religious thought. But St. Thomas is above all a deeply religious, deeply Catholic soul. He founded his teaching on Scripture and on the tradition of the Fathers of the Church, especially the works of St. Augustine. St. Thomas wanted to pursue the work of his predecessors and to carry it on in the light of the intellectual revival of his age. His personal genius enabled him to produce a synthesis which, in its perfection, remains the necessary point of reference for all Catholic thinkers.

Still, if we omit St. Bonaventure and St. Thomas, the Scholastic period did not have the brilliance of the fourth century. The form of instruction, with its rigid outlines, was not adapted to the wealth and variety of expression which give the first intellectual expansion of Christianity its charm and brilliancy. The severity of Thomist doctrine could not win the support of the masses. The value of this synthesis lies in its inner power, which enabled it to impregnate Catholic thinking gradually, without ever introducing such emotional elements as the works of an Origen, Augustine, or Chrysostom. The importance given to logical and reasoned organization of doctrine, together with the strictness peculiar to the technique of the schools, limited its appeal.

This expression of Christian thought also contained the germ of a disease that was soon to infect the rivalry between the religious orders. Between St. Bonaventure and St. Thomas there was competition rather than a real contrast. But subsequently, in a battle for prestige, Franciscans and Dominicans dug in for a defense of the doctrine of their respective teachers, and what should have become a flood of fresh intellectual activity soon dwindled away in stale, repetitive, formal discussion.

But it would be unjust not to mention a few thinkers who, with St. Bonaventure and St. Thomas, contributed to the grandeur of this period. Robert Grosseteste, who died in 1253, won fame for the University of Oxford and distinguished himself as an excellent translator of the Greek Fathers. St. Albert the Great taught at Cologne and was the teacher of St. Thomas. Siger de Brabant played an important historic role in the development of Scholastic thought. And finally, Roger Bacon, a pioneering genius condemned to isolation because of the originality of his scientific and philosophical conceptions, left a work whose importance was only to be revealed later.

The fourteenth century, compared with the preceding era, is often regarded as a period of decadence. The complex evolution of historical facts makes it difficult to justify such a comparison. While it is true that theoretical thought was in decline, there were still great minds, such as the Franciscan Duns Scotus, whose teaching, which was heavily criticized, was inspired by the most authentic Catholic tradition.

The influence of the German masters, Tauler and Eckhart, was important in the domain of mystical thought. The thinking of the Franciscan, William of Occam, also played a considerable role in pre-Reformation times.

MODERN TIMES

Decadence of Scholasticism

The disturbances that marked the beginning of modern times should not have caught the Church unprepared. In themselves, the discovery of new lands, the Renaissance, the discovery of printing, political and social evolution could not hurt the development of Catholicism. In fact, the Church showed itself receptive to the new spirit and in the beginning contributed to the development of the modern world. Missionary zeal accorded very well with the adventurous spirit of the explorers, and religious were not the last to plow the seas. The invention of printing brought an unexpected means of reaching souls, and religious publications increased considerably. Moreover, almost all printers were anxious to begin their work by first issuing the Scriptures or Books of Hours. Most of the great humanists turned eagerly to Catholic literature and published with extreme critical care the texts of the fourth-century Fathers. So the misfortunes of the Church which were to result in the Protestant crisis could have been avoided. They came from internal causes rather than from a lack of adaptation to the new ideas.

The Church was not lacking in fine men and superior minds. For more than two centuries learned scholars were to make an inestimable contribution to Christian thought, while the spiritual life would have its period of glory with the great mystical authors. Nonetheless, this scientific and spiritual expansion would not compensate for the doctrinal sterility of Christianity in this era.

There were many good theologians, such as Cajetan, John of St. Thomas, and Suarez, but their thinking was stifled by the Scholastic limitations, which destroyed all their creative drive. A St. Augustine or a St. Bernard was needed to give the necessary stimulus to the theologians. St. Thomas had been able to make use of the rediscovery of the work of the Greek philosopher Aristotle in producing his marvelous synthesis of Christian thought. One can imagine what he would have done with the riches unearthed by the Renaissance. Unfortunately, the pontifical court was dozing in the delights of a profane Renaissance, and the theologians were neglecting the treasures of the Fathers of the Church, for the least of which a St. Thomas would have gladly exchanged all Paris.

Far from being a goad, the Protestant crisis hampered Catholic intellectuals, and for several centuries the great fear of the innovators led everyone to retreat into a debilitating apologetics that employed old arguments lacking in conviction. The juridical framework of doctrinal presentations impeded all fruitful research.

On the other hand, the Catholic humanists were able to bring together their thirst for culture and their profound faith in the scientific study of Christian origins. Their capacity for work still amazes modern scholars. One after another, the works of the Fathers of the Church were exhumed from the dust of the libraries and put out in editions many of which are still authoritative. This lengthy enterprise—it continued for almost two centuries—was carried on in the centers of the Port Royal movement and the famous Benedictine Abbey of St. Maur. The Belgian Jesuit Bollandus undertook the gigantic task of a critical history of all the saints. Le Nain de Tillemont, one of the "Gentlemen" of Port Royal, published his *Memoirs for the Ecclesiastical History of the First Six Centuries.* Thus Christian scholars were quietly piling up treasures of erudition which, unfortunately, their contemporaries were unable to make use of. One had to await the twentieth century to appreciate the real value of this work and to draw from it the documents needed for a basic return to the authentic tradition of Christian thought.

Preaching Becomes a Form of Literature

The decadence of Scholasticism represented the end of an epoch, but not the ruin of thought. The sixteenth century saw the development of the preaching that made the following century the age of eloquence. Then the sermon became a genuine element of civilization, and it would have been possible to hope for a renewal of thought in a pastoral form, as in the fourth century, if the preachers had not been slaves to worldly literary conventions.

The struggle with Protestantism in the sixteenth century eliminated the trivial, the pedantic, and the affected from preaching. A St. Francis de Sales or a Father Bourgoing knew how to speak with an eloquence that was sturdy and homely but still dignified in its simplicity.

Some years later, preaching had become a type of literature and was exemplified by Bossuet, Bourdeloue, Fléchier, and Massillon. It must be admitted that these great orators were inspired by a deep faith, and they never abdicated their pastoral duties to yield to the art of pleasing. But they subjected their ministry to rules of taste that remarkably weakened its effect. This was the case with

Bossuet, the greatest of them all. Some have chosen to see him as closely related to the fourth century Fathers if not their equal. He was at best a remote inheritor. Decent and virtuous, the Eagle of Meaux, whose faith had been nourished on the thought of the Fathers of the Church, always retained a high conception of his priesthood. Never a court bishop in the pejorative sense of the term, he possessed that balanced sort of thinking and urbanity of expression that disciplined his ardor and veiled to some extent the strength of his convictions. A great bishop—the greatest of his age—he acquired a just reputation in the history of French literature and deserves commendation for his righteous life. While he had the gift of eloquence, he lacked that of prophecy. His work, in spite of its magnitude, has left no appreciable trace on the development of Christian thought.

The Dull Century

Would, though, that the Church had had nothing but Bossuets in the eighteenth and nineteenth centuries! With the conclusion of the eighteenth century the Church seemed to have lost all its intellectual vigor and entered an era of incurable decline. Until then the Church had been distinguished in one domain or another, and even in the darkest years of the Middle Ages clerics, in spite of their meager education, were learned men in comparison with the ignorance of their contemporaries. On the other hand, from 1750 to 1850 there is nothing to justify the extreme poverty of Christian thought, and nothing to explain it except the universal mediocrity of the clergy and of Catholic leaders, all of them more concerned with defending temporal privileges than in maintaining the Church's spiritual patrimony intact.

It would be useless to look for a name worth remembering in this immense wasteland in which Christian thought was mired. In France, at the beginning of the nineteenth century, the intellectual baggage of every churchman included two elementary manuals, Lyon's *Philosophy* and Bailly's *Compendium of Theology*. It is in this context we must consider the eloquence of Lacordaire and we will understand how he was able to command the attention of his contemporaries. He had courage and a certain talent. But what can we say of his imitators, all of whom believed they were heirs of Bossuet! To offset this riot of "illustrious" preachers who flooded the nineteenth century with their verbiage, Providence raised up a humble priest, St. John Vianney, the Curé of Ars, who gave the Christian elite a severe but sound lesson. This poor priest, lacking all the intellectual qualities of which the stars of the pulpit availed themselves, worked relentlessly and kept a keen sense of his responsibility as a priest charged with teaching. Intense faith combined with constant effort easily made up for his intellectual difficulties and assured him a well-deserved success with throngs eager to hear the word of God.

A New Spring

Newman in England and Möhler and Döllinger in Germany were the initiators of the brilliant intellectual restoration of the Catholics during the second half of the nineteenth century. The French, hampered by political squabbles and the last gasps of Gallicanism, were longer in returning to the tradition of the medieval University of Paris. Only an eccentric, Abbé Migne, in 1849, amid general indifference, undertook and successfully completed the colossal work of re-editing the texts of the Fathers of the Church. Not until Renan's *Life of Jesus*, in 1863, was there a worthwhile reaction. Then France quickly resumed a more than simply honorable rank in the Catholic intellectual renaissance.

At the beginning of the present century, Monsignor Mercier, at Louvain, in philosophy, Monsignor Duchesne, Abbé Hefele, and Dr. Pastor in history, and Father Lagrange in exegesis enabled Christian thought to resume its place in the intellectual and scientific world.

The condemnation of Modernism brought a halt, regrettable but necessary, in this movement. Among many other factors, the principal cause of this Modernist crisis was certainly the intellectual mediocrity of the clergy. There was too violent a contrast between the scientific effervescence of the new generation and the rigid and often ignorant dogmatism of the old. Thus Modernism was found almost exclusively in cultured milieux and was especially rife in France and Italy, where the intellectual awakening had been longest delayed. In Germany and England, the movement attracted only a few individuals. Personal questions and malicious suspicions, inspired and sustained by an "integrist" group, embittered the conflict and resulted in regrettable obduracy, both among the Modernists and in the hierarchy. But condemnation was imperative. The Modernist attacks, which were justified when they were directed against prior defects of instruction, soon went beyond this objective and, rejecting the pontifical magisterium, tended to deny the Church any right to control its own doctrine. As the intellectual revival became more general, Modernism quickly lost its virulence and soon had the character of an outmoded movement. Instruction of high scientific quality checked the evil at its roots and provided the best reply to the Modernists.

At present in the midst of expansion, Catholic thought is making a new effort to create a synthesis between modern attainments and Christian culture. While it is not possible to foresee the results of this attempt, serious hopes are warranted since, with few exceptions, study is being carried on with constant reference to the authentic

tradition of the Church. The impassioned debates, often
interrupted by calls to order, are in no way sensational
but are evidence of splendid vitality. Evil lies in loss of
unity, not in research, which in its striving for results
leads, more or less inevitably, to numerous dead ends. It is
the right of the magisterium to point out these dangers.

Two aspects of the present flowering of Christian
thought should be stressed: the birth of a Catholic social
doctrine and the importance given by the bishops to their
pastoral teaching role.

The Church has never been disinterested in the social
problem and it is easy to pick out "prophetic" texts from
the fourth-century Fathers. Inasmuch as justice and charity and the absolute equality of all men are inscribed in
the heart of the Gospel teaching, the Church's doctrine
has always defended the poor against the rich, the weak
against the strong, and has attacked all egotism in order
to promote a perfect community among mankind. However, the Fathers of the Church obviously could not take
a stand with relevance to a specific historical problem,
namely the social question born of the Industrial Revolution. The Church has to adjust to this new dimension of
the modern world while drawing from its tradition the
principles of a solution compatible with its mission.

Social Catholicism was born in France about 1830. The
pioneers of the movement—Buchez, Ozanam, Albert de
Mun, Abbé Maret—had to carry on a long and difficult
struggle against the interests and prejudices of a majority
of the clergy and the Catholic laity. The episcopacy's
support of the Second Empire cut short the first promising
efforts and gave social Catholicism a conservative, paternalistic orientation from which it has not yet completely
freed itself. The high authority of Pope Leo XIII was
needed to permit Léon Harmel to try to release the movement from this impasse. In addition, Leo XIII published
in 1891 the encyclical *Rerum Novarum*, a genuine revolu-

tionary document, both in its positions on the social problem and in the introduction of social Catholicism into the official teaching of the Church. Since that date the social question represents an important department of Church doctrine, and all the pontiffs who have since occupied the throne of Peter have carefully supervised its development.

For a century, moreover, the data of the problem have altered considerably. At first the principal objective was to win respect for a certain social justice in defining and defending the dignity of the worker. Subsequently, the development of a genuine theology of work made necessary a new study of property rights and a doctrinal evaluation of various economic theories. In a homogeneous working class, impelled by a special mystique, the Catholic labor movement and various movements of Christian inspiration developed. The last war brought out clearly the problem of evangelizing the working world. But is this only a problem of the working world? The breadth of the movement and the reactions to it seem to show that the Church today is facing a major challenge—its integration in an industrial and atomic civilization in the course of expansion.

The bishops' teaching role was never completely neglected, but since the Middle Ages bishops have preferred administrative duties, leaving to theologians of all complexions the initiative of research. Modern means of communication have given a new importance to the teaching role of the pope and the bishops. Now they can easily and quickly address the entire Christian world. The rapid course of events forced the popes themselves to take the initiative in doctrinal progress and the intellectual orientation of the Church.

Also, since Leo XIII, the popes have developed the happy practice of addressing the whole Church by means of encyclical letters. It is true that the procedure itself was quite old and the encyclical letter has always been the traditional means used by the popes to address the Catholic world. But the new interest of this form lies in the fact that the popes now use it as the regular instrument of the teaching they want to convey. Thus, each pontiff has produced a body of encyclicals which constitute a veritable doctrinal treatise on the problems that concerned Christendom during their pontificates.

It should be noted, also, that the encyclical letter, the pope's ordinary means of instruction, in no way involves his infallibility. The juridical conditions that give a text a dogmatic character are very strict and can never be extended to anything as complex as a encyclical letter. At the same time, the teaching dispensed in the encyclicals must receive the serious attention of Christians. Their author holds directly from Christ the normal power of teaching in the Catholic Church. Except in rare cases, the pope does not pretend to settle a question, but he recommends a direction for research, protects against the danger of certain opinions, condemns certain dangerous positions, and sets up the guideposts needed for the orientation of Catholic thought. This raises the question of the apostolic magisterium and the way in which Catholic thought has been defined in the course of the ages.

2. The Magisterium

The richness and variety of Christian thought expresses an aspect of the Church's vitality. We can also understand that, left to itself, this force can become a source of anarchy and death. It is important then that this activity be disciplined, directed, and, if necessary, defined, in order to become a seed of life. Unity of faith must insure the cohesion of the teaching effort.

Moreover, this mission of controlling comprises manifold aspects: now it is concerned with designating those Christian authors who combined with eminent knowledge a sturdy orthodoxy and exemplary holiness (the Doctors of the Church are so defined); again, it must give a positive sanction to essential points of doctrine—these are the professions of faith and dogmatic definitions; yet again, during periods of agitation it seems necessary to establish limits beyond which thought ceases to be orthodox. These definitions of a negative type are called anathemas. The entire body of these positions, both positive and negative, constitutes the dogmatic synthesis, belief in which is required of every Christian.

The magisterium of the Church must also be active constantly, though less strictly, in pointing out to Christians opinions that are dangerous or hardly compatible with Catholic faith, but without defining any official teaching, whether because the problem does not seem essential or because the matter has not been studied thoroughly enough to be made the subject of an official decision.

Whatever its form, this control belongs solely to the Church's magisterium, that is, to the pope for the universal Church and to the bishops for their individual dioceses. The pope and the bishops are, in effect, the depositories of the faith and the guardians of Apostolic Tradition.

Granted the importance of this matter, it seems necessary to retrace its history at this point. There is no intention, of course, of taking up all the doctrinal positions of the magisterium, but rather of indicating the outlines of the exercise on this jurisdictional power which the pontifical primacy dominates.

In the Beginning

The Book of Acts and the Epistles show us the Apostles explaining the faith to new converts in preparation for Baptism or denouncing the errors that were already being preached by certain innovators. However, the unquestioned authority of the Apostles did not imply a juridical organization. They held their power directly from Christ. For an entire century this function of the Church was exercised empirically, as circumstances required, and we are not clearly informed on the matter. The Apostolic Fathers and even their immediate successors did not worry about describing problems with the scientific exactness that our modern authors might desire. They are witnesses to the faith in their age rather than theoreticians or constructors of syntheses. In their writings, however, numerous allusions indicate that this episcopal prerogative was being used even though its nature is not clearly discernible. Thus, about the year 100, Clement of Rome, one of the early successors of St. Peter, reminded the Corinthians of the need of following the guidance of their Pastor and intervened authoritatively in a dispute that was disturbing this Church. The other Apostolic Fathers were also to insist, on occasion, on the importance of tradition and on the power of the bishops in this domain.

As early as the second century—St. Irenaeus is the authority for this—the principle of the Church's magisterium was recognized universally, and none of the following generations ever contested it. This principle is the following: Doctrinal authority is the attribute of the bishops, who are linked to the Apostles through an uninterrupted succession. The apostolic Churches and particularly that of Rome enjoy a privileged position. In this era, moreover, Pope Victor, a powerful personality, loudly proclaimed his right of control over the universal Church and vigorously intervened in a conflict between the Church of Asia and that of Rome. At this time, also, the elements of the traditional Catholic faith were summed up in a short profession of faith required of all those who wished to receive Baptism. The Apostles' Creed goes back to very remote antiquity. Again, pope and bishops dealt severely with heretics, relying on the idea of tradition in refuting the innovators.

The religious unrest of the patristic period and the violent conflicts that resulted from it led the Church to solemn definitions of certain essential points. At this time the bishops developed the custom of gathering in assemblies called councils or synods. These gatherings, which at that time were innumerable, came to a great number of doctrinal or disciplinary decisions. However, the important decisions were made in the councils called ecumenical, in which, as a rule, representatives of the entire Church took part, particularly the pope or his legate. Now—and this is important—only those councils were regarded as ecumenical which were ratified by the pope. The Council of Nicaea in 325 formulated the Nicene Creed, still recited in our day. The Council of Constantinople, in 381, put an end to the Arian controversy and defined the doctrine of the

Trinity. The Council of Ephesus, in 430, put an end to the heresy of Nestorius, and that of Chalcedon, in 450, condemned the Monophysite heresy. Four other councils meeting at Constantinople and Nicaea are key events in the patristic period and completed doctrine defined previously.

It would be futile, however, to seek here for a dogmatic formula defining the role exercised by the pope in his relations with the various councils. In this period the function was exercised without any formula. It was manifested as circumstances required, though its domain was not clearly defined. However, the work of Pope St. Leo shows us that the pontifical primacy was admitted universally at the end of the patristic period. The pope had his eye on the whole Church. There was nothing important that took place in which he did not feel his responsibility was involved.

The Middle Ages

The Middle Ages were to bring no significant modification in the exercise of the pope's doctrinal power. His primacy was asserted more and more, without any notable objection being raised. Besides, in the intellectual stagnation, no important doctrinal problem arose. Regional councils increased, however, in order to insure the moral and disciplinary reform of the clergy. When this reform entered its decisive stage, under the influence of St. Gregory VII, five ecumenical councils—four at Rome and one at Lyons—sanctioned the pontifical undertaking with their decrees, without any intention of questioning the Roman primacy. It was the pope himself who took the initiative in these meetings, in order to give greater solemnity to their decrees. In 1274, another council meeting at Lyons was to achieve a short-lived union with the Orthodox

Church. During this entire period, pontifical authority increased remarkably and under Gregory VII and Innocent III attained a degree of power unequalled in the history of the Church.

The Greek Schism

The Patriarch of Constantinople attempted to shake loose from the Roman primacy and, for the first time, a discordant voice was heard on the subject of the exercise of doctrinal power in the Church. The patriarchal claims, moreover, were not openly flaunted, which, in its way, proves the traditional character of the pope's power over the whole Church. But various maneuvers attempted to sap the pope's authority in the East.

In 381 the Bishop of Constantinople had the ecumenical council concede him a "primacy of honor" second to the Bishop of Rome. At the time, it is true, the measure aimed at offsetting the infringements of the patriarchs of Alexandria, without challenging the traditional rights of the Bishop of Rome. Sixty years later the situation changed. This time the Patriarch of Constantinople aimed at obtaining a right of jurisdiction over all the Churches of the East. Unable to appeal on the basis of the age of his see, established in the third century, he did not hesitate to alter radically traditional teaching on the apostolicity of the Churches. He forgot that the pope holds his pre-eminence from the Apostle Peter, and at Chalcedon, in 450, he obtained decrees granting him prerogatives equal to those of the Bishop of Rome, but recognizing the latter's precedence, "because this city is the residence of the emperor." Pope St. Leo denounced the trap and recalled the doctrine regarding the apostolic origin of the Churches. Continuing his oblique maneuvers, the Patriarch of Constantinople, in 588, gave himself the title of "ecumenical

Patriarch," the equivocal sense of which relieved the
Byzantines' thirst for domination. Finally, a plot in 681
used a tendentious interpretation of a formula to show a
pope as appearing on a list of heretics. Thereby the East
counted on re-establishing an uneasy equilibrium, for the
see of Constantinople had the sad distinction of including
among its dignitaries thirty-two patriarchs formally condemned for heresy.

Still, until the eleventh century, even though in practice
it strove to limit the Roman primacy, Byzantium never
challenged the principle. At this particular time, however,
the Patriarch of Constantinople tried to make Rome acknowledge that he had a sort of higher jurisdiction over
the Eastern Churches, as a lieutenant of the Church. This
device made no frontal attack on any dogmatic truth. But
it involved a serious danger for the maintenance of unity
and would have constituted a serious precedent. It is obvious that the momentary importance of such and such an
episcopal see closely depends on the size and vitality of
the Christian community and is thus connected with historical conditions. Communities come and go. It will be
so until the end of time. The case that could have been
made for Constantinople could subsequently have been
made just as validly for Paris in the thirteenth century,
for Madrid under Charles V, for Vienna under the Haps-
burgs, for New York in our own time. But authority in the
Church cannot depend on historical fluctuations of communities. And, even more so, the spiritual primacy cannot
be subordinated to certain political conditions without
bringing on the breakdown of the Church into numerous
national communities, which would soon become so many
sects. In fact, it was not until after the separation of 1054
that the Orthodox openly contested the exercise of the
Roman primacy, without, however, ever completely denying it.

In the West

If the popes failed to win respect for their authority in the East, this was by no means the case in the West, where from the time of Innocent III, the pontifical primacy was universally recognized. The omnipotence of pontifical power then attempted to express itself in ways that may be justified or at least excused on the basis of the historical situation but which, from the standpoint of the Gospels, must be viewed with serious reservations and even reproval.

The need for an internal reform in the Church thus led the popes, particularly Innocent III, to certain methods and certain sanctions that were legitimate in principle but that soon degenerated into flagrant abuses of powers. The papacy fixed upon three sanctions, related to its spiritual aims: suspension, a sanction which deprived an ecclesiastic of the right of exercising his ministry, wholly or partly; excommunication; and interdict. This last sanction forbade the exercise of Christian worship in a specified area. In early times these weapons were found to be formidable. The interdict, in particular, which deprived the faithful of religious marriage and burial, was an effective threat against princes and sometimes provoked violent uprisings of the people. History has recorded many examples of kings who were thus forced to bow before the pontifical power. But the abuse of this sanction soon weakened its effectiveness, the more so since the popes too often used it for purposes rather remote from religious concerns, such as the collection of tithes from recalcitrant populations. So, soon after Innocent III, these outmoded weapons were merely theoretical methods of pressure.

In the thirteenth century, when medieval Christendom attained its height, a violent heretical current spread through the Church, particularly in the south of France.

This heresy was at the same time a doctrinal and social danger. Its revolutionary character threatened religious and civil institutions. In the beginning the Church employed traditional methods to fight it: preaching, spiritual sanctions, excommunication. All in vain. The circumstances and the authoritarian temperament of Innocent III led him to resort to weapons that were less traditional in the Church. He started the Albigensian Crusade, which soon acquired an atrocious character. The northern lords plunged into the south with intentions that were not at all religious. The campaign that began with the sack of Beziers, in which seven thousand people were massacred, dishonored the princes and the Church through the extortion practised. But from the religious viewpoint, it was a failure. The princes pursued their political aims and, at the conclusion of the battles, the heresy was just as lively and was finally put down only through the apostolic zeal of Dominic and his companions.

It was at this time that one of the successors of Innocent III, Gregory IX, employed the popes' and bishops' traditional powers for justice and reorganized ecclesiastical tribunals for the suppression of heresy. Thus, in 1231, on the banks of the Rhine, was born the infamous Inquisition. Entering France in 1233, it gradually became general throughout Christendom, through the support of the Holy See; unfortunately, due to the concerted action of the temporal power and of some clerics deprived of religious sense, it often functioned at the expense of elementary human rights and rules of justice. It is true that historical circumstances can explain the creation of these courts of special pleading; it is true, too, that the Holy See attempted to limit abuses which it had neither desired nor commended. Nevertheless, such an institution stands as a fault. Repression is always a dangerous method of restoring order and when it is openly accompanied by the right of informing, exorbitant rights for judges, and the impossibility of the accused to defend themselves, one may expect all sorts of abuses. The Inquisition did not escape this tragic logic. Later, when it was normalized, when it became a canonical institution, strictly regulated and closely controlled by the pope, it was too late. The Inquisition was to be stigmatized forever, not only in the eyes of the pagans but also of the faithful.

There is no excuse for reducing the exercise of the pontifical power to a disorderly use of various means of coercion at its disposal. But while we may have to charge them with these abuses, the popes of the Middle Ages were still great popes. These abuses represent only a small part of the role they performed.

It was indeed in the Middle Ages that the Church's juridical *Corpus* was developed. Never was the pope's authority so solidly established. Long and patient efforts accomplished the centralization of the Church and assured the pope a direct and immediate means of control over all Christendom.

The Council of Constance

However, the sojourn of the popes in Avignon, followed by the Great Schism, resulted in a serious question of authority within the Church. The situation seemed hopeless, since one schismatic pope was replaced by another. It seemed necessary, therefore, to arrange for a meeting of a universal council to resolve the difficulty. Convoked by Pope John XXIII, the last of the antipopes in the Great Schism, the Council of Constance, in 1414, proclaimed conciliary supremacy and declared that a council held its power directly from God and that everyone, including the pope, had to submit to its decisions. Beyond this, it decided the principle of the periodic meeting of councils. The situation was becoming critical. This power of assembly was incompatible with the traditional position of the

Catholic Church. In 1451 the pope was forced to summon a new council at Basel, successively transferred to Ferrara and Florence. After some dramatic scenes, the council reconvened and even achieved a reunion—only temporary, unfortunately—with the Greek Church. In any case, throughout the Council the pontifical primacy was universally recognized, and the conciliar theory would never again receive serious support.

The Protestant crisis led to the meeting of a new council, after much procrastination, for the troublesome Council of Constance was still fresh in men's minds. Pope Paul III resigned himself to the task for the good of the Church. Summoned by the pope to resolve the Protestant controversy, the Council of Trent gave official confirmation to the unquestionable power of the sovereign pontiff in doctrinal matters. The pope was to keep close control over the council's projects through his legate, and the directives needed for the reform of the Church were to be left to his discretion. The juridical reorganization confirmed the centralization of the power of the Church. From this time on, doctrinal errors were to be dealt with solely by the pope in bulls, briefs, letters, encyclicals—all letters issuing from the pontifical chancellery. In addition, the pope was to organize the Congregation of the Holy Office, the purpose of which was to defend the faith and ecclesiastical discipline by promulgating dogmatic decrees, by defining as rash, erroneous, or heretical, any tendentious proposition. Likewise, in 1543, there was the first publication of the *Index of Forbidden Books*, which advised against or forbade the reading of certain books because of their subversive ideas.

Under Louis XIV and Louis XV, the Jansenists attempted, though vainly, to make a subtle distinction between the question of fact and the question of law and thus to resume under another form the ideas put forth at the time of the Council of Constance, appealing from an ill-advised pope to a pope who was better informed by means of a national council. This was much discussed, and since then papal supremacy has not undergone any attack.

Among the various condemnations and censures brought by the pontifical power since the sixteenth century were the Bull *Unigenitus* against the Jansenists in 1713; the *Syllabus*, in 1860, against modern errors; the various condemnations of the Modernist movement; the condemnation of the *Sillon* in 1910; and the condemnation of *Action Française* in 1926. In addition, three events of universal importance marked the exercise of the pontifical primacy. These were, first of all, the solemn proclamation of the dogma of the Immaculate Conception in 1853 and of the Assumption of the Virgin Mary in 1950, a doctrine whose unanimous acceptance by the universal Church attests the present ascendancy of the sovereign pontiff.

The third event was the meeting of the Council of the Vatican in 1869-1870. Actually, a council was not a pressing necessity at this time. But a number of reasons gradually increased the desire and the need for one. First, Pius IX cherished the desire for an ecumenical council which would deal with rationalism as the Council of Trent had dealt with Protestantism. There was no certainty, however, that the success of the Council of Trent would be automatically repeated. This former success, moreover, had been paid for dearly in the prolonged delay of all doctrinal progress in the Church. However, those around the pope also favored the proclamation of papal infallibility and of the complete primacy of the pope. This definition was no more urgent than the council itself, for this doctrine presented no difficulty among Catholics. While Gallicanism questioned some pontifical claims and demanded a degree of decentralization, it in no way attacked the principal of Roman supremacy. Still, it appeared to its proponents that this definition of infallibility would completely neutralize Gallican tendencies and also recompense the pope for the destruction of his temporal power. The council opened therefore on December 8, 1869, and as might have been foreseen, the first question discussed was that of pontifical infallibility. There was a warm debate between supporters and opponents, centering on the timeliness of the decision, the principle of which was not questioned by anyone. The council adopted a constitution *De fide* and then unanimously adopted the constitution *Pastor aeternus*, which defined pontifical infallibility. Interrupted by the war, the council was adjourned, and was never resumed. The personalities of the popes who have since succeeded to the throne of Peter have conferred on the pontifical power, both within and without Catholicism, a prestige unequaled in the history of the Church. In our own time, the impact of Pius XI and Pius XII on the minds and social consciences of all men is well-known. Most recently, the impact of the warm personality of John XXIII on the hearts of men, within and without the Church, his kindly and humble regard for all faiths and peoples, his innovations in favor of "non-Catholic" observers at the Second Vatican Council has not merely commanded respect for the papacy throughout the world but has given strong impetus to ecumenical hopes for reunion.

Part IV

"... but they remain
in the world ..."

The mission of teaching, in spite of its primordial character, does not comprise the Church's entire vocation. This teaching is only a means—undoubtedly necessary—to maintain the presence of Christ in the world and to call all men to sanctity. A Church as a mere coming together of all those who witness to Christ—so some would have it who wish to give the ecumenical movement this meaning—would lose its divine character and become merely another philosophic and spiritual system. But the Church is not a teaching brotherhood, it is the continuation of Christ, the Life and the source of Life. The fruitful reflections of its thinkers therefore represent only one of its dimensions.

One of the most distressing—and most topical—questions deals precisely with the Church's incarnation, its presence in the world. According to Christ's own words, the Church is not *of* the world, but it is to be *in* the world. From this sort of internal contradiction rise endless search, suffering, and conflict. The extremely fine balance point between the continuing effort of purifying the Church and its involvement in the temporal realm demands vigilance at every instant. This is why the history of the dangers that have beset the Church in its incarnation, and the history of the means used to overcome them, constitute a particularly important page. Through it we can better discern the Church's role in the world and better understand the task reserved for Christians in the evangelization of modern humanity.

The incarnation of the Church presents two series of delicate problems: those which concern the Church community, that is, the sociological aspect of the Church, and those that arise from its relations with the world, that is, the coexistence of the Church and the civil powers.

It seems best, for greater clarity, to consider these two points in succession.

1. The Church of the "Pure" or of the Masses?

The First Centuries

Since its foundation the Church has been unceasingly occupied with extending its field of activity while at the same time seeking to remain faithful to the ideal of the Gospels. Thus this problem of adaption has always existed: to strive for perfection and to reach out to all humanity, that is, to incorporate, necessarily, all into one. ✓

In the days that followed the pouring out of the Spirit at Pentecost, the preaching of the Apostles led to the conversion of a certain number of Jews. Some were natives of Palestine, others came from various parts of the Roman Empire. The latter were called Hellenists. Now, in the Jewish community it was customary to form into groups according to ethnic origin. The first converts naturally resumed their ancestral habits; this did not take place without seriously damaging the material interests of the Hellenists who, on pilgrimage, could not adequately contribute to the support of the poorest among them, especially the widows. The Apostles' reaction was immediate. They created deacons responsible for an equitable distribution of funds and thus re-established the unanimity of the Christian community, which cannot put up with a system of favoritism. But the Apostles' gesture abolished only a single particularism among the Jews and did not solve the problem—still a delicate one—of the integration of pagans in the Church of Christ.

The Jews could not associate with pagans, who were regarded as impure. In spite of the explicit teaching of Christ, the boldness of which astonished even His disciples, the Apostles must have hesitated to take up this venture. Then an event of capital importance decisively influenced the Church. A Roman officer named Cornelius, who was sympathetic to the Jewish religion but was still a pagan, miraculously received the command to go to Peter. At the same instant, Peter had a vision during which God intimated that he was not to regard any man as defiled or impure. Thus the direct intervention of the Holy Spirit basically settled a particularly nettlesome case of conscience for the head of the Church. Cornelius was baptized.

The conversion of St. Paul was to be oriented entirely to the call of the pagans, who entered the Church in greater and greater numbers as it expanded into the Roman Empire. However, in spite of the miraculous conversion of Cornelius, Christians of Jewish origin maintained a certain reticence, if not hostility, toward their brethren who had come over from paganism. During one of the first meetings of the Apostles at Jerusalem, where the question was raised, Peter settled the discussion in the way the Spirit desired. All men are called to the faith and everyone, though he has the right to retain his legitimate customs, must respect the conscience of others. But this was not the end of the matter. Some time later, Peter met Paul at Antioch. At first everything went along smoothly. But under the influence of a group of Christians of Jewish origin, Peter changed his attitude. "When they came," writes Paul, "he began to withdraw and to separate himself, fearing the circumcised. And the rest of the Jews dissembled along with him, so that Barnabas also was led away by them into that dissimulation. But when I saw that they were not walking uprightly according to the truth of the Gospel, I said to Cephas before them all: 'If thou, though a Jew, livest like the Gentiles, and not like the Jews, how is it that thou dost compel the Gentiles to live like the Jews?" (Gal. 2:2-14). Peter sided with Paul, thus settling the dispute at its outset: the great community of the Church brings all men together—Jews or pagans, slaves or free men, without distinction as to their orgin—into the same faith of Christ. Certain dissident sects, called Judeo-Christians, would not accept the basic decision of the Church, which nevertheless was never altered: it remains open to all, without distinction of race, sex, or social rank, in fact and by right.

But a related question was left standing: Did entry into the Church imply renunciation of all traditions and the unification of customs and usages? Two texts answered this. But the application of the principle, as we shall see, was to receive diverse interpretations throughout the ages.

The first basic text was, in fact, that of the Council of Jerusalem. It did not oblige pagans to adopt Jewish customs on entering the Church, and still permitted Christians who had come over from Judaism to retain their legitimate usages. Thus, side by side with the Judeo-Christian sects, an authentic Catholic Judeo-Christian Church existed for a time in Palestine and the adjacent regions, made famous by the Apostle St. James and his successor, Simeon.

The other text is found in the Epistle to the Corinthians and centers upon pagan customs. To a question raised by the community of Corinth, Paul replied that only customs imcompatible with the Christian faith were forbidden. "Do not be a stumbling-block to Jews and Greeks and to the Church of God" (1 Cor. 10:32).

Another problem was soon to be presented to the growing community. The early Christians could not all be mod-
els of virtue. Had not the twelve Apostles included one
traitor? What should the Church's attitude be toward
those who slip; not those guilty of the little weaknesses
that are the price of mediocrity, the traditional baggage
of faithful Christians, but toward those guilty of faults
which, in their seriousness, jeopardize the Church's ideal
and its expansion in the world—adultery, crime, apostasy?
We don't know what became of Simon the Magician after
the severe reprimand from Peter. The hand of the Lord
struck dead Ananias and Sapphira when Peter caught
them in the act of lying. But the divine intervention in this
exceptional case was intended to emphasize the power entrusted to Peter; the God of mercy could not thus pursue
the guilty. The Corinthian guilty of incest presented the
first real test-case of this kind. Paul's recommendation was
quite clear, and we may call it excommunication: Let the
community drive from its midst those who offend Christian dignity. With our weakened faith, we find the Apostle's condemnation harsh; but this severity, understand-
able and necessary, seems to be stressed still later on. In
the years that followed, the Church did not envisage the
possibility of repentance, or, at any rate, of reintegration in the community. Thus, the first communities, in
spite of their fervor, also experienced the default of
some of their members. Nevertheless, in the enthusiasm
of expansion individual lapses must have been rare and
their severe repression presented no problems for more
than a century.

The relations of Christians with profane society presented no greater difficulties. "We Christians," wrote Tertullian at the end of the second century, "do not live apart
from the world; we frequent, as you do, the forum, the
baths, workshops, stores, markets, the public squares; we
follow the professions of sailor, soldier, farmer, merchant;

we put at your service our work and our industry." It is true that, in a way, the Christians had to stay on the limits of social life when it required certain religious gestures or certain activity incompatible with the faith. With rare exceptions, however, Christians took part in the activity of their contemporaries without incident. Only a certain inner detachment from temporal possessions, varying according to the individual, emphasized their membership in Christianity as well as the dignity of their life and their fraternal charity. As, in any case, recruitment was being carried on from door to door, so to speak, the moral requirements for admission to the Church were not officially established.

In the middle of the second century a definite stand was taken with regard to forgiveness and the nature of the Catholic Church.

As it developed, the Church began to enter seriously into Roman society. The Christians then experienced the two temptations of those who aspire to a more perfect Church and seek to escape the limits imposed on the Church on earth. Marcion, the one who wanted to reject the Old Testament, created a Church of "pure" Christians subject to a rigorous asceticism and proclaimed that salvation was reserved for a very restricted elite. Montanus, on the other hand, preached a prophetical Christianity, declared the time of Christ had come again, and announced the reign of the Holy Spirit. Consequently, he founded a spiritual Church in which the faithful maintained that they were inspired directly by the Holy Spirit. Both of these movements, which had notable success, rejected the episcopal hierarchy, and favored excessive rigorism as well as anarchy. Advancing from one restriction to another, the innovators led their followers to a veritable hysterical exaltation. Condemnation of sex relations and marriage frequently brought on an abnormal sexual obsession that resulted in the worst excesses.

Catholic reaction was immediate, and the hierarchy universally repudiated these two dangerous deviations. But Montanism and Marcionism still continued for a long time in the Church, producing new outbreaks in small fanatical groups.

But the advance of the Church was tending daily to a gentler attitude to be adopted toward erring Christians. About the year 150, Hermas, a brother of Pope Pius I, in his *The Shepherd,* a small book that was soon well known, brought up for the first time this difficult question of the reconciliation of sinners. For this author, as for all his contemporaries, one principle remained sacrosanct: Baptism remits all sins and the baptized should never again stain his robe of innocence. Nevertheless, he added, "if someone yields to the temptation of the devil, he has a right to repentance." This did not refer to a privilege that could be used repeatedly; the sinner had a right to repentance a single time. While Hermas thus attests to the possibility of reintegrating a fallen Christian into the community, he sheds no light on the conditions of this reconciliation. The first official decision that we know of emanates from Pope Callistus who, about 220, declared the sins of adultery and fornication were remitted for those who did penance for them. There was a great outcry of indignation at this. Tertullian, who had become a Montanist, composed an indictment in which he drew a touching picture of a repentant sinner who lost the benefit of his tears through reconciliation. Hippolytus, who instigated a schism against Callistus, was more violent and charged the pope with teaching concubinage and infanticide. Against all the rigorists, Callistus set tradition and the authority of Chirst who, in the parables on the Kingdom of God, indicates that the Church on earth must tolerate the promiscuity of the good and the wicked.

Thirty years later, shortly after the persecution of Decius, the dispute resumed with terrible severity. Through fear and sometimes under torture, many Christians had relapsed. With the return of peace, certain of these apostates—often the least worthy—demanded reconciliation, depending on the surety of a Christian who had been imprisoned for the faith and who had remained faithful. Cyprian, Bishop of Carthage, and Pope Cornelius granted pardon to apostates who had accepted the Church's penance. Representatives of extreme tendencies—the rigorist Novation at Rome and Novatus at Carthage, who asked for unconditional reconciliation without pardon—united and produced a schismatic movement that soon spread throughout the Church. This conflict gave Cyprian the occasion for writing his great treatise *On the Unity of the Church*. After some hesitancy, the East wholeheartedly supported Catholic unity. Only the West was long disturbed by the schism of Novatus and Novatian.

The question of apostates was raised again in the great persecution at the beginning of the fourth century. There was regret at Rome for a large number of renegades. As soon as the danger had passed, the fearful and cowardly demanded their unconditional reintegration, while the pope imposed the traditional penance. Some disturbances and an incipient schism followed but were soon quieted. This was not the case in Africa and Egypt. A party of rigorists opposed the merciful attitude of the bishops, and schism was established in these two regions for two or three generations, with serious consequences for the spread of the Church.

Nonetheless, mercy prevailed in the Church as a whole. Thus this sensitive question was solved in the spirit of Christ. The Church granted pardon after penance for the sin of apostasy, the most serious of all sins in those times of persecution. The principle having been established, the practice of forgiveness after penance was to advance steadily in the direction of mercy.

But peace was already creating new cares for the

Church. During the third century the number of Christians had increased considerably and at the same time
there had been a general decrease in the fervor of the
communities. After the peace, the mass of those undecided rushed to the security of the victorious side, and
throngs resolved to become Christians. The clergy, overwhelmed by this untimely flood of neophytes, reduced the
severity of the preparation for Baptism. Besides, even if
there had been the desire to be more strict, it would have
been impossible to give full attention to these groups of
thousands of people. In these circumstances, the masses
of the faithful were Christian mainly in name and appearance. For the first time in its history the Church was fully
incarnate: its limits coincided more or less with those of
Greco-Roman civilization. There was no lack of critics to
point out the shortcomings of this incarnation and many
historians have echoed their lamentations, basing themselves on texts selected from the best authors of the period.
Yet, when we make allowances for rhetorical excesses in
these writings, we have to admit that the dominant note
was one of joy and enthusiasm. No authoritative voice
was raised to challenge the merits of this unprecedented
expansion, and history vindicates the enthusiasm of the
Fathers. This vast Church with its share of failures and
individual lapses, marks the high point of the primitive
Church. From these throngs motivated by good will if
not by energy sprang an intellectual and spiritual leadership that imbued society with the evangelical ideal and
in less than thirty years engendered almost all of the
great Doctors of the Church. This must be acknowledged:
only a fully incarnate Church could support Athanasius,
and Hilary, Ambrose and Augustine, the Gregories, Basil,
and Chrysostom; in a group of "pure" Christians these
powerful personalities would have lacked the foundation
needed to bring their talent to the level of exceptional
genius.

The Middle Ages

At the end of the fifth century, then, the Church had solved certain problems dealing with its incarnation. The admission of the faithful and their reconciliation were now definitely regulated in principle, and henceforth would undergo only modifications of details. But the breaking down of the Roman Empire and the succeeding upheavals concretely influenced the establishment of the Church by leading to a factual situation full of consequences for the future.

The Church had been propagated in the Roman Empire, which possessed a certain cultural unity. As the faith expanded into the more intellectual and cultured circles, differences in language and behavior became more noticeable but in no way weakened the profound sense of unity and Catholicity of the Church. Great Churches were established on the basis of homogeneous doctrine but with notable peculiarities in their usages. Thus, from the third century, the Churches of Rome and Africa used the Latin language, while the Churches of Alexandria, Antioch, and Jerusalem employed the Greek language, in which, as it happened, the Christian message had been spread. The situation seemed so normal that when Christianity developed at the limits of the Empire, the Church adopted the customs and language of the converted peoples. Thus there were successively Syriac, Coptic, Armenian, and Arab communities. The Church made itself all things to all men without creating the slightest difficulty in the matter of unity. These various communities still exist today within the Catholic Church, with their own liturgies, languages, and juridical codes.

The invasions of the fifth century, which broke up the Empire, modified this state of things and created serious difficulties. The propagation of Christianity among the barbarian peoples was the work exclusively of missionaries of Latin language and customs. This came about naturally, for the barbarians' belated achievement of civilization took place in the Gallo-Roman cultural framework. This historical conjunction would not have led to any serious consequences if it had not produced the breaking away of the Churches of the East.

As early as the seventh century the Patriarch of Constantinople raised difficulties regarding the jurisdiction of the provinces of Illyricum (these provinces corresponded more or less to the territory of Yugoslavia and part of Greece), located on the linguistic frontier. About the same period, dissension between Rome and the East increased, and the interminable quarrels that followed, interrupted by transient reconciliations, produced more ill feeling at Rome than the definitive break in the eleventh century. It should be recognized, moreover, that the initiative for the attacks came mainly from the patriarchs of Constantinople, who affected a disdainful condescension toward the Latins and vehemently denounced supposed ritual and liturgical errors of the Westerners. In any case, without altering its position in principle, the Catholic Church showed itself very reluctant to introduce new rites. In the ninth century, Sts. Cyril and Methodius had already encountered enormous difficulties in securing acceptance for the Slavic liturgy they promoted. The rallying of the Slavs to Orthodoxy marked the final point in this attempt at adaptation. Thereafter the Catholic Church stuck to the Roman rite in its expansionary activities, regardless of the ethnic origin and the civilization of the peoples evangelized.

While the geographical extent of the Catholic Church became progressively restricted during the Middle Ages, it became more deeply rooted in the world from day to day.

Even in the period of its splendor, in the time of the Roman Empire, the Church actually remained outside the world. It was concerned with spreading the ideal of the Gospels and worked actively for the reform of morals. But the direction of civil matters remained exclusively the province of the prince, or of the laity, who were still mostly pagan. Law, customs, teaching, culture remained Hellenistic. Basil, Jerome, John Chrysostom, and Augustine thus received an education identical with that of their pagan fellowmen. On the other hand, during the Middle Ages, circumstances forced upon the Church the responsibility for numerous temporal tasks. As it was the sole refuge of culture, law, and civilization, in this barbarian world, it was normal that its ascendancy should be manifested in all domains.

Gradually there came to be constituted what was called "Christendom," that is, that world in which the civilization and administration were to some extent a function of religion. Of course, this did not take place in a day. Several centuries were required for this churchly impregnation in the West, and the foundations of Christendom were not really discernible until the age of Charlemagne. But from this time on, the influence. of the Church constantly increased, reaching its height at the beginning of the thirteenth century. Not only was civilization then impregnated with Christianity, but the Church secured or controlled the essential machinery of society. It thus had an actual monopoly of instruction and numerous disputes arose as to the jurisdiction of its tribunals. It exerted a strict doctrinal and moral control, which was accompanied by both spiritual and material sanctions. The autonomy of the two cities immortalized by St. Augustine thus gave way to a dynamic unity dominated by the Church, in which the diversity of nations fused and harmonized. This conception, postulated in large part by historical circumstances, was explicitly expressed by St. Bernard and Pope Innocent III. The latter almost fulfilled the ideal completely, by providing its political climax.

But to achieve the ideal it would have been necessary to ignore the deficiencies of human nature. The Fathers of the fourth century were profoundly aware of the real opposition between the pursuit of a temporal ideal and the perfection of the Kingdom of God. The bolder reformers, such as St. John Chrysostom, professed no illusion on the subject, persuaded that the perfect city would be achieved only at the end of time. In principle, surely, St. Bernard and the theologians shared this view. But they took advantage of the historical situation in order to try to create a society really animated by the Christian spirit. Between the age of the Fathers of the Church and medieval Christendom—both periods of culmination—there is, properly speaking, no contradiction. They were merely two expressions of the same' ideal, differing in their historical incarnation. The error in vision was not to develop until much later, when Christians, once more colliding with the misunderstanding of "the world," withdrew into sterile contemplation of an ideal, mythical Christendom. Bernard and his contemporaries never fell into this error; and with good reason—they knew better than anyone else the defects of this Christendom.

Christendom is, nonetheless, an important stage in the history of the Church. It was one of the historical moments when the ideal of Christ was most profoundly incarnate in humanity. A certain number of dangers led later to serious reactions in the Church. But this spiritual outpouring brought to the Church and the world an equilibrium that is rarely attained.

The Coming of the Modern World

Contrary to an idea that is too often prevalent, the Church had not installed itself in this civilization with the firm desire of opposing the coming of the modern world. Such a reaction could have been manifested in the fifth century, when the Roman world was crumbling under the blows of the barbarians. In the Middle Ages this attitude was inconceivable, for the coming of the modern world was not marked by any cataclysm of this scale. On the contrary, what took place was a slow advance in which the Church took part rather than opposing it.

The Church had nothing to fear from the discoveries of science, no more than she had from the great discoveries of new lands. A new field of activity was opened to her missionary activity and the invention of printing insured an unprecedented distribution for Christian thought. The Church could not fail to be interested in the thirst for culture that obsessed the West, as it favored the development of both religious knowledge and profane culture. A large number of fervent Christians and even churchmen were "distinguished humanists." The Renaissance marked a return to the ancient Greek and Latin culture, but it also found expression in a return to the Bible and the Fathers of the Church. The Church found support against the claims of princes in social and economic evolution.

Therefore the crisis that was to shake the Church did not have its immediate origin in a more or less reactionary attitude of the Church. On the contrary, the cause must be looked for in the compromise of the responsible members of the Church who established themselves "in the world" and disdained the mission assigned by Christ.

The Roman court itself led the way in enthusiastic acceptance of the neo-paganism of the Renaissance. Wealth, display, and luxury reigned at Rome, with their concomitants of disorder and corruption. Officials who were deeply involved in material concerns directed the Church like a temporal society and used the Christian ideal for questionable purposes and to secure their own material interests. The people, whose religion was still alive, were no longer receiving adequate spiritual nourishment because of the lack of dynamism of an ill-informed and poorly educated clergy. In such disorder as this it was inevitable that the Christian elite (including humanists whose culture had made them aware of the demands of Scripture and Tradition) should forcefully manifest their desire for reform. The Reformation was less an explosion of new forces repressed by the weight of tradition than the opposition of an elite to a debasement of the Church, caused by the intellectual mediocrity and moral weakening of the clergy. As ill luck would have it, those responsible were too late in undertaking this reform and thus completely lost control of it for some time.

Nevertheless, the bond between the Church and the world had become so close that from its beginning the Reformation comprised social and political aspects that soon transformed it into a revolutionary movement. It ended in violent armed conflicts and permanent intervention of the civil power in the religious controversy. And when the acute crisis eased, the various antagonists, beginning with the Catholics, found themselves more subject to temporal contingencies than at any other time in the history of the Church. The adage "to each region its religion" practically had the force of law and prevented any possibility of tolerance of diverse customs.

The Reform Program of the Council of Trent

Still, the Protestant crisis had not jeopardized the influence of the Catholic Church. While the internal reform of the Church developed too late to ward off catastrophe, it still managed to clear the air and to give back to all Catholics the understanding of their mission. Then came a veritable reconstruction, dominated by the Council of Trent, and though the seventeenth century lacked the luster of either the patristic or the scholastic periods, it was, nonetheless, a great age of expansion. The efforts of the missionaries were reflected in the establishment of the Church beyond the seas and in a religious reconquest of tradition-ally Catholic nations. Thanks to religious orders and to great preachers, the Church organized a way of life that was still its own at the beginning of this century.

But then the Church lost its position as a dynamic leader. The struggle against Protestantism had been so violent that the Church never stopped mobilizing its forces against this danger. It thus failed to keep in touch with the general evolution of society, in particular the rational-istic intellectual trend that developed during the seven-teenth century and the social evolution that was already presaging the birth of the industrial era. The deeper causes of the French Revolution completely escaped it. The Church entrenched itself in a conformity that eventually took on a reactionary character, both in the domain of thought and that of concrete achievements. Beginning with the eighteenth century one could observe a progres-sive hardening of the Church's organization. The cause was not some vague desire to return to the past, but the intellectual and spiritual stagnation of the clergy and the faithful.

Again, the Protestant crisis emphasized the latinity com-plex, which had been latent since the Greek Schism. From 1054 to the Council of Trent the Church had striven to re-establish unity. But from this time on, it became estab-lished in its juridical position and accepted the situation, vainly awaiting the return of the prodigal children. The Protestants' return to a vernacular liturgy ended all efforts at adaptation of the Catholic liturgy, which remained Latin. Reaction to this use of the vernacular was so violent that it was forbidden to translate the liturgical books into a living language. For spiritual nourishment the Christian people had nothing available but paraphrases, usually in-sipid and unrelated to the official forms of worship. This defensive attitude extended to intellectual life as a whole, for the clergy insisted on closely controlling the biblical and religious culture of the faithful. The results were all the more regrettable in that the mediocrity of the clergy permitted nothing more than weak doctrine dominated by legalistic arguments from authority to filter down to the faithful. Thus the Church gradually lost the intellectuals' and the ruling class, who took advantage of the social power of Catholicism but did not accept its doctrinal or moral imperatives.

The shock of the French Revolution could have had helpful results, but none developed. At the time, Catholicism lacked men who were sufficiently informed and discerning to draw a lesson from events. However, the Church's structures stood up against the storm, and in many places the faith of the people, which was still lively, halted the official attempt at dechristianization. Unfortunately, the clergy wasted its efforts in the reconquest or desperate defense of material positions that were definitively weakened. The Church did not hear the appeal that reached it from the emerging working classes. The defense of the papal states, the struggle for freedom of instruction, political quarrels, absorbed the vital forces of Catholicism, which lost contact with the masses of the people as early as 1851.

Modern Perspectives

The awakening of Catholicism coincided with the beginning of the twentieth century. Leo XIII laid the foundation stone of a social doctrine for the Church with his encyclical *Rerum novarum* in 1881, and also strove to renovate culture and science within the Church and the clergy. It is true that these pontifical documents may seem rather moderate to us today because of the accelerated evolution of human history. But the work of Leo XIII has a revolutionary character, for it deliberately led Catholicism toward a more adequate adjustment to modern society. His successors continued his work with perseverence and, with some difficulty, were able to free the Church from an excessive temporal involvement, restore its full independence, and reconcile it to a role that was exclusively religious.

Thanks to this influence, the Christian people have once again an awareness of their responsibilities and their mission. The result has been a more intense desire for religious culture and a more and more noticeable concern for introducing the Christian ideal in modern civilization. This activity is not proceeding without argument, and indeed without some mistakes. But these manifestations are signs of vitality, preferable to the deadly silence of mediocrity.

2. The Church and the City

The Church's presence in the world inevitably raised the problem of its relations with the civil power, a problem that is always current because of the constant evolution of societies. The Church's acquisition of an effective temporal power merely added to the complexity of a particularly difficult situation.

The Church and the Roman Empire

Rome, which exercised a policy of religious tolerance toward colonized peoples, ignored Christianity during its first fifty years of existence. The Christians' first official contact with the Roman authorities took place in 59, when Paul, attacked by the Jews in the presence of the Procurator Festus, appealed to the Emperor. We do not know the outcome of this recourse to imperial justice. But in his Epistles, Paul recommended submission to the established power and recalled, in accordance with the spirit of the New Testament, that Christianity had no political aims.

This was the common attitude during the early centuries. The Church, as such, did not possess enough power to disturb the Roman government seriously. The authorities persecuted Christians as members of a subversive sect, but they did not undertake the systematic destruction of the Church. Nero's persecution, in the year 64, the result of a ruler's folly, remained limited in scope and cannot be considered as a suppression of political character.

It should not be deduced from this that the Christians led a peaceful existence. A hostile world hated them, the state ignored them except when circumstances made a different attitude more advantageous, and it permitted the worst violence to break out. This was the case in the persecution of Nero and, later, in 177, of the martyrs of Lyons, to mention only two examples. We can understand the bitterness of the apologists in their early writings, when they protested against the unjust lot of the Christians, even with regard to Roman law. Such a man as Tertullian could never imagine that the state would one day be converted and cease to persecute.

Relations altered during the third century, for several reasons. The sectarianism of some Christians, particularly members of the Montanist and Marcionite sects, was in direct opposition to authority. The appeal for universal celibacy and the conscientious objection advocated by these heretics went counter to the imperial policy of the time, which was engaged in ardent propaganda to increase the birth rate, and was striving to raise forces to resist the barbarians. The arguments of Tertullian, the first theoretician for conscientious objection, were taken up by many Christian intellectuals, among whom were Origen and Láctantius. In practice, refusal of military service did not become common, but nevertheless, this idea was the origin of a fairly large number of martyrdoms.

Finally, the Church became so solidly established that the imperial power became alarmed. A confrontation took place for the first time in 250. The Emperor Decius attempted the extermination of Christianity. In spite of its universal extent and a fairly significant number of apostasies, this persecution ended in failure. The martyrs' example strengthened the Church. In 257 Valerian attacked the clergy exclusively, attempting in this way to get at the heart of Christianity. Pope Sixtus, his deacon, Lawrence, and the bishop, Cyprian of Carthage, were the most famous victims. The savage persecution of Diocletian, from 304 to 310, came too late. The Church had already entered into all the machinery of Roman society, and paganism capitulated. In April of 311, the Emperors issued a decree of toleration, an unequivocal admission of the failure of the persecutions. After many vicissitudes, Constantine, who had become sole emperor in 313, opened a new era in the history of the Church.

The Peace of Constantine

After three hundred years of hostility that had almost persuaded Christians of the impossibility of an understanding with the civil power (besides, had not Christ told the Apostles that they would be ridiculed by the leaders of this world?), Constantine brought the faithful immense relief, and some bishops even believed that the Kingdom of God had arrived.

But official recognition of the Church resulted in numerous ticklish problems. First of all, according to a well-established tradition, the emperor wanted to meddle with ecclesiastical questions. He did so with the awkwardness of an amateur, and his desire of quieting disputes led to more, rather than less, dissension. But if one is acquainted with the religious role of the emperors under paganism, Constantine's interventions seem relatively minor. His successors, particularly Constantius, severely handicapped the advance of the Church, issuing numerous orders for exile and annoyances of every kind. But, apart from several obsequious bishops, the Church had in Athanasius, Basil, Ambrose, Gregory, and John Chrysostom incorruptible leaders, able to win respect from the despotic Caesars. Thus, considering the customs of the time and in spite of the state's interference, the Church remained relatively independent and used the "secular arm" only to the extent approved by custom. The situation deteriorated in the East in the beginning of the fifth century. There John Chrysostom paid with his life in defense of the Church's independence, threatened by the combined forces of the Empire and clericalism, but he was unable to halt the dangerous trend toward collusion of the emperors and the patriarchs of Constantinople.

In the West, the collapse of the Empire momentarily suppressed the question of the relations of Church and state, though such men as Ambrose and Augustine were interested in the matter. Some, with Jerome, viewed this debacle as the end of the world. Others, while they lamented the ruin of the Empire, did nothing to prevent it. It was at this time that Augustine wrote his immortal *City of God* and reminded men that, in spite of upheavals, the Church would endure until the end of time.

Can the State Govern the Church?

Other dangers than persecution were awaiting the Church, and in the midst of Christian society. The two most serious ones were the subjection of the Church to the civil power and the involvement of the Church in affairs of the state. The balance between these two contradictory but equally dangerous positions was admittedly so delicate that the Church could not always avoid both extremes.

The Eastern Church was the first to learn, to its cost, the dangers of a Christian government. Caesaro-papism is the name of this system in which the emperor—Caesar— appropriates the prerogatives of the pope. In this situation the state substitutes for the regular hierarchy of the Church, assumes absolute power over spiritual matters, and finally aims at recognizing the Church as a mere po-

litical force subordinate to its own interests. Certainly, the
limit between the legitimate relations of the Church and
the civil power and certain forms of Caesaro-papism is
sometimes difficult to determine. The exercise of civil or
religious power includes a large range of gradations. In
judgments on the past, we should take account of the historical context. Thus, when Constantine and his immediate
successors meddled on various occasions in the government of the Church, they did not think they were exceed-
ing their rights, and no one dreamed of challenging the
emperor's action. Did not this correspond to the traditional practices of Roman religion? Besides, the various
popes who succeeded each other then were, at best, lacking in personality. The first, Leo the Great, did prove
himself capable of establishing a spiritual primacy—which,
in principle, no one questioned. His successors used it
sparingly. Constantine and his successors came to the
assistance of the bishops, often at their request, which
implied a choice, for the most part ill-advised, between the
various opposing factions. They did not pretend thereby
to be substituting for the legitimate religious authority.
While they exerted pressure, sometimes forcefully, on the
bishops, they did not supplant them.

On the other hand, the fragmentation of the Greek
Church, ravaged by endless disputes and the evolution of
imperial power inevitably led to Caesaro-papism, which,
at the end of the sixth century, became a well-established
institution—established to such an extent that the Christians' adversaries called them "the Melkites," that is, "the
Imperials." They have kept this surname.

Caesaro-papism reached its height with Justinian, who
legislated for the whole of ecclesiastical life and made
himself a name in theology. The religious policy of this
great emperor was admittedly catastrophic, for it established the subservience of the Greek Church to the civil
power. All of his successors maintained control over the
progress of this faction of the Church, and this must be

seen as one of the determining causes of the schism consummated under Michael Cerularius. The Orthodox
Church could never free itself from this control of the
civil power. Even after the ruin of the Byzantine Empire,
in 1451, the patriarchs still bore the mark of the yoke and
the Eastern Church broke up into national Churches, the
most important of which was the Russian Orthodox
Church.

Facing the Barbarians

There was no danger of Caesaro-papism in the West,
because the Empire was foundering. An imperial phantom
was still roaming between Rome and Ravenna, but the
disappearance in 476 of Romulus Augustulus, that child
with the fateful name, practically passed unnoticed. The
barbarian chiefs, still uncertain of power, were hostile toward the Church, if not persecutors of it.

In this chaos of the early Middle Ages, when Europe
experienced the greatest stirring of populations in its history, only the Church retained a stability of power and a
definite culture. Rome then had two of its greatest popes:
Leo and Gregory, who gave the pontifical see a luster and
power that befitted its predestined role.

Leo had the painful mission of presenting the barbarian
Genseric with the capitulation of the Eternal City. Undoubtedly, his grief was intense on that dramatic occasion.
But this remarkable man, both a theologian and organizer,
was able to win respect for his decisions everywhere—at
Chalcedon, where the Nestorian and Monophysite errors
were brought out, in Gaul, where he limited the infringements of the jurisdiction of bishops. Beyond all this, he
was the only man capable of impressing Attila and
Genseric.

Gregory, another Roman of the old school, gave up a
brilliant career to become a monk according to the rule
of St. Benedict. Raised to the pontificate by the voice of

the people, he established in the Church disciplinary and liturgical rules which, for the most part, have remained in use up to our own time. He, too, had to deal with the Lombard tribes, and through his prestige saved the city of Rome. In every city, bishops imitated Leo and Gregory and popular recognition was shown to all these defenders of the city, such as Aignan of Orleans, Loup of Troyes, Hilary of Arles, Germain of Auxerre. When things became stable, the Church appeared not only as a religious force but also as the guardian of order and culture. Subsequently, the new princes manifested an increasing interest in the Church. Clovis and his successors maintained close relations with the episcopacy and often employed bishops as counsellors in order to insure the proper operation of the kingdom. The king's intervention in the nomination of bishops replaced the traditional elections with more and more frequency, a development that was later to lead to serious conflicts.

Charlemagne

The consequences of these relations between the temporal power and the Church appeared at the advent of Charlemagne. He finally achieved the political unity of Europe and dreamed of restoring its former grandeur. In this case, Christianity was not grafted on a civilization that had reached its peak, as in the time of the Fathers; but it was Christianity which, after having prepared the way for the birth of the Carolingian world, supplied the impetus for this renaissance. The delineation of the proper domains of Church and state was obviously difficult under these conditions. The legislation was based—more or less imperfectly, indeed—on the great directives of the Gospel and on Catholic tradition. The prince, following a tradition that was already ancient, did not scruple about entrusting certain duties of general administration to men of the Church. On the other hand, he assumed the right of intervening in Church appointments, and made the bishops and even the pope aware of his power. The Church had a monopoly on teaching, but the prince made himself defender of morality, discipline, and the Catholic faith. This alliance of Church and state was to give birth to a new form of Caesar-papism, quite different from that of Constantine or Justinian. To use modern terminology, we might say that the Church, in religious matters, retained the legislative and spiritual power, while the prince kept in his hands the entire executive power. In fact, under Charlemagne, this alliance of the throne and the altar was rather beneficial. This depended on the harmony that reigned between the pope and the emperor. They were able to achieve together a vast plan of reform, which permitted the Church to discover a new brilliance, the prelude to a Western world imbued with Christianity.

This mixture of the spiritual and temporal achieved under Charlemagne was made even more concrete by the creation of a pontifical state. The author of this innovation, Pepin the Short, gave territories to the pope in 756. In 774 Charlemagne solemnly renewed this donation. It was to weigh heavily on the life of the Church for over a thousand years. Although the pope was not a vassal of the emperor, the latter regarded himself as the protector of the pope's temporal power. Thus was achieved in all its complexity the involvement of the Church in the Western world at the time of the latter's gestation. From this situation flowed perpetual conflicts and a constant temptation for the Church to neglect its fundamental mission.

My Kingdom Is Not of This World

The political and religious anarchy that followed the Carolingian age defies description. What definite line of behavior can be found in this iron age in which laymen

made and unmade popes? For a century the Church was
in agony. But the Spirit was watching. On April 22 the
people placed on the chair of Peter the monk Hildebrand,
who firmly established the reform timidly initiated by his
predecessors. St. Gregory VII proved a worthy successor
of Leo and of Gregory the Great. His personal sanctity
intensified his severe personality and his conception of
his mission. With extraordinary courage, he undertook the
reform of the Catholic Church. Through example, word,
and, when necessary, through sanctions, he succeeded in
getting the clergy to appreciate their dignity and to respect their duties. He also attacked the traditional privilege of the civil power in naming bishops. Thus began the
dispute on investiture in which the pope opposed the
princes, especially the emperor of Germany. Gregory
again strove to destroy the Caesaro-papism inaugurated
by Charlemagne and claimed for the pope exclusive sovereignty in the Church. He also proclaimed the superiority
of the spiritual over the temporal power and the right of
the pope to free subjects of an unjust prince from the duty
of fidelity. Drawing practical conclusions from his teaching, Gregory did not hesitate to excommunicate King
Philip I of France and to depose the emperor of Germany,
who came to beg his pardon at Canossa. But the latter
subsequently resumed the fight and raised an anti-pope,
whom he installed at Rome by force. Gregory VII died in
exile at Salerno in 1085, but his work survived. Nothing
could stop the reform of the Church.

Bernard

Five years later St. Bernard was born, the disciple of
Gregory and continuer of his work. With the mind and
temperament of Gregory VII, Bernard had a spiritual affinity with Athanasius and Basil. His multifarious activity
clearly puts him in the line of the Fathers of the Church.

Thus he could not fail to adopt the ideas of reform of Gregory VII and Urban II. In fact, his life was to be a perpetual struggle to consolidate pontifical power and to defend the doctrine of the Roman primacy. For forty years this unquestioned master of the Church had such power that he was even assigned to arbitrate a contested pontifical election. Bernard had this responsibility, unique in the history of the Church, of designating one of two claimants as the legitimate pope. Later, one of his spiritual sons from Cîteaux ascended the papal throne. However, Bernard always acted in the name of the pope and in accord with him. His renown and activity contributed greatly to establishing pontifical authority and spreading the theocratic theory of Gregory VII, the foundation stone of medieval Christendom. This was a world of which men made God the king.

Innocent III

Innocent III deduced all the inferences of this doctrine and led Christendom to its highest point. Whatever may have been said of it, his teaching did not differ essentially from that of Gregory VII or St. Bernard. In spite of some unfortunate expressions, he entertained no temporal ambition and only sought for recognition of the pontifical authority already set forth by his predecessors. But he laid down the principles with absolute strictness and applied himself to expressing them in deeds. The restored prestige of the papacy made his action more effective and significant. Thus he was able to win respect from the German Emperor, the King of France, Philip Augustus, and the King of England, John Lackland. The ecumenical council he summoned in 1215 was the climax of an age. More than four hundred bishops and eight hundred abbots, with ambassadors and delegates from all the courts of Europe, synthesized Roman Christendom in this gathering. This

Council of the Lateran achieved the most important ecclesiastical codification prior to that of the Council of Trent.

Thus from St. Gregory VII to Innocent III a doctrine was developed that began with a mere spiritual primacy and culminated in the desire for a political unity of Christendom, under the hegemony of the pope. Severe and often unjust judgments have been made regarding the work of these popes. Undoubtedly, theocracy, considered abstractly, is hard to reconcile with the teaching of the Church as it appears in Scripture and Tradition. But in the overlapping of spiritual and temporal that marks the Middle Ages, the Church could not free itself from the ascendancy of the emperors except by tending more and more toward a theocracy. Practically inevitable, this form of society contained the seed of numerous abuses which Innocent III, for one, and his successors, especially, could not or would not avoid. Men—even when they belong to the Church—can be deceived. The mistake here consisted in clinging to this theocracy when progress called for a new style.

The Crusades

Some see in this movement a religious epic, others the utilization of the spiritual for political and economic ends. In reality, the Crusades were both of these. There is often a misunderstanding of the judgment that the Church itself has implicitly made of this undertaking. No crusader, not even Peter the Hermit, has received public veneration. Bernard and Louis IX were canonized for other reasons. The Church thus shows that it sees in the Crusades, not a universal gesture but a manifestation of Christendom, that is, of this quite specific medieval society. With all this, religious fervor undoubtedly had a preponderant place in most of the Crusades.

Pope Urban II took the initiative of the First Crusade.

This act of high religious policy was developed in the pattern of the reforms carried out by Gregory VII. Wishing to end the unceasing wars that divided Christian princes, to the great detriment of the Church and the poor, Urban II sought in the East for an outlet for the bellicose passions of the knights. The deliverance of the Holy Places newly occupied by the Turks presented an ideal objective.

A seriously considered undertaking, the First Crusade was to include a disciplined military expedition. It also aroused the enthusiasm of the crowds and, under the influence of preachers who were more ardent that thoughtful, such as Peter the Hermit in the north, it turned into a people's crusade, ending in brigandage and massacre. The following expeditions were better prepared, both on the diplomatic and military level, and became more and more important politically. There could hardly be any point in relating here the story of the Crusades, which belong more to general history than to that of the Church. Besides, the Crusade idea became generalized: a Crusade in Spain against the Moors; one in France against the Albigensians; in Prussia against the pagans; in England against John Lackland; in Germany against Frederick Barbarossa; soon there were crusades everywhere, except in Palestine. All of these expeditions were accompanied by pillage, murders, and extortion, which discredited them. Thus perished the grandiose project of Urban II: to achieve the unity of the Christian world against the Moslem world.

Although the Crusade was lost, some men—saints—restored the profound vocation of the Church with regard to Islam: Francis and Dominic sent missionaries to the East.

The Death of Christendom

Christendom required as fundamental conditions the peaceful coexistence of states or at any rate the explicit acceptance of the arbitration of the pope, and in the case of the latter a total detachment and a purely spiritual concept of his mission. This was too much to ask of a human institution. Christendom soon disintegrated under the blows of the princes, combined with the weakness of certain popes.

The existence of the pontifical states remarkably hindered the popes' freedom in the exercise of their mission. From the middle of the thirteenth century the protection of these states made the pope lose the universal sense of his mission, of which his predecessors had been so conscious. For forty years, absorbed in the question of the Two Sicilies, the papacy sought to become a temporal power, to the great detriment of its spiritual ideal. Thence came the development of an increasingly demanding ecclesiastical fiscal system and nepotism, that concern for entrusting important posts to one's partisans, preferably to members of one's own family.

The knell of Christendom began to toll with the coming of Boniface VIII in 1294. A violent person, he intended to continue the policy of the pre-eminence of the Church but came into conflict with the king of France, Philip IV, called the Fair. Boniface died in 1303. The residence of the popes in Avignon, from 1309 to 1367, and the Great Schism, from 1378 to 1417, increased the disrepute of the papacy at the very moment when it needed an especially bold and clearheaded leader to confront a situation that demanded a new form of relations between the Church and the civil power.

From the middle of the thirteenth century, conflicts of jurisdiction increased between the bishops and lords jealous of their authority. The communal movement set the middle class at odds with the bishops and abbots, who were great landholders. The rebellion broke out over the multiple taxes imposed by the pontifical fiscal bureau, which was ever more insatiable. Thus was expressed a mood of independence, even hostility toward the papacy, a mood whose manifestations were at first sporadic but became general with the strengthening of the powers of the national governments. The progressive laicization of society was also reflected in doctrine. Minds were freed more and more from ecclesiastical influence. In particular, the royal "jurists" developed juridical theories incompatible with the theses of Innocent III. As early as the fourteenth century, Pierre d'Ailly and his disciple, Jean Gerson, who were, as it happens, men of great virtue and deep piety, recommended the constitution of a federal Church, within which each national Church would enjoy a great autonomy. Their system further restricted the Roman primacy by the "conciliar" thesis, according to which an ecumenical council was superior to the pope.

Naturally, the princes gave full support to these tendencies, which would have permitted them to exert direct action on the Church. The Pragmatic Sanction of Bourges, in 1438, which sided with the conciliar theory and gave legal sanction to the main provisions of the schismatic Council of Basel, was the most conclusive example for France. This Pragmatic Sanction continued in effect until the Concordat of 1516, and its provisions, apart from the conciliary theory, were subsequently often revived by the kings.

Finally the pope settled a rather desperate situation, but his prestige had suffered considerably. Thus the Council of Basel-Florence sanctioned the death of a Christendom that had been wasting away since the time of Boniface.

Sin in the Church

The most striking element was not so much tension between modern society and the Church but these worldly tendencies of the Holy See that were soon to bring it to the ultimate stages of decline. After Avignon and the Schism came the Borgias! This name in itself suggests the mass of deceit, scandal, and vice then gathering around the Roman court. The reputation of the popes of the Renaissance remains a stain on the Church. At the present time, some attempt is being made to excuse them by placing Roman depravity in its historical context. In fact, the court of Rome was no more depraved than the other European courts. But this is precisely the fault of the popes. Their crime consisted in managing the Church like a temporal society and completely ignoring the law of Christ. Under the pontificates of Innocent VIII and Alexander VI, with whom we may venture to place Julius II and Leo X, the Holy See failed in its mission and reduced Rome to the rank of one of the many Italian principalities. Indeed, one of their successors, Paul IV, did not hesitate to admit that, except for special assistance from the Holy Spirit, the Church would not have survived such a blow.

At the death of Leo X nothing remained of the grandiose dreams of Innocent III nor of the sanctity of a St. Gregory VII. The pope conducted himself like one of the ostentatious noblemen of the Italian Renaissance, a friend and grand patron of the arts, but unworthy of occupying the chair of Peter. Christians were overcome by immense disgust. This was expressed, unfortunately, in the Protestant outburst. But it is surprising that this catastrophe did not take place on an even broader scale, and that Catholicism did not break down into a multitude of national Churches. The fact remains, nevertheless. After much discussion and many difficulties, the Council of Trent managed to salvage an apparently desperate situation and, under the direction of popes of great merit, restored the Church's honor and dignity. Now it remained for the pope to establish his authority over the state on a new basis.

Gallicanism

Religious wars rent France in particular at this time and stirred all Europe with the exception of Italy and Spain.

When peace returned, the Church's position had altered considerably. Catholicsm had been driven out of England, the Scandinavian countries, a great part of Germany, and a number of the Swiss cantons. The pontifical supremacy inaugurated by Innocent III no longer existed. For two centuries, the Pope had gotten into the habit of dealing with other states as a sovereign political power. Such customs had reactions on the spiritual level. The convoking of the Council of Trent, its development, and the promulgation of its decrees thus became the subject of numerous negotiations with the various sovereigns. Unquestionably, this procedure represented a debasement of the pontifical primacy, which was to recover its independence only after several centuries of persevering effort.

Now Gallicanism had its period of ascendancy and became the malady of Christian states. The civil power, while granting the Catholic Church the privilege of being the state religion, demanded in return the right of exercising strict control over that religion. There were, actually, two forms of Gallicanism. One, professed by the civil power, refused the pope any interference in the state's affairs. Without denying the pope universal primacy and the right of legislating for the whole Church, the king subordinated pontifical jurisdiction to his own will and claimed to be the sole judge of the timeliness of publishing any particular Roman decree. On the other hand, ecclesiastical Gallicanism, emphasizing the fullness of the bishops' priestly power, tended to subordinate the decisions of the pope to episcopal acceptance. This amounted to admitting to the pope that he had universal jurisdiction but denying him the means of exercising it. As a consequence of the overlapping of canon and civil law, state Gallicanism and Church Gallicanism tended to intermingle. This confused situation could be cleared up only through schism or through the complete independence of the Church.

The Gallican crisis reached its climax in the Jansenist dispute, and on two occasions, under Louis XIV and Louis XV, there was extreme tension between the pope and France. The matter of the *Regale*, the king's right of collecting the resources of vacant sees, led to the summoning of the Assembly of 1682. Bossuet delivered his speech on the unity of the Church there and strove to take the leadership of the movement in order to moderate it. He did not prevent the Assembly from adopting the Four Articles, which practically limited pontifical power throughout the kingdom of France. Of course, Gallicanism soon became an item for export and its theories, taken up by the principal courts of Europe, were to result in continual conflicts between the Church and the Catholic sovereigns.

A Concordat

With its equivocal nature, Gallicanism could be no more than a transitory phenomenon. The Revolution failed in its attempt to create a schismatic Church. Napoleon unintentionally gave episcopal Gallicanism a mortal blow by demanding the collective resignation of all the bishops of the Old Regime in order to set up an episcopate more submissive to his instructions. Recognition of the universal primacy of the pope became the only way of evading the Emperor.

Thus the Concordat of 1801 marked a decisive date in the history of the Church. From this time on, the Church freed itself more and more from these temporal handicaps, to the advantage of its universal vocation. But numerous obstacles still barred the road to freedom.

The ideas of this period, particularly the rationalist trend that prevailed throughout the nineteenth century, led to a view of Catholicism as a temporal society of the same kind as the various states. While affecting anticlericalism in principle, the governments actually tried to keep the Church's existence under the strict control of the state, for in their eyes religion represented a moral force valuable for maintaining order.

In the Church, the clergy rebelled at the idea of relinquishing certain traditional privileges and freely accepted compromises which, without affecting essential principles, assured them of some material advantages at the cost of some of their freedom. Rome was unable to find a practical solution to the dilemma posed by papal states. Thence developed, in the course of the nineteenth century, that incoherent attitude which split up ecclesiastical power among opposing factions.

These various reasons thus forced upon the Church the necessity of dealing with the government according to the norms of diplomacy. Between 1801 and 1841 the Pope signed no less than fourteen concordats, which had the dubious fate of all international treaties. In itself, this policy, which was needed at the time, brought the Church certain advantages by guaranteeing it freedom to function and by regulating its inevitable relations with the state. But, in a way, the concordats established the recognition of the Church as a temporal society, to the detriment of its spiritual nature. They were to transform the clergy into a group of functionaries bound by their allegiance to the State.

Christians themselves, recognizing this social force, united to obtain certain political rights. Their attitude, legitimate from a certain point of view, gave the impression that the Church was forming a state within the state. Some certainly had such a desire. The nostalgic memory of Christendom reflected a more or less conscious desire rather than a regret for a past that was largely unknown to most of those sighing for it. The defense of the papal states from 1850 to 1870 aggravated the situation. Some, such as Louis Veuillot, would have liked to give this defense the character of a crusade. But times had changed.

This conflict appeared merely as the desperate defense of the temporal interests of the Holy See and as a manifestation of reaction to a changing world.

The loss of the papal states in 1870, and France's Separation Law of 1903, in spite of the violent reaction they produced, marked two great dates in the history of the Church. Catholics keenly regretted these apparent defeats. In retrospect, however, it appears that from this time on, the Church, fully independent, attained a prestige that was probably unique in its history. A series of popes of exceptional quality enabled the Church to win the respect of the world in crucial times. The refusal of Pius XI and Pius XII to join the League of Nations or the United Nations shows the important evolution that has taken place in Catholicism since the nineteenth century. The Church no longer claims to exercise "leadership" among the nations, as she did in the Middle Ages. It has no need of political representation or of action on the political level. As Jesus prescribed, it is *in* the world but not *of* the world. Its prestige and its action cannot be limited to the political sphere. A spiritual leaven in the world, it has no direct role in establishing political or economic policies.

This is the basic principle that now governs the relations of the Church and the various nations. The prestige and attention given the see of Peter demonstrate more effectively than any other argument how faithful the Church is to its vocation.

3. A Community Established upon Earth

The Church's incarnation still requires a certain internal organization. Its vocation of teaching already implied the necessity of a magisterium responsible for the control and orientation of doctrine. Prayer, the duty of dispensing the Lord's grace, and simply good order in the community likewise demanded concrete rules, rules which have been made specific in the course of time. It will be useful, therefore, to trace the general evolution of the Church in the exercise of its functions, with regard to the administration of the sacraments, the liturgy, and rules needed for the proper functioning of the community.

The Primitive Church

In the very beginning the Church appears in history with an organization that is concise indeed, but essential. Using the image of the organic harmony of the human body, Paul, in his Epistles, constantly stressed order as an indispensable condition for the proper functioning of a community. Again, the Acts of the Apostles shows us the Apostles' concern with taking care of the various needs of the emerging communities and fighting against the anarchical tendencies that might penetrate the Church. The office of deacon was created to provide help for the Apostles in their administrative work. A corps of widows and virgins was organized. Numerous rules were drawn up regarding the administration of Baptism and the celebration of the Eucharist.

The theologian is interested in these various measures, which enable us to discover the apostolic origin of certain practices of the Church. But they also reveal the Apostles' way of doing things, which was to become, moreover, the traditional practice of the Church. The Apostles decreed no abstract juridical or liturgical rule to be imposed as law for the whole Church. Conscious of the power of the Spirit, they let the community manifest its vitality and intervened only after an event, to guide, discipline, and co-ordinate the various manifestations of the Christian faith. In these circumstances we can understand the diversity of practices in the first communities. Agreement was demanded only on essentials. Two important incidents that occurred in the early centuries illustrate this attitude of the Church, which was torn between its duty to safeguard the faith and the desire of respecting traditional practices.

Whereas the Churches of Asia celebrated Easter on the fourteenth of the month of Nisan, the Church of Rome waited until the following Sunday. This difference in date probably reflected a profound divergence on the meaning of the Paschal feast. Asia celebrated the death of Christ, Rome particularly commemorated His resurrection. This duality of customs, as old as the Church itself, originally presented no dangerous difficulties. But the practice of the Quahtordecimans, as those who celebrated Easter on 14 Nisan were called, resulted in an annoying confusion with Judeo-Christian customs. Sensing the seriousness of the situation, Pope Victor called for regional meetings of bishops to settle on the date of Easter for the whole Church. Agreement was reached everywhere except in Asia Minor, where the bishops decided to keep their own tradition. This went back to St. John the Apostle. The

pope, irritated by this resistance, wanted to excommunicate the dissidents, but St. Irenaeus, the Bishop of Lyons,
smoothed over the dispute. Pope Victor tolerated the observances of the Churches of Asia which, in any case, disappeared during the fourth century. The Easter dispute
raised for the first time the painful conflict between legitimate individual usages and the higher interest of the
Church. Unfortunately, there was not always a St. Irenaeus to prevent shocks dangerous to unity.

A hundred years later, another conflict developed between Pope Stephen and Cyprian, Bishop of Carthage.
This time the dispute involved the validity of Baptism
administered by heretics. Contrary to the universal tradition that accorded Baptism a value in itself, Cyprian, basing his opinion on African usages, declared that the baptism of heretics was invalid. This dangerous opinion
brought into question the basic nature of this sacrament
and, consequently, of all the others. The conflict soon
became bitter; the pope even thought of excommunicating
Bishop Cyprian. Persecution brought an end to the quarrel
and reconciled the two antagonists, both of whom glori-
ously suffered martyrdom; St. Stephen in August of 257 and
St. Cyprian on September 14 of the same year. Meanwhile,
Bishop Dionysius of Alexandria had attempted to prevent
the conflict from extending to the whole Church. Soon,
moreover, as Catholic doctrine was more fully defined,
usages became standard.

In spite of persecutions liturgical life was organized and
the territorial organization of the Church was gradually
outlined. In the heroic ages of evangelization, worship
took place in private homes. We should not see in this anything more than a practical measure, for the Eucharistic
celebration had had from the beginning a clearly defined
liturgical character. The rites celebrated in private homes
and, especially, those in the catacombs, were carried out
in this way for lack of any better arrangements. As soon

as the size of the community permitted it, regular places
of worship were set up. Thus, in several places in the
Roman world, vestiges of Catholic basilicas prior to the
year 250 have been discovered. While details of the office
varied from one church to another, the basis remained
identical: psalms, prayers, readings, and celebration of the
Eucharist. Traditional regulations likewise applied to the
preparation of postulants for Baptism, the catechumens.
Even in this period, Church organization was established
under the authority of the bishop, assisted by priests and
deacons.

Next came serious controversies regarding the reintegration of those who had been excluded from the community.

The Church was troubled by the decrease in fervor that
followed its rapid growth in Roman society. While it
sanctioned forgiveness, penance was still remarkably severe. Penance, it is true, applied to only a limited number
of faults, regarded as extremely serious: fornication, adultery, homicide, and apostasy. New Christians, fearful of
the rigors of penitential discipline, got into the habit of
putting off the reception of the sacrament of Baptism until
the time of their death. This custom even became widespread among Christian families, who delayed longer and
longer in having their children baptized. Thus, John Chrysostom and Augustine received Baptism very late. The Fathers of the fourth century resolutely fought this abuse,
which transformed Baptism into a magic formula for eternal salvation and removed its basic meaning of entry into
the Church, the body of Christ.

The fourth century was that of the development of the
liturgy. Now victorious, the Church was able to display
its splendor in ceremonies which sometimes brought together thousands of the faithful. Rites acquired the structure which, in its main lines, is still in use today. The liturgical cycle was increased with a large number of new

feasts. In addition, Christians began to honor the martyrs by celebrating the Eucharist at the site of their tombs. Thus was born the veneration of the saints, both to honor their memory and to obtain their intercession with God. Athanasius was the first bishop who was not a martyr who became the subject of official veneration.

At this time, too, the Church made a large number of disciplinary decisions. But, these were adopted as circumstances required and were not part of a code. At best, we might speak of a certain harmonization of decrees which preceded the development of a common law, a law elaborated through the centuries from a nucleus of a few essential principles.

The Christian communities were not satisfied with merely organizing worship. From the beginning, the Church considered the care of the poor and the protection of the weak as among its essential duties. Mutual assistance was established in the communities, and the early Christians even attempted the bold experiment of a common possession of material goods. St. Paul himself collected alms to care for the needs of the poorer communities. This kind of charity always remained active in the Church of the early centuries. It was normal, therefore, to see charitable institutions develop. Indeed, the Fathers, following the example of the Apostles, were to remind the faithful emphatically that the bishop's role is not to manage institutions, even charitable institutions, but that this task falls to the laity. However, faced with neglect by both civil power and laymen, the bishops of the fourth century did not hesitate to create the first charitable institutions. The promoter of the movement, Basil, established hospitals, soup kitchens, hospices, overnight shelters, and even a workers' city. St. John Chrysostom, St. Augustine, and many others followed in his footsteps. Basil and Chrysostom were innovators in creating a corps of medical monks and nurses to insure the proper operation of their hospitals. Chrysostom also encouraged the development of nursing sisters.

On the other hand, the matter of secular teaching did not interest the Christians of the Empire. It is true that the Church jealously watched over the religious instruction of her faithful, safeguarding it through her pastors and, in certain places, by something like schools of theology and exegesis. But with regard to general education, the Church never considered any other solution than that of letting young people attend the traditional schools. Indeed, in 362, when the Emperor Julian the Apostate tried to oust Christians from teaching positions in these schools, the Catholics reacted violently. They rebelled against this measure, which they regarded as discriminatory and humiliating, and they refused to create a sectarian school. In 364 the imperial edict was withdrawn, and Catholics resumed their place in official education. It seems, however, according to certain texts of St. John Chrysostom, that the imperial persecution, which particularly afflicted Antioch, aroused certain circles there to a reaction in favor of instruction given under the control of the monks and the Church, but this movement had no practical results.

The Middle Ages

By the end of the fourth century, the Church had reached its characteristic form. Liturgical and juridical patterns underwent no further basic modifications, and the way of life of Christians was established in its main outlines. The history of its institutions is still continuing, and every age will contribute its own peculiar coloring in this domain. The evolution of society will create new problems, which the Church will have to face with new solutions.

Two incidents involving worship shook the Church during the Middle Ages and aggravated the latent tension between East and West.

The first incident produced profound disturbances in the patriarchate of Constantinople and is known in history under the name of the Iconoclastic heresy. Unlike the Jews and the Moslems, Christians have never forbidden the representation of Christ or the saints. Magnificent paintings already decorated the catacombs and the basilicas. The Fathers of the fourth century do not seem to have been seriously concerned about this question which, in any case, presented no difficulties then. However, as early as the fourth century, Christians began to preserve the relics of the martyrs and to venerate their tombs. This deserved recognition of the best of Christ's servants accompanied traditional belief in the power of the saints as intercessors. Unfortunately, abuses of this practice were not slow in developing. False images became numerous. The veneration connected with the saints or their images was imitated in superstitious practices which had a disturbing resemblance to the worship of idols. It appeared necessary to define clearly the nature and limits of the veneration to be given the saints. The job seemed an easy one considering the unity of Catholic thought; no Christian could pretend to adore the saints, even if it were the Virgin Mary; nobody seriously thought of attributing a magical power to representations of Christ or the saints, even though popular piety and the ill-timed enthusiasm of the monks contributed to reprehensible practices.

But as often happens in such cases, passions became involved, encouraged by the imperial power. For over a century, from 725 to 843, a terrible persecution took place in the East against those who defended veneration of the saints. This persecution affected the monks especially, and they suffered violence and tortures as frightful as in the age of Diocletian. Finally, reason won out, and veneration of the saints kept its rightful place in the Catholic religion. But there was an unpleasant page left standing in the history of the Church, a page in which so-called Christian emperors, sometimes assisted by bishops, massacred their brethren with a sadistic fury worthy of the most barbarous ages.

(2) The second incident was not a violent one. The problem, apparently quite trivial, concerned a liturgical innovation introduced in certain parts of the West, probably during the seventh century. With the probable intention of better explaining doctrine, certain Churches added to the Credo of the Council of Nicea (the one we recite at Mass) the word *filioque*, which was not found in either the original Greek text or in the Latin text in use at Rome. This addition gave explicit expression to the belief of the Church according to which "the Holy Spirit proceeds from the Father *and* from the Son." Charlemagne tried to extend this usage to the whole Church and provoked a conflict with the Eastern Church. Pope Leo III, called upon by the emperor of the Franks to take a position, stated the Catholic teaching with regard to the Holy Spirit. Seeing no need for intervening in a minor question, he refused to require the use of the *filioque*. The pope's wise decision eased their minds. But some years later the patriarch of Constantinople, Photius, brought up the question again and tried in his turn to forbid the use of the *filioque* in the West. Endless discussions ensued. The *filioque* was extended to the whole Latin Church and still remains an item of dispute between the Catholic Church and the Orthodox Church.

The disputes over images and the *filioque* illustrate the subjective importance that certain apparently harmless terms can assume when they become symbols of the conduct and religious expression of the Christian community. It was natural that in view of these facts the Church attempted to unify usages in order to strengthen Catholic solidarity.

The initiative for this evolution came from the theological situation created by Charlemagne. There is much reservation about the emperor's religious policy. But he possessed the merit of restoring intellectual culture in the Frankish world and, with the help of a distinguished group of men, of undertaking the reform of the Church. His efforts bore fruit, especially after his death, when they continued to strengthen the Church.

Three questions interested the Carolingian reformers: reorganization of the ecclesiastical hierarchy, re-establishment of discipline among clergy and laity, and unification of the liturgy.

Reorganization of the ecclesiastical hierarchy was essential. The barbarian invasions and the Christian conquest of the new empire had disturbed basic patterns. The political unification achieved by Charlemagne permitted a new distribution of episcopal jurisdiction. It was effected with a view to centralization. The bishops' sees were regrouped into ecclesiastical provinces under the authority of a metropolitan. There was undoubtedly some evidence of a tendency to a regional and federal organization of the Church. But the pope was alert to the importance of maintaining his primacy and never recognized in the metropolitan anything more than a mere administrative function, as it still is today. Furthermore, elections of bishops, which had already fallen into disuse, disappeared almost completely and the emperor reserved for himself the selection of nominations. This intrusion of the civil power into ecclesiastical organization subsequently brought serious abuses and the strong hand of St. Gregory VII was needed to suppress them. The emperor also was interested in the education of the clergy. He required candidates for the priesthood to have theological knowledge, knowledge that was still quite rudimentary but which represented a considerable advance in comparison with the mediocre level of the Merovingian clergy.

Organic reform implied a liturgical reform, for a certain anarchy had entered into the celebration of rites. The greatest diversity had been introduced into the usages of the Frankish churches. This diversity did not go back to an ancient tradition, as in the case of the great Churches of the East, but to a more or less accidental deformation of Gallo-Roman usages. Charlemagne, in his forceful way, attempted to bring back order in this anarchy. The pope could not but praise an attempt that brought the Roman liturgy into general use in the Western world. Certain legitimate usages or certain traditional practices continued, however, and contaminated Roman customs, resulting, in the eleventh century, in the Latin liturgy that is still in use. The disciplinary reform, moreover, brought about the need for a harmonization of the various juridical texts promulgated by the previous councils. This led to the development of ecclesiastical law, which reached its full expansion in the twelfth century. Legislation on the sacraments became stabilized, in particular the regulations on penance. This advance of juridical science had a curious repercussion in the ninth and tenth centuries. With the intention of securing the Church's freedom and of ensuring the pope's authority in a particularly troubled era, anonymous jurists, living in the period about 850, brought together collections of apocryphal documents. These "False Decretals" became of amazing importance in the Middle Ages and contributed to strengthening the pope's authority both inside and outside the Church.

Christendom

The Carolingian Renaissance had no extended success, but it achieved decisive results in the various fields that it explored. The anarchy of the Iron Age hardly encouraged progress in ecclesiastical organization. Again, however, the establishment of Christendom in the eleventh century, brought the Church a large number of interesting developments. The interior life of the Church underwent only alterations of details, for liturgy and ritual were by then firmly established. The changes applied mainly in the disciplinary and juridical domain. During the feudal era, simony, traffic in ecclesiastical appointments, and moral depravity of the clergy wrought havoc. General and local councils increased in the eleventh and twelfth centuries in order to correct these defects and to re-establish a healthy discipline among the clergy.

The particular result of this effort was to modify profoundly the system of nominating the pope and bishops. From the beginning of the Church, the episcopacy was closely linked with ordination. The ordination ritual and that of episcopal consecration had long since become fixed, and no one dreamed of any innovations on this point so solidly established by tradition. However, the method of selecting the future bishops required a profound reform. In principle, the election of the pope and of the bishops belonged to the clergy and to the Christian people of the diocese to be filled. The intervention of princes and of powerful families produced many scandals.

In 1040, Pope Nicholas II entrusted the election of the pope to the cardinals alone. A century later, in 1179, the ecumenical Council of the Lateran required a majority of two-thirds of the votes for this election. Finally, the ecumenical Council of Lyons, in 1274, set up the rules for the conclave. These provisions, completed in 1621 by Pope Gregory XV and in 1904 by Pope Pius X, still regulate the pontifical election today.

The reform of episcopal elections proved to be more difficult. St. Gregory VII and his successors, in the twelfth and thirteenth centuries, had to engage in the long controversy on investiture to try to win respect for the Church's independence. One of the first phases of the reform entrusted the election of bishops to the cathedral chapter, excluding all other persons, whether lay or clerical. However, the pope reserved the right of intervening in order to insure the regularity of the election. These interventions subsequently became frequent and, from the fourteenth century on, the pope became the sole dispenser of bishoprics. Since that time, the pope alone names all bishops. He may recognize certain particular arrangements, such as consent of the government, but these arrangements may always be revoked.

This disciplinary reform resulted in a real advance of canon law. Until this time, the various rules had been distributed in councilar archives and in the records of the Holy See. The codification begun in the Carolingian era continued during the eleventh and twelfth centuries, and is exemplified by Burchard of Worms and Yves of Chartres. About 1140 the Decretals of Gratian established the basis of canon law until the twentieth century.

While it was strengthening its structure, the Church did not neglect the organization of its work. Continuing its great mission of charity, it created and managed through its religious orders, hospices, hospitals, benevolent efforts. But the most striking achievements in this period were the creation of the "leagues of peace" and the organization of teaching.

The Fight for Peace

The struggle for peace remained the most tangible proof of the vitality of the Christian ideal in the dark days of the Iron Age. According to traditional doctrine, it was for the king to maintain peace and justice, to defend the weak and oppressed. In fact, the anarchy of the feudal period hardly favored the application of such a principle. The king's authority was disputed, if it existed at all, and the princes indulged in endless little private wars or in mere highway robbery. Through all the means in its power, the Church attempted to establish peace and justice.

At the end of the tenth century the Church pronounced an anathema against plunderers of ecclesiastical possessions and the goods of the poor, or in the language of the period, of the peasants. The Council of Puy, in 990, excommunicated all those who exploited the peasants and merchants. Beyond this, the Bishop of Puy invited the lords of the region to subscribe to a peace pact. It is true that, considering the princes' ill will, the bishop made them take their oath under compulsion of the episcopal army and that he held hostages in order to make them keep the pact. But what other means could be used in a society where violence was the law? Nevertheless, the idea caught on, and bishops everywhere obtained, with more or less reluctance, the lords' adherence to the peace pacts. As a large number of princes violated their oath, certain bishops took the initiative of their colleague, Aymon de Bourges, and created peace leagues, directed by the bishop and supplied with an armed force that hunted down the perjurors.

In the middle of the eleventh century, a council decreed the "truce of God," that is, the forbidding of any act of private warfare from Wednesday evening to Monday morning. In November of 1095, at the Council of Clermont, Pope Urban II extended the "truce of God" to the universal Church. Various councils subsequently elaborated and extended the obligations of peace and of the "truce of God."

The results of these measures were not immediate, but undoubtedly they contributed to the disappearance of the private wars that infested feudal Europe and they prepared the way for the restoration of order under the rule of the principal kings.

Teaching

Taking up the tradition of the monks of Lérins and Marseilles, the monk Paul the Deacon, an advisor of

Charlemagne, had required each monastery to open a school. In spite of enormous ravages, the disorganization of society in the tenth century did not completely wipe out the work of Charlemagne. At the beginning of the eleventh century some cultural centers existed here and there, very unobtrusive and very poor. However, they had the advantage of existing and they were preparing for the future.

A considerable evolution affected intellectual life at this time. Teaching spread beyond the cloister, which lost control of it.

True, the Benedictine monks, St. Anselm and St. Bernard, were representative thinkers at this time. But the Abbey of Cluny was never an intellectual center, and devoted its efforts more to the liturgy. And the Cistercian rule excluded any idea of a monastic school. At the moment when the monks abandoned teaching and turned to the spiritual life, a thirst for culture and learning obsessed the West.

It was at this time that the episcopal schools developed, and some of them—Chartres, Rheims, Paris—acquired great renown in the tenth century. Placed under the jurisdiction of the bishop and intended mainly for the education of clerics, they saw a large influx of students and, during the twelfth century, became intellectual centers. Gerbert (the future Sylvester II), St. Fulbert, Bernard of Chartres, Gilbert of Porrée, William of Champeaux, and Peter Lombard taught in these schools. Paris prided itself on the famous school of St. Victor and the School of Saint Genevieve, where Abelard became famous.

At this time, various developments completely altered the teaching structure. The political events of the twelfth century favored intellectual contacts between the West and the Arab world and permitted the Latins to rediscover Greek culture. Social evolution upset the methods of the schools. The more advanced centers crystallized intellectual life, and Paris soon became Christendom's metropolis of learning. Furthermore, following a general trend, those engaged in studies organized autonomous corporations, thus giving rise to the first universities.

The pontifical power could not remain indifferent to this transformation. In 1134, Pope Innocent II intervened in an incident involving the School of Saint Genevieve and the Bishop of Paris. As it turned out, the pope supported the corporate movement, which favored his policy of centralization, and gave the university many privileges. The development reached its height by the middle of the thirteenth century. Independent of both the civil and episcopal powers, the university was under the direct control of the Holy See. The mendicant orders ensured a supply of monks and furnished a top-flight professional body more adapted to the new ideas.

The Council of Trent

Christendom reached its full growth in the middle of the thirteenth century. At this time, not without some difficulty, the Church managed to stabilize its internal organization and its integration in the medieval society of which it was the heart and brain. Such was the harmony of the institutions that they resisted all ensuing shocks. This aspect of the Church was to remain practically unchanged, in its main lines, until the beginning of the twentieth century; thus the stability of the Church was guaranteed, but it became more and more difficult for it to adapt to a constantly evolving society.

Called upon to sanction the reform of the Church after the disturbed period of the fifteenth century, the Council of Trent took numerous disciplinary steps to restore the clergy and to get completely rid of simony, those two wounds of the medieval Church. After legislating, the Council left to the pope the application of the reform measures. Now the papacy really had control of the Church's destiny, to the Church's great advantage. Some great popes—Pius IV, Pius V, Gregory XIII, and Sixtus V —worked energetically to carry out the Council's program.

The Pontifical administration was reorganized into large ministries called "congregations," each of which was responsible for watching over a particular sector of Catholicism: faith, sacraments, missionary activity, the episcopacy, etc. Rome thus had at its disposal a remarkably effective instrument, which contributed considerably to strengthening the Church's centralization and which is still in operation in our day.

This program was accompanied by an effort to unify the customs and practices of Catholicism. Pius V published the Catechism of the Council of Trent, which became the model for all diocesan catechisms, as well as a missal and a breviary that were obligatory for the whole Church. Gregory XIII reformed the calendar and created many colleges at Rome, which enabled the pope to guide the education of the leaders of the clergy directly. Sixtus V, founder of the modern organization of Roman administration, produced the official edition of the Vulgate, standard biblical text for Catholics.

Finally, these popes carried out one of the pledges of the Council and created diocesan seminaries, which marked an important step in the history of the Church. Thanks to this institution, the Church had a means of testing priestly vocations and making a selection among candidates. All future priests could thus receive the necessary intellectual and spiritual formation and learn to live the kind of religious life indispensable to their priesthood.

These pontiffs completed their work by reforming and rebuilding various religious orders.

In this way, beginning with the Council of Trent, the organization of the Church was completed. The clergy constituted a coherent and disciplined unit, dominated by pontifical authority. In addition, the harmonization of rites and usages accentuated the uniformity of the Catholic Church.

I have mentioned the danger of rigidity that went with this over-perfect organization. Also, the reform spirit, which was dominated by concern for order and discipline, resulted in a clericalization of the Church. The laity became minors, as it were, and could not enter into the areas of theology and Church discipline except with great caution. Thus a gap opened between the clergy and laity, with the latter feeling that the Church was no longer an integral part of their being but only an institution responsible for satisfying their religious aspirations. The situation was accentuated by the evolution of society, which gradually reduced the influence of the clergy by clearly distinguishing their role from that of the laity and by separating the spiritual from the other areas of life.

The difficulty reached its peak when civil society made claims on certain social sectors traditionally entrusted to the Church.

Although, for over fifteen centuries, the Church alone had provided for the care of the sick and other charitable works, state participation and control in this area produced no serious conflicts. It is true that these social projects had never been the object of Church organization as such, and it was, therefore, easy to find practical solutions to insure harmony in a field in which the interests of Church and state could meet without conflict.

On the other hand, the matter of education created constant tension between the Church and certain states during the nineteenth century. Each power claimed the monopoly of teaching. Loaded with dangerous emotion, the matter remains an issue of discord, awaiting the day when the Church, freeing itself from outworn structures, and the state, rid of an equally outworn anticlericalism, find a bold and original solution in harmony with modern society.

Problems of Today

In spite of the urging of certain gifted pioneers, the Church of the nineteenth century was primarily concerned with protecting its institutions and did not understand all that was involved in the development of a working class. Refusing to follow the pioneers of social Christianity, the clergy tried to confront the problem according to rules that had become anachronistic in this respect, using works of charity and philanthropy. The organization of social clubs and societies were palliatives that could only disappoint their founders.

However, with the lucidity that characterized his pontificate, Pope Leo XIII understood the gravity of the social evolution. The encyclical *Rerum Novarum*, promulgated May 15, 1891, insured the progress of social Catholicism, which developed in spite of enormous difficulties. But soon the problems raised necessitated a more direct action by the Church, which was gradually becoming aware of the need of evangelizing the working world and of the modern world in general. At this stage the matter was a Church problem, for it involved certain measures capable of profoundly altering the Church's organization. The various Catholic Action movements, with their own organization paralleling the traditional organization of the Church, raised delicate problems of jurisdiction and required an adaptation to diocesan and parish structure that was sometimes difficult. Moreover, Catholic Action once again gave the laity a place in the organization of the Church itself. The consequences of this development are still incalculable today.

The popes themselves, who were alert to this outburst of vitality and were aware of their heavy responsibility, regularly took steps intended to direct, assist, and, occasionally, to awaken this new development in Christianity. Thus, the encyclical of Leo XIII became part of a doctrinal series that touched in particular on philosophical studies, the relations of Christians with politics, biblical studies, Christian democracy, the unity of the Church, Christian marriage. Pius X attacked Modernism especially, but he also achieved an important liturgical reform that was destined to renovate Christian fervor, and he reorganized the Roman congregations. His successor published the Code of Canon Law. Pius XI made decisions that were fundamental for the development of the native clergy and gave the support of his authority to emerging Catholic Action. As for Pius XII, the postwar upheavals forced on him the superhuman task of being everywhere at once and of making decisions—often daring decisions—in widely varying fields: education, doctrine, exegesis, the nature of the Church, the missionary problem, and the reform of the liturgy. In the present time Pope John XXIII, while already having added new dimensions to the social doctrine of the Church through his encyclical, *Mater et Magister*, has convened the Second Vatican Council for the purpose of "union and renewal," and for the bringing of the Church "up to date" with the atomic age. It promises to be an event of far-reaching significance for renewing the Church from within, and for reaching out to the "separated brothers" from without. His last encyclical, *Pacem in terris*, addressed to all men in the interests of world peace, has in turn received the favorable attention of all men everywhere. These measures attest more than ever the vitality of the Catholic Church.

Part V

The Church, Source of Life

For every Christian the Church constitutes a mystery: the mystery of Christ's presence in the world. It is true that the Church seems to be a society really incarnate in the world, with temporal obligations. It has its doctrine, its government, its morality, and its laws. In these aspects, however, the Church would not be basically different from other religions unless it drew humanity to greater spiritual heights and to a deeper knowledge of divine reality. But this would not be enough to prove its irreplaceable role as the sole means of salvation, responsible for all humanity. Its basic nature, its *mystery*, derives from the fact that it is Christ on earth. All its activities, its dogmatic or moral preaching, are directed toward making humanity assume the form of Christ. While there are souls to be reached, civilizations to be affected, the Church cannot remain quiet and must introduce and develop in the midst of humanity the leaven of holiness of which it is the custodian.

This sublime mission implies that there is in the Church's teaching and way of life a new dimension that really expresses the essence of this unplumbed mystery of faith. It is the imprint left in history by this aspect of the Church which must now be described.

But, first, some observations of a general nature.

At first glance, it would appear that, as a principle of perfection, the Church must elude the historian. But since its very purpose is the salvation of humanity, the mystery of the Church is integrated in history. Each generation has reflected on this calling of the Church and has attempted to express it in deeds.

These concrete achievements, deeply affected by their historical context, have emphasized one or another aspect of Christian perfection. Each generation has brought its own contribution to this effort and has insured through this means the redemptive work of Christ. There is, therefore, a history of Christian perfection, marked off into sections by the unique character of the spirituality of each era. The age of the Fathers was dominated by the expectation of Christ's return. The medieval era gave more stress to the mystery of the Incarnation and strove to imitate the incarnate Christ. Modern times have been influenced by the Redemption, by the question of individual or collective salvation. This is merely a matter of emphasis, of course, and in no way excludes for these periods the other aspects of the Christian religion.

Certain ascetic authors have attempted to determine the means of attaining Christian perfection. Others have confided their intimate experience of communication with God, and, in spite of the exceptional character of their message, have given the Church a matchless wealth and vigor. Mystical authors, in effect, communicate to others the ardor that animates them.

Ascetic and mystical authors thus contribute to narrowing down the problem of the perfection that is demanded of every Christian. Quite often, moreover, they have encouraged spiritual tendencies that have given rise, for example, to a Benedictine, Franciscan, Dominican, or Carmelite spirituality. Here, again, there is no question of determining the superiority of one over the other but of noting a particular variety of manifestation of the Church's prodigious fertility.

The history of spirituality has been dominated by three crucial problems on which a position must be taken in order to avoid any ambiguity: the superiority of the religious state over ordinary life, of celibacy over marriage, of the contemplative over the active life. I have no intention of entering into a theological study of these questions —this is for more competent people—but of stressing a few points that are indispensable for a sound understanding of this history of spirituality.

In the broadest sense, the superiority of the monk over the layman is explained by his essential role in the life of the Church. A completely theoretical perfection would have no effect on the world. It is necessary, therefore, to establish a link between the evangelical ideal and the people called to practice it. By vocation, the Christian must be that "salt of the earth" that Christ demanded. However, since the Church must integrate all men and be normally a Church of the masses, a leaven would seem necessary to arouse the community and keep it from falling asleep. Such is the role of the monks. There is also a close connection between ascetic or mystical authors and the religious life. Nearly always, they have expressed their message by establishing a religious society that has deeply influenced the Christian community. In effect, the religious takes on his full significance when he takes his place in the mainstream of the Church and the Church will unceasingly denounce the man who egotistically seeks for personal perfection, even though he does so at the cost of the greatest renunciation.

One of the essential criteria of the religious life—one which aroused much discussion in the Church—is celibacy. Its superiority, affirmed by Christ, is unquestionable. The discussion has always arisen over the false problem of the contrast of celibacy and marriage. Now, as the greatest Doctors of the Church have clearly demonstrated—John Chrysostom, for example—religious celibacy is meaningful only with relation to marriage. In effect, it can constitute a criterion of perfection only if marriage is acknowledged as something intrinsically good, for, as John Chrysostom justly remarks, one can legitimately renounce only that which is good, since adherence to evil is excluded. Marriage, therefore, is the ordinary way of salvation for men and is an efficacious means of sanctity, for it is a sacrament. The superiority of celibacy thus arises in comparison with marriage and not in contrast to it. By voluntarily renounc-

ing marriage out of love for Christ, the religious gives
proof of a special generosity toward God and His Church.
This positive motive of love is what gives value to continence freely accepted. This preliminary renunciation implies the promise to live an exemplary life. Thus, through
his celibacy, the religious helps to maintain the perfection
of Christian marriage by keeping alive in the Church the
virtue of chastity, which is obligatory for everyone. Moreover, his independence permits him to enter into the vital
tide of spirituality which must insure the development of
Christian perfection. Celibacy is, as it were, the supreme
distinction of a life given wholly to the service of Christ.

Similar reasons justify the need for a contemplative life.
Since prayer is an imperative obligation for Christians and
a vital function of the Church, it is important that women
and men devote themselves exclusively to this task. Besides the value of prayer in itself, their life helps to keep
alive the meaning of prayer.

Thus, in spite of the failings of some of its members,
the religious life, with its obligations of celibacy and contemplation, is not confined to the margin of the Christian
community. Its place is, rather, in the vanguard. Quite often it marks the orientation of a new generation or gives
its impetus to a new advance of the Church. Its history
is quite as vital to Christians as the history of ideas or
doctrine.

1. The Early Centuries

Virgins, Widows, and Ascetics

A current opinion would have it that the search for Christian perfection is related to a weakening of the Church's fervor. Thus, religious are forced to go outside the community, or at least to its borders, in their search for conditions adequate to their thirst for the ideal. In reality, this call to the ideal is heard in the very heart of the Christian community and especially in the midst of the most fervent groups. The religious life is closely associated with the generosity of the community, for it develops its most sublime aspect. So the existence of a religious life appears as early as the founding of the Church.

Thus, widows brought to the Church the contribution of their sorrowful freedom, women consecrated themselves to the Lord through their virginity, and men too, according to St. Paul, himself a bachelor. In effect, St. Paul gave up marriage for the sake of asceticism and not because he was an Apostle. Several Apostles were married. Priesthood is one thing, the religious life is another. The priest exercises a social function, as it were, in the midst of the Church. Celibacy is the result of an individual call to perfection. We shall see, moreover, how, in the course of history, the Church came to entrust the priestly responsibility only to souls that were already called to a more perfect life.

These ascetics, who were distinguished by their continence, were for the first Christian communities an active ferment in the religious life. Their influence was the greater since they lived in the midst of the community and made no change in their way of life unless it was in their assiduous pursuit of prayer and a stricter observance of the evangelical counsels. Their existence seemed natural to the early communities, which were themselves imbued with a generous fervor, and they did not feel the need of establishing a rule for their behavior. Only widows and virgins merited particular attention from the Church. It seemed necessary to watch over them and protect them in a society in which women's status was especially difficult.

St. Paul intervened on many occasions to regulate forms of spiritual life and get rid of abuses. In his Epistles it appears that the various expressions of Christian perfection—religious life or mystic impulses—should be exercised under the Church's control and in its service if they are to acquire their full value. Paul is not evincing mistrust here, for he himself has given us in his writings certain sublime aspects of his inner life and experience. But he declared that the life of union with God can be conceived of by the Christian only in and through the Church. Later, Clement of Rome was to remind the Christians of Corinth of this: "Let the body that we constitute in Jesus Christ be kept in its integrity; let each be subject to his neighbor, according to the grace that has been given him . . . let him who is chaste in his flesh be not prideful, knowing that it is another (the Lord) who gives him the gift of continence."

Thus, the religious life, an eminent but natural function of the Church, would almost completely escape us during the early centuries if certain abuses had not crept into this search for perfection.

The Foolish Virgins

In a world as depraved as Roman society, the Church was proud of its ascetics and its virgins, who constituted a glorious manifestation of the Christian ideal. So, this division of the faithful soon took on a greater and greater importance, a development that did not take place without seriously disturbing the leaders of the Church. Some practiced this more perfect life as a way of sanctity gratifying to their own self-respect, and were led into a certain insubordination with regard to the hierarchy. This was an endemic ailment, a normal temptation connected with the religious life. The first ascetics did not completely escape it. All the authors of this period—Clement, Ignatius, Polycarp, Tertullian, Origen—had, like St. Paul, to call upon the ascetics and virgins to submit to the bishop, the head of the community.

The practice of celibacy soon raised difficult questions. While the obligation of celibacy was incurred through a free choice, the breaking of this obligation did not take place without scandal in the community. Therefore, the ecclesiastical authority soon had to intervene to settle this question and decide on the circumstances and procedures needed for the return to ordinary life of those who had rashly blundered into the religious life.

The solution of this purely disciplinary question was simple enough. A false conception of the religious life led to serious troubles of another kind. The practice of continence was regarded as the most obvious external sign of the perfection of the ascetics. From this position, the confusing of perfection and continence was only a step away, a step that was blithely taken by a certain number of virgins who ventured to live a life in the world and were satisfied with merely guarding their physical integrity. Tertullian and Cyprian took a strong stand against this abuse, which threatened not only to discredit the bands of virgins but to squander the spiritual treasure of the Church. They recalled that chastity, a completely interior virtue, and a particularly fragile one, could not be respected without the practice of a large number of other virtues, among the first of which were charity, piety, and modesty.

Again, the hierarchy had to suppress certain erroneous conceptions which were gaining acceptance by Christians. An entire trend of thought, designated as "encratist"—from a Greek word meaning continence—sought to impose on Christians renunciation of marriage and abstinence from meat and wine. Paul had already had to put his followers on guard against this false conception of asceticism. As a matter of fact, according to the constant mind of the Church, mortification is an interior thing. It is true that it must be expressed by certain renunciations and certain practices, but no food, nor any natural object can be forbidden in itself. Therefore, while we may deprive ourselves of certain goods, and while it is even recommended that we do so to discipline our will, this is no reason for saying that the use of these things is bad for others. From the beginning, the Church has been suspicious of ascetics who sought to impose their own mortifications on others. This disease—encratism—was propagated in the Church, as was already mentioned, through the influence of the Montanist heresy.

The Lord Shall Return

If the ascetical life was highly favored in the Church's beginnings, this was because it was supported by an intense spiritual life of the communities, dominated by the hope for an early return of Christ. This belief in an early end of the world, numerous echoes of which are found in the letters of St. Paul, was to extend well beyond the first Christian generation. Undoubtedly, this illusion was soon dissipated and Christians understood that the Church would have to struggle and suffer for a long time to come. Yet, this idea of the return of Christ, stripped of the simplest expectation of an immediate, universal upheaval, animated the spiritual life of the early Christians. It was expressed in the feeling of the permanent, though invisible, presence of the Lord Jesus in the midst of the community and the hope of each of the faithful of soon being united with Him for all eternity. The sense of the precariousness of the world, still strong in the preaching of the fourth-century Fathers, provided an excellent ascetic basis for this desire of union with Christ. In effect, the renunciation of goods here below appeared easier for the Christian who regarded himself as a traveler responsible for bringing the good news of salvation. An inner life based on these two notions sustained heroism during persecutions. Far from being depressed in this world that hated them, the Christians, in spite of their precarious lot, lived in enthusiasm and hope. Death did not frighten them and, in many cases, the Acts of the Martyrs show us that tortures assumed for them the appearance of a triumphal sacrifice. The Church even had to deal severely with the intemperate zeal of some who, under the influence of Montanist excesses, voluntarily offered themselves to the executioner. Martyrdom, the bishops opportunely recalled, must be accepted, not sought for.

In any case, the communities of the time lived in a state of intense fervor which began to fall away only during the third century, when the number of the faithful substantially increased. The end of the persecutions, with a sudden increase of the resources of the Church, while it guaranteed their security, weakened that striving toward the ideal that had been maintained by the fervor of the communities and by the ever-present possibility of martyrdom. Another attitude was required of souls dedicated to a more complete perfection. Then monasticism appeared for the first time in the Church.

The Monks

For a century there have been increased efforts to seek out the origins of monasticism in religious movements anterior to, or parallel with, Christianity. I see no need for lingering on this question, which is a negligible matter from various points of view. Since Christianity assumes all human values, it is not only possible but inevitable that there should be found among some of its rites and customs a correspondence with other similar customs of mankind. No one will question, for example, that the need for silence, meditation, and an often intense asceticism is intimately related to the religious instinct. Therefore, these things had to be found in Christianity. It matters little whether this behavior arose spontaneously as a normal development of humanity or whether it was more or less acquired from some already existing source. The special character of Christian monasticism does not depend, in fact, on any particular style of life, but on the guiding principle of a response to the Gospel that involves the development of authentically Christian spiritual values.

Monasticism appeared, then, toward the beginning of the fourth century. The exact date is unknown to us, for this was not an institution created by authority but by a sort of impulse that arose in Egypt, soon spread throughout the East, and in less than fifty years invaded the entire body of the Church. This movement, our knowledge of which is incomplete, represents in its scope and variety a major advance in the history of the Church.

The first hermit we learned about—thanks to his friend and admirer Athanasius—was the great St. Anthony, who may be regarded as the father of monasticism. A native of Egypt, he sold his possessions on the death of his parents and began to live as an ascetic. Some fifteen years later, being drawn by the desert, he lived in the most complete solitude. Subsequently, some disciples settled near him, and visitors, attracted by his sanctity, became numerous. Then he plunged still deeper into the desert. He died there about the year 336, at the age of 105.

Thus, the father of hermits supplied the example of

complete detachment and of a life devoted solely to prayer and penance. For all that, he was not without interest in the life of the Church, and he twice left his solitude. On the first occasion, during the persecution of Diocletian, Anthony went down to Alexandria to support the martyrs and strengthen their courage. His second trip to the capital was for the purpose of lending assistance to Athanasius in his struggle with Arianism by officially offering him the support of his own renown and of all the monks following his example. Athanasius showed his gratitude by writing, in the evening of his life, the biography of his friend. This life of Anthony had a prodigious success and contributed in large part to the spread of monasticism in the West. Anthony the Great, with his temptations, remained one of the most popular figures in the Catholic Church.

The example of Anthony was contagious. In Egypt, the desert became the retreat of all men drawn by perfection. Thus, the spiritual posterity of a certain Amon, who retired into the frightful valley of Nitria, reached the astonishing number of five thousand monks in a few decades. Anthony's disciples at Scete and Tabennensi in the desert— likewise numbered in the thousands. All was not perfect in these hermits' republics where an independence neighboring on anarchy prevailed. Emulation often degenerated into a veritable contest of virtuosity, which had only the most remote connection with Christian perfection. The existence of these gatherings of men who no longer felt they were subject to any regular authority presented a real danger for the Church. As a matter of fact, at least in this period, the monks of Egypt remained faithful supporters of the Bishop of Alexandria, who encouraged this movement and strove to provide the monks with spiritual centers where they could meet and benefit from a more regular life. However, the hermits subsequently caused a great deal of trouble for the ecclesiastical authority, which encouraged this sort of life only as a special exception.

About the same period, another Egyptian hermit, Pachomius, also acquired great celebrity. A former military man, he had kept a liking for discipline. He naturally attempted, therefore, to organize his disciples to lead a common life. He thus founded the first monastery. Soon he recruited hundreds of postulants to the monastic life and had to found nine branches to satisfy all the requests. We still have his rule, which is fairly endurable and is quite moderate in comparison with the practices of the hermits. Inaugurating another tradition, Pachomius had his sister come to him to establish, under his counsel, the first women's monastery.

From Egypt, monasticism swarmed, under various forms, into Palestine and Syria. The Syrians exceeded the bounds of reason, going far beyond the austerities of the Egyptians. The Stylites distinguished themselves by spending a large part of their life perched on columns on the top of the sugar-loaf hills of the region, to the great displeasure of the ecclesiastical authorities, who condemned these practices.

However, the old form of asceticism was still held in honor. In each community one found men and women who continued to devote themselves to the service of the Church in silence and prayer. At Antioch, Diodorus and his friend Flavian organized in the very midst of the Church a community which appears to have been of a more refined and intellectual type than the Egyptian monasteries. They introduced into the Church singing with two choirs, so that the faithful could take a more active part in prayer. Their ascetic group became a kind of nursery for bishops and priests, some of whom gained great renown in the Church.

Then came a development of vital importance: the encounter of the great masters of Christian thought with this spiritual movement. The particularly fruitful outcome gave monasticism its permanent place in the Church.

The Fathers and the Monks

All (or practically all) of the Fathers of the fourth century spent some time in monastic life. This was not the culmination of their religious life but, on the contrary, the starting point of their activity, while they were still in their youth. There is nothing surprising in this. These chosen souls could not fail to be attracted to this unusual way of life, entirely consecrated to the Lord. This ascetical experience, while not the climax of an active life but a time of probation that enabled souls to deepen their spiritual life before beginning action, thus fulfilled its normal role.

Each of the Fathers practiced asceticism according to his temperament and aspirations. There is need for a study —and a particularly fruitful one it would be—of the religious life of their early youth. The move toward the desert had just begun when Athanasius appeared in history, and his bishop, Alexander, hastened to bring this promising young man into the service of the Church. But subsequently his many dealings with the great of this world enabled him to return frequently among the monks and to draw from his contact with them new strength to resume the struggle. Ambrose did not have the opportunity of living with the monks, who were as yet non-existent in the West, but when he became a bishop he promoted their way of life. Hilary learned to like them in the East and lived with the famous St. Martin. Augustine, after a far from ascetic youth, tells us himself of the influence of the life of St. Anthony on his conversion. His long retreat at Cassiciacum offered a peaceful solitude that was perfectly adapted to his intellectual temperament. Later, he organized his bishopric like a monastery. Basil and Gregory Nazianzen, after visiting the monks of Egypt and Palestine, retired to a quiet and verdant valley in Asia Minor. The impulsive and restless temperament of John Chrysostom led him to try

all possible forms of ascesis, from the community of Diodorus to the excesses of the Syrian hermits. As for Jerome,
his extraordinary personality, full of contrasting elements,
led him to follow an entirely individual way of life. All his
life long he was "the Monk." He traveled through the deserts, became a hermit, and quarreled with all his neighbors until the day when he returned to Rome and at last
ruled his own monastery, which was a community of
women!

This hasty glance is enough to show that monastic life
was not just an intellectual problem for the Fathers of
the Church. They participated with their entire being in
this religious movement.

Therefore, when they were called upon to assume responsibilities, they could not remain indifferent, and they
left their mark on this essential aspect of the life of the
Church.

Without openly intervening, Athanasius did all he could
to discipline the Egyptian monks and keep them under the
control of the Church. In the absence of documents, however, we cannot determine the significance of his periods
in the desert and the advice lavished on the followers of
Pachomius. His *Life of St. Anthony*, through his choice
of incidents and the sayings attributed to his good friend,
became of great importance in the Church's spiritual life.

The influence of Basil was basic. Introduced to the ascetic life by Eustathes of Sebaste—some of whose errors,
unfortunately, had to be suppressed by the Church—he
made journeys among the ascetics of Egypt and Palestine
with his friend Gregory Nazianzen. There he learned the
grandeur of monasticism, but he also learned its dangers
and its failings. Though still convinced of the importance
of this institution in the very heart of the Church, Basil
undertook to reform it. The excesses of the solitaries quite
reasonably made him suspicious. He therefore attempted
to promote a form of community religious life, fairly close

to that of the Pachomian monasteries. But he brought these innumerable and practically ungovernable republics down to dimensions within the range of human possibilities. Thus he favored monasteries with smaller complements of monks, and he forbade the superiors to extend their authority over a number of foundations. Moreover, he set up a rule that was directly inspired by the Gospel and in which he gave an important place to prayer, work, obedience, and silence. Complete continence and poverty were taken for granted, since they were basic elements of the monks' asceticism. All these prescriptions, scattered through a number of works, were brought together in a special collection that became the code of the Eastern monasteries and later regulated those of the Greco-Slavic world.

The influence of John Chrysostom was decidedly different. He had a rather unhappy recollection of his attempt at life as a hermit. The empty performances of the solitaries seemed to him to ruin the body without any spiritual benefit. On the other hand, he retained great respect for the school of asceticism of his master, Diodorus. So his work undoubtedly represents the most faithful echo of the ascetic ideal of Antioch. Lacking Basil's administrative talents, he established no rule. But he wrote out a number of ascetic counsels, which were brought together in a collection and became one of the favorite books of Eastern and Western monks. Apart from the virtues professed by Basil, on whose works he had certainly meditated, John Chrysostom was the apostle of chastity, moderation, and joy. His remarkably vigorous psychological analyses brought everyone counsels of great use in the spiritual life.

John Chrysostom also was generous in his advice to certain followers who subsequently played an important role in the development of monasticism, especially Cassian, who introduced the common life in the West.

Basil and John Chrysostom did not confine their spiritual activity to the perfecting of monasteries. Chrysostom in particular constantly stressed in his work the need for the presence of ascetics within the city, mingling in the life of the people, in order to make Christ's ideal shine forth. Through his homilies we learn of the existence at Antioch of nursing nuns, who went into homes to care for the poor and aged. The two bishops also founded hospitals at Caesarea and Constantinople, entrusting their management to medical and nursing religious. We should also stress again Chrysostom's attempt to send religious missionaries among the barbarian tribes and to institute teaching monks. Let it suffice to recall that these two great saints saw no limits in the spiritual life and that they strove to increase its expressions.

Gregory Nazianzen, surnamed "the Theologian," often inspired the ascetic and mystic authors of the Greek Church; Gregory of Nyssa also had considerable influence, but their work merges with and was dominated by that of their brother and friend, Basil.

The Monks of the West

The influence of the Western Fathers was less significant. In their time, monasteries in this part of the world had not developed as much as in the East. The contribution of Ambrose of Milan and of Jerome was, rather, on the doctrinal level. But, all through his episcopate, Ambrose fought to insure the development of women's religious vocations and he must have had to combat family prejudices in this matter. Jerome, who was too much of an individualist to live in a community, nevertheless directed and advised a group of holy women, with whom he had prodigious success. He introduced them to exegesis and even taught them Hebrew in order to have them join in his works of erudition. The association of Jerome and his religious, too unusual to serve as a model, was a highly colorful episode and remarkable for its sanctity, but it was not a school of spirituality.

Augustine himself experienced a sincere desire for withdrawal after his conversion and retired to Tagaste with some friends, but the service of the Church called him to a higher destiny. Following a usage established in Italy by Eusebius, Bishop of Vercelli, and perhaps inspired by the comments of Diodorus, Augustine organized his see in the style of a monastery, in which he led a community life with his clergy under a strict rule. Much later, about the ninth century, this practice was resumed in the West and placed under the patronage of the "rule" of St. Augustine. From this development was born an important religious family, which has continued, with varying fortunes, down to our day.

The spiritual writings of Augustine, like those of his colleague, John Chrysostom, had a decisive influence on ascetic life.

Many reasons of a sociological type—and therefore difficult to pinpoint—were involved in the slow spread of the ascetic life in the West. Geographical conditions and the customs of the inhabitants of these regions did not favor an increase in the number of hermits. However, Ambrose, Jerome, and Augustine showed they were interested in protecting and encouraging virginity in the Christian community.

But popular enthusiasm for the Easterners could not fail to affect the Western part of the Church. There were frequent contacts between the two communities through pilgrimages to the Holy Places by the faithful, periodical meetings of bishops, or simply through political events in the Empire. The exile of Athanasius at Trier and that of Hilary of Poitiers in the East were influential in introducing monasticism in the West. Athanasius made the Latin world acquainted with the fervor of the Egyptians, while

Hilary had the opportunity of living with the Eastern monks, and on his return he joined the famous St. Martin as a companion.

St. Martin played in the West the role of St. Anthony in the East. His father, a veteran of the Roman legions, had forced him to serve a military enlistment. At the end of his service, Martin joined Hilary and founded the monastery of Ligugé, near Poitiers. Elected Bishop of Tours, he founded in the vicinity of the city, the monastery of Marmoutier. But this love of perfection was united with a lively apostolic desire. Riding a donkey, living a rough life, dividing his time between prayer and preaching, Martin crossed and re-crossed Gaul and made himself the apostle of the rural populations, still impregnated with paganism. He thus accomplished the conversion of the country, inspired in it a love of monastic life, and became its most popular saint. However, he remained only an originator. He lacked administrative gifts for organizing a spiritual family.

About the same time, Eusebius, Bishop of Vercelli in Italy, developed a form of asceticism that was very close in spirit to that of Diodorous in Antioch. Although this movement has not yet been sufficiently studied, it is very clear that it encouraged monastic life among the parish clergy. This development had great success in Gaul and in Africa. St. Augustine and St. Caesarius of Arles became ardent promoters of community life among the clergy.

Following the rule of St. Pachomius, there was established in the island of Lérins a famous monastery that furnished a large number of holy bishops to this region.

However, the real promoter of monastic life in the West was John Cassian, a priest of Marseilles, originally from Eastern Europe, probably from Rumania. After a stay of some ten years among the Egyptian monks, Cassian came to Constantinople, where his close friend, John Chrysostom, ordained him a deacon. Cassian went to Rome to in-form the pope of the dramatic events that had led to the deportation of Chrysostom. Some years later, at Marseilles, he founded the abbey of St. Victor. Between 410 and 425, Cassian put out books of spirituality, the *Institutions* and the *Lectures*, that supplied material for meditation for monks of the Middle Ages. In these works Cassian related his conversations with the monks of the Egyptian desert, but he inserted into them the instructions of his illustrious master. Besides the traditional virtues of ascetical life, Cassian repeatedly recommended discretion, patience, fraternal friendship, fidelity to promises, peace—and in these things we find reflected the spirit of John Chrysostom. Unfortunately, Cassian put forth some erroneous opinions on the role of divine grace, and this gave a certain discredit to a work which is most attractive in other respects.

With Cassian the patristic age ended in the West.

Saints Are Not Angels

Nonetheless, this quest for perfection was not free from deviations and errors. But unlike heresies, the errors concerning problems of spiritual life were manifested especially in the West, where they subsequently gave rise to profound disturbances.

In the East, Eustathes of Sebaste, St. Basil's teacher of asceticism, was suspect for some time. Criticism was aimed not so much at practices he encouraged—his asceticism seemed to be relatively moderate—but at the tendency he had of presenting his ascetical practices as obligatory for all Christians. In the same region and more or less in this same period the sect of the Messalians developed. These wandering monks were a serious danger because of their eccentric habits. Their doctrine was based on prayer and absolute detachment from earthly goods. Roving through hills and valleys, sleeping in the open, men and women side by side, living only on alms, these ascetics regarded themselves as angelic beings. Obsession with ideas about demons led them to grotesque, if not magical, practices. The Church took a strong stand against this movement which discredited asceticism. But, nevertheless, the movement had a certain success and continued for a long time in Asia Minor and Armenia.

The West was not forced to deal with such eccentricities, but, nevertheless, was much concerned with the problem of sanctity.

Pelagianism, in the fourth century, almost eliminated real spiritual life, substituting for it a morality and asceticism which were more profane than religious. The semi-Pelagianism of which the good abbot Cassian became guilty, was rather the unfortunate result of an unbalanced mixture of Greek and Latin conceptions of perfection. Abetted by human passions, semi-Pelagianism long disturbed the ascetic communities of Gaul and Italy.

Other errors attacked the very principle of perfection. In Spain, Priscillian, a preacher of asceticism, was accused of reviving Manicheism and of preaching an immoral doctrine. The emperor intervened and Priscillian was condemned to death. Thereupon passions were stirred up and Priscillianism continued for a long time.

At the same time, in Rome, a certain monk named Jovinian, weary of excessively ascetic practices, returned to an ordinary mode of life, and to justify himself, taught that there was no religious difference between celibacy and marriage and that mortifications were useless. The Church, obviously, could not tolerate such teachings.

Pelagius, Priscillian, Jovinian, and their followers thus led the Church into a controversy that abounded in consequences for the future of Latin Catholics. The defenders of orthodoxy, Augustine, Ambrose, and Jerome, who were strong enough to crush the enemy, reacted excessively. In the heat of the struggle, Augustine, a great champion of the theology of grace, made some unfortunate remarks that were often quoted subsequently, especially at the time of the Protestant Reformation. Moreover, some of his extreme positions introduced a pessimistic view of human nature, which acquired in the West a place which it certainly did not have in the total thought of the great Doctor. Ambrose became the champion—a little on the extreme side—of virginity. As for Jerome, he took delight in discharging upon Jovinian all his rancor against the worldlings of Rome who had persecuted him so much. His violent polemics frightened his own friends. According to him, marriage was only a necessary evil. Dytherambic praises of monastic life animated his teaching, which was, nonetheless, orthodox. He never fell into encratism, but his position was still dangerous: it introduced into clerical circles a condescension toward marriage that was more harmful than downright hostile.

In all fairness, in dealing with the controversy, we must admit that there was nothing in common between the exaggerations of Ambrose, Jerome, or Augustine, and the ideas of their adversaries. We must regret, however, that in succeeding centuries, certain intemperate defenders of virginity and monastic life found support in the most extreme texts, the most unfortunate phrases of these men, at the risk of falsifying the traditional teaching of the Church.

None of these Fathers claimed to make perfection the exclusive property of monks and ascetics. Their sole desire was to have all men advance in the evangelical ideal. To this end they preached to their people a remarkably rich doctrine which drew a limited number to enter on the road to perfection.

The Spiritual Life

How can the vast flow of life in the fourth century be summed up in a few lines? So numerous, so varied, so de-

voted were those shepherds who, each with his own qualities, inculcated Christian ideals in his people! Nevertheless, we can discern in their teaching a common character
and certain typical aspects of religious life proposed to the
faithful of the time.

First of all, Christians nourished their interior life by
reading and meditation of Holy Scripture. The Fathers
never conceived of teaching except in the form of an explanation of a verse of the Gospel, or very often as an
extended commentary on various books of the New Testament, which went on for several weeks, or indeed, for several months. The faithful were thus constantly comparing
their thought and life with revealed doctrine. The heated
discussions that ensued still surprise us today, for the entire Christian community took an active part in theological
controversies.

To this instruction was added a keen sense of community prayer, likewise nourished by Scripture. The piety of
the faithful was ordinarily expressed in religious offices
and in the recitation of the Psalms, which were regarded
as the Christians' bedside book, along with the New Testament, a collection of prayers and a condensation of elementary instruction. Indeed, this tradition survives in the
Mass, which is interwoven with Psalm verses, that are,
at the same time prayers and summaries of the doctrinal
meaning of the feast day.

Among all the virtues, the Fathers put the emphasis on
charity whether in giving alms or in sharing in the suffer-
ings and joys of one's neighbors and on conjugal fidelity,
exemplified not only by their struggle against adultery and
divorce but especially by their reminder of the essential
harmony that must unite spouses and impregnate their
daily lives.

All of this spiritual life was animated by the intuition
of mankind's salvation. The work of the Fathers seems
like a perpetual song of thanksgiving to God, who saved

humanity by sending His only Son, and of gratitude to Providence which permitted them to live in this "advent of the Lord," a prelude to His return at the end of time. True, the Fathers did not develop a theology of the Church: they did not sense the need of putting into formulas the fundamental principle of their special life. They felt that they were bound to the Church by a physiological bond. For them, the Church, the spouse of Christ, His Mystical Body, was, above all, the Mother in which the soul acquires a new life to rise again in Christ.

The spiritual progress of the Christian consequently became an imperative necessity, whether he was a monk or layman. What the Fathers proposed to their faithful, then, was an ideal little different from that of the monks: an insistence on the importance of chastity and continence, of total renunciation of all material goods, of the perpetual obligation of prayer and the apostolate, and of the importance of the contemplative life. And this teaching did not reflect an extreme rigorism or nostalgia for monastic life. The Fathers' correspondence attests to the sturdy good sense of their teaching, together with their profound faith, which prevented them from preaching a second-rate Christianity, one that encouraged mediocrity. Their demanding spirituality staggered the mediocre and stimulated the ardor of the elite.

Their own sanctity was splendid. Quite often, led away by their zeal for Christ, these shepherds forgot the subject of their discussion and revealed to the public the intense inner life that animated them. Their mystical life, which they did not seek to analyze, ascends to heights on which faith, hope, and charity are fused in an immense cry of love. And it is perhaps here, rather than in their teaching, properly so-called, that the secret of the matchless value of their message is to be found.

2. The Middle Ages

Eastern Monasteries

The Greek Church did not know the brutal shock of the barbarian invasions. The vague frontier that separates the period of the Fathers from the Byzantine period, is practically nonexistent in the field of spirituality. The religious life continued to be nourished directly by the texts of the Fathers of the Church. However, creative effort noticeably diminished until, in the eleventh century, there was veritable spiritual and intellectual paralysis.

Monasteries continued to increase—there were already no less than a hundred in the vicinity of Constantinople at the beginning of the sixth century—and the various forms of asceticism prospered. All this did not take place without some disadvantages: numerous wandering monks were tramping through the East, and not all the monasteries were disciplined. Therefore, Justinian, in the middle of the sixth century, decreed numerous laws to organize the monasteries and thus unified the various ascetic institutions which, from that time on, were based almost exclusively on the precepts of St. Basil.

The extent of the movement gave the monks a preponderant influence in the Eastern Church: they intervened in the great doctrinal conflicts, and most often, inflamed them, for these troops of monks, more excited than scholarly, were powerful forces in the hands of the various factions.

It would be unjust, however, to think of them all as ignorant and turbulent. Many of their religious centers proved to be sources of intense religious culture. The monks specialized in a type of literature that was destined to have a great future: the writing of the lives of the saints. Continuing the tradition established by Athanasius, the monks maintained their fervor by having circulated in the monasteries collections of anecdotes and pious remarks made by the most notable ascetics. Sometimes these were real biographies, but most often the desire to edify prevailed over the concern for historical exactitude. Some of these collections such as the *Historia Lausiaca* of Palladius and the *Spiritual Meadow* of St. John Moschos, had an immense success and can still be read with interest in our own day. In the tenth century, a monk, a dependent of the emperor of Constantinople, Simeon Metaphastes, condensed this entire literature into a series of *Lives of Saints*, arranged according to the order of the calendar, which became an inexhaustible source of all pious biographers.

Besides this edifying literature that fed the simple and robust faith of the most ignorant, the monastic centers deepened the roots of the spiritual life, and published ascetical works intended to increase the fervor of the elite. These were most often collections which grouped together or summed up the ascetical works of Basil, Chrysostom, Gregory Nazianzen, and other Fathers. Original works of great value also appeared.

Thus, Diadocus, Bishop of Photike, wrote a little treatise on spiritual perfection. St. Anilus, a great admirer of Chrysostom, wrote books and many letters of advice for the use of monks and laymen. But the most popular was St. John Climacus, whose *Ladder of Paradise* had a great success for a thousand years. John explained to his brothers in religion the various steps to be taken in order to advance on the road to perfection. He gave great emphasis to the struggle against vices and to the importance of penance and solitude. The austere path that he pointed out to religious could not fail to win the sympathy of generous souls, who drew courage and comfort from his work.

About the same period a mysterious personage put out, under the patronage of Dionysius, a disciple of St. Paul, some mystical treatises which impregnated the spirituality of the Middle Ages. According to this "pseudo-Dionysius," the transcendence of God sets narrow limits on the rational knowledge that man can have of Him. Only mystical theology enables him to penetrate deeper into knowledge of God, through a sort of supernatural and inexpressible intuition. Man can and must prepare himself to receive this veritable gift of God by prayer and by an attempt at moral and spiritual purification. There is then established a tenuous and silent contact, a "mystical union," between God and the soul, sealed by a mutual love. Thus Dionysius gave to contemplation and the quest for this "mystical union" a preponderant place in the spiritual life. This doctrine prevailed in the religious centers of the Middle Ages and opened the way to mystical theology.

We should also mention St. Theodore the Studite and his friends of the Studion, a famous monastery of Constantinople, who fought the good fight in the Iconoclasm controversy. Finally, St. Maximus the Confessor, a bold defender of Catholic doctrine against the demands of the emperor, was cruelly mutilated because of his faith and died in 662 as a result of his torture. His work, completely imbued with the doctrine of the Cappadocian Fathers, likewise tends to draw souls toward the contemplation of God but gives great importance to the Incarnate Word. For Theodore, the Incarnation is the great event of the world; also, Christians must imitate the Savior through prayer, effort, and contemplation. Thus, through this doctrine of the imitation of Christ, Theodore was heralding a spiritual tendency that was to continue to increase until the seventeenth century.

The Monks in the West

Although the monastic life in the West during the fourth century did not compare in fervor with that in the East, it nevertheless left an indelible imprint on the Church.

During the first four centuries, ascetics lived in rhythm with the community. Their life, closer to the evangelical counsels, required of them certain more severe efforts, such as celibacy and exercises of mortification, and conferred on them certain privileges. But, otherwise, they participated in the life of the community and received, on the whole, the same instructions as the faithful.

The monasteries, by setting the ascetics apart, produced a decisive transformation of spiritual life. In the East, the spectacular flight to the desert had few repercussions on the progress of the community, at least in the early years. In the West, on the other hand, geographical and climatic conditions did not favor such a radical exodus. Some ties remained—though very tenuous ones—between the monks and the Christian community, and these bonds led to a parallel evolution of the Church and monastic institutions.

With their organization, the monasteries became autonomous institutions in the Church and tended to take over the direction of spiritual life. Even when they were established in out-of-the-way places, they remained relatively accessible centers of attraction. Thus, the Churches gladly found their bishops in neighboring monasteries. Currents of spirituality arose in connection with the appearance of the great religious families and the monastic institutions fulfilled their role as a source of ascetic and mystical life for the Catholic Church as a whole. On the other hand, the community, through its own needs and aspirations, inspired the reform of the old orders and the creation of new forms of religious life. Thus was established a harmony between the Christian community and its spiritual elite, which the Church attempted to discipline within an institutional framework.

St. Benedict

The great figure of St. Benedict dominated the first stage of this interpenetration of monasteries and the community.

The rise of monastic life in the West coincided with the unloosing of the barbarians upon the Empire. Following the example of St. Martin and the Provençal communities, men began to live the monastic life, either as hermits or in communities. Cassian, the monks of Lerins, and, some years later, St. Caesarius of Arles, had outlined regulations for the life of their communities, but their routines were manuals of asceticism rather than real regulations. There was no authority to impose these rules on other communities and, hence, no possibility of co-ordinating monastic development. The greatest variety reigned among the monastic foundations.

Abuses, inevitable, in such an anarchic situation, showed the need for organizing this vast ascetic burgeoning, at least on the disciplinary level. It even seems that Pope Hormisdas, a contemporary of St. Benedict, was interested in doing this, but the latter had the honor (and the genius) of composing a rule which became established as the most powerful source of Western spirituality.

Benedict of Nursia lived in the beginning of the sixth century. Sprung from a well-to-do family, he received an education proper to his social rank. He soon felt called to the ascetic life and fled to the wilderness of Subiaco. After various unfortunate episodes, he established himself on Monte Cassino and founded a monastery there, where he died about 550.

Benedict did not attempt to innovate. He had long meditated on the writings of his predecessors and was explicitly dependent upon St. Augustine, St. Basil, and Cassian. However, his Rule is neither an extract nor a resumé, nor a condensation of earlier ascetic texts. Benedict, indeed, had experience with the advice given by these great masters of spirituality to souls eager for perfection. He gave to his monks and to posterity the result of his experience and of his prayer in a little work of seventy-three articles which remains one of the masterpieces of spiritual literature.

The originality of the Rule—if such an institution can be summed up in a few words—springs from its simplicity, its moderation, and its flexibility. Its simplicity is apparent even in the way it is written, embellishments and literary digressions being passed over for the concise and rather severe style of Roman juridical texts. A superficial reading does not reveal its greatness. No sentimental or picturesque element holds one's attention in this manual and code of the monastery's interior life. As St. Benedict declares, the monastery is "the school of the Lord's service" and the Rule is the indispensable guide in this school. To appreciate the spiritual wealth of the Rule, it is necessary to meditate on it. Then one discovers, behind the concrete prescriptions, the evangelical spirit that animates it. A person of moderation, Benedict shows himself anxious to bring souls to perfection through gentleness and not through constraint. He systematically avoids methods that are too harsh and presents an ideal that is always capable of development but is accessible in principle to all men of good will. Finally, Benedict refused to draw up detailed regulations. Through its flexible and often indefinite provisions the Rule aims at creating a community which is not a barracks, but a great family animated by prayer, obedience, stability, humility, and the sense of hospitality.

The Rule Conquers the West

Thus, the Rule of St. Benedict, which achieved a harmonious and balanced combination of the vitality of the great monastic traditions, imported from the East, would claim predominance over all the Western monasteries. However, its progress was slow and its success, which eventually would be undeniable, was not complete until the tenth century. How is this phenomenon to be explained? The monasteries were already solidly established at the time when St. Benedict appeared, and the inertia of institutions is well enough known for us to understand the difficulties of changing their direction. But two other more important factors also operated as restraints. The Rule represented a stage of spiritual development that was in advance of the civilization of its time. For a long time the Franks and Germans were to be attracted more by the cruder conceptions of a St. Columban, for example, than by Benedictine gentleness. Besides, in spite of its perfection, the Rule had not assumed the "canonical" ideal, as Dom Rousseau called it, which constituted an essential, although different aspect of the monastic tradition and religious perfection in the West.

Until the ninth century therefore, monastic rules remained composite; many monasteries, such as Saint-Croix of Poitiers, founded by St. Radegund, adopted the Rule of St. Caesarius, but the most popular rule was that of St. Columban.

Ireland had experienced in the sixth century a monastic fervor that was remarkable for its quality and originality. The Irish monasteries, like those of Egypt, comprised hundreds and sometimes thousands of religious—rough men, capable of a rigorous asceticism, but quite hard-headed. The rules then in use seem extraordinarily harsh to us. The fasts were very strict and were more or less perpetual; prayers were excessively long and were recited in the most uncomfortable positions. The whip and the rod were the standard means of enforcing discipline. We are surprised at these things. But Benedictine sweetness and Latin moderation would have proved incapable of conquering these rude but generous natures.

Circumstances, love of adventure, and their missionary sense led the Irish to evangelize the continent. Pioneer monks spread into France, Germany, and Holland and undertook the conversion of the Franks and Germans, establishing the reign of Christianity as it prevailed in Ireland. The most famous of these monks, St. Columban, founded about 590 the Abbey of Luxeuil, in Burgundy. His rigorous method was acceptable to these people with their savage ways, and Luxeuil had an extraordinary success. This popularity continued to increase until 610, when the celebrated Brunhilda, whom Columban had soundly rebuked for her misconduct, expelled her critic and his monks. Following the splintering of Luxeuil, the Irish monks spread to the four corners of Europe.

However, the rude Irish vitality could prevail only for a time. While it stirred up the faith of the people, it could not perpetuate itself through violence. About 630, the abbot of Luxeuil took the wise step of tempering the Rule of St. Columban by combining it with that of St. Benedict.

About the same period, the Benedictine Rule spread into England, under the influence of St. Augustine, a monk sent by Pope Gregory, himself a disciple of St. Benedict, to evangelize the Anglo-Saxons.

Thus the abbeys multiplied during the Middle Ages, with either the Benedictine Rule observed, as in England, or, more often, a composite rule in which there was an intermingling of Benedictine precepts, canonical traditions, and various monastic customs. However, as in every institution, the ascetic fervor of the first communities and the apostolic zeal of the Irish were gradually diluted as comfort and luxury were introduced into the abbeys.

Charlemagne showed some desire of making monastic observance uniform and tried to transform each abbey into an intellectual center, but his practical and political mind did not clearly discern the importance of the manifestations of the inner life. So he had little concern for the monks and did not encourage their expansion. On the other hand, his son, Louis the Pious, raised in the monasteries and endowed with a contemplative spirit, took the reform of the monasteries very seriously.

In the south of France, at Aniane, there was then living a young nobleman named Benedict, who in 782 had reestablished Benedictine life in its original spirit in a little monastery built on his land. Manual work, poverty, and prayer constituted the essential lines of this restoration, which abandoned the teaching favored by Charlemagne in order to devote itself more to the ascetical life. Benedict was ordered by the emperor to reform the monasteries, and in a diet at Aachen, in 817, decided upon the extension of the Benedictine Rule to all the abbeys of the Empire.

The same assembly determined to organize the various chapters of canons according to a community that had been originated by the Bishop of Metz, Chrodegang, some fifty years before. This rule was based on that of St. Augustine, implemented with certain Benedictine prescriptions.

Thus, from this day forward, the spiritual tradition of the Church appeared in two types which, under various forms, have continued to our own time. On one hand there is the ideal of St. Benedict, combined with certain forms of canonical life, and on the other the ideal based on the thought of St. Augustine, implemented with certain Benedictine traditions. The profound unity of Christian spirituality, however, shines through diverse forms and practices.

In less than a century feudal anarchy swept away the patient efforts of Benedict. Norman pirates, Saracens, and

Huns struck at the monasteries, pillaging, killing, stealing. But these ravages were not the worst misfortune, for the abbeys which survived fell into a lamentable condition. It was no longer a question of mere decadence! The lord-protectors installed themselves permanently in the monasteries with their attendants, to the great detriment of religious life; but could one still speak of religious life when, as only too often happened, the monks themselves were marrying and setting up house in the cloister with their wives and children to live on the products of the abbey? But this sort of situation was not what the avaricious abbots and the lord-protectors wanted. So they transformed a large number of abbeys into communities of canons, not out of concern for perfection or the apostolate but because the canons, endowed with a personal patrimony, lived on their own resources and thus left the revenues of the abbey intact.

Many Christians and fervent monks—there were still some—were distressed by this shameful condition. Gradually, a spirit of reform was introduced into the Church. In time, the Church tore itself free from feudal barbarism to expand into Christendom. And the Benedictine monks were the chief artisans of this renovation. As always happens in such cases, once the proper atmosphere was established, only a few courageous men were needed to awaken and develop the movement, which soon rallied others behind it. Reform centers arose on all sides, chiefly in Lorraine and in Italy. But because of a lack of organization, these developments remained ephemeral; only Cluny and Cîteaux, because of the strength of their institutions, achieved an enduring work.

Cluny

The first artisans of this reform were a layman, William the Pius, Count of Auvergne and Duke of Aquitaine, and his friend the Abbot Bernon. They founded together the Abbey of Cluny on September 11, 910. After Bernon, Cluny had the privilege of being headed by a series of abbots whose longevity was equalled by their virtue. Bernon, Odon, Aymard, Maieul, Odilon, and Hugues— these six men alone directed Cluny for two hundred years. All of these virtuous abbots were honored as saints and they were well deserving of it. William, the layman, was evidently forgotten.

The Abbot of Cluny did not attempt innovations. He simply reorganized the life of his monastery according to the rule of St. Benedict, which had been restored in its purity by St. Benedict of Aniane. He restored emphasis on prayer, silence, individual poverty, work, obedience, and humility. His successors did not attempt to reform the Church, but they greatly contributed to this by their example, through the influence of their sanctity. Very soon the spirit of Cluny won over all of the monasteries, which rediscovered an authentic monastic life. At the end of the twelfth century more than a thousand abbeys bore witness to the spirit and discipline of Cluny.

However, Cluny, in spite of its fervor, retained, like every human work, a fault which led to a rather rapid decline. Primarily preoccupied with directing the monk's activity toward the contemplative life, the abbots of Cluny neglected manual work, and, furthermore, did not encourage intellectual activity. They strove to fill this gap with a multitude of vocal prayers. Offices were amplified excessively in order to keep the monks occupied, but the fine Benedictine balance had been lost. Soon the fatigue resulting from long services alternating with periods of inactivity brought about a decrease in fervor and the monks settled down to a life of gilded leisure. Thus, without falling into their earlier depravity, the Cluniac monasteries, which for more than two hundred years had been leaders in reform, became buried in a comfortable mediocrity.

Cîteaux

But someone was at hand to pick up the torch. On March 21, 1098, the Abbot Robert of Molesmes founded the Abbey of Cîteaux. This foundation was not aimed simply at opposing the relaxation of discipline at Cluny. Robert of Molesmes was thinking more of setting up a monastic regime in opposition to the profane culture then in full development. He inaugurated at Cîteaux a tradition that was so austere that recruiting proved difficult until in April, 1112, St. Bernard knocked on the monastery door, bringing with him thirty-two companions. At 22, he already had extraordinary influence. Three years later, the monks named him abbot of Clairvaux. Another twenty years, and seventy-five abbeys bore witness to the tradition of Cîteaux. As a matter of fact, this tradition remained authentically Benedictine: it again stressed manual labor and insisted upon absolute poverty, not only of the individual but of the community. Moreover, the rule of cloister was strengthened and practices of mortification were reinstated. The influence of Bernard insured the Cistercian movement an extraordinary development across all Europe, from Portugal to the confines of Russia.

Chartreuse

Paralleling the Benedictine renovation, less sweeping reforms developed in many localities. Gerard de Brogne and St. Peter Damien produced movements of an excessive austerity that did not outlive their authors. The solitary life, on the other hand, returned to favor, especially in southern Italy, which was still in contact with the Eastern Church. A hermit named St. Nilus became very famous there. St. Romuald likewise undertook an ascetic experiment combining the hermit's life with Benedictine practices; his foundation, the Camaldolese monks, had a certain success. Similar experiments were attempted at Grandmont near Limoges and at Sauve-Majeure in Aquitaine.

So far, however, no one had succeeded in solving the difficult problem of organizing the life of hermits and making an enduring ecclesiastical institution of it. St. Bruno and his disciple Guigues achieved this remarkable feat and reconciled the legitimate aspirations of souls attracted to solitude and the requirements of a freely accepted discipline. A canon of Rheims, Bruno was discouraged by the behavior of his bishop and decided to live as a hermit. This austere man, intelligent and well-balanced, meditated upon the various rules then in use and upon the history of his predecessors. Then he organized a strict order which harmoniously combined principles of absolute and particularly austere solitude and certain community practices, such as celebration of the Divine Office and a weekly meeting. The disadvantages of solitary life were thus notably reduced. Moreover, Bruno and his successors gave a privileged place to intellectual work, thus preventing the dangers of perpetual reverie. The Carthusians thus constituted an original institution, capable of absorbing vocations to the solitary life. The order was an unquestionable success: the only religious order which, in the thousand years of its existence, has never stood in need of reform.

The Canons of St. Augustine

The priestly community life favored by St. Augustine and St. Caesarius of Arles had likewise maintained its followers in the course of the preceding centuries. As early as the Carolingian age, the canons of certain churches lived in community. This movement, after a period of decline, was prominent at the time of the reform of St. Gregory. The canons adopted a rule inspired by

St. Augustine, based on a community of goods, humility, and charity. Pope Urban II had particularly interested himself in this reform. This practice inspired, in the twelfth century, an original institution: the Canons Regular of St. Augustine. At this moment, indeed, the reform of the monasteries was tending to restore the rule of cloister in its full severity. While this practice strengthened the monk's fervor by preserving them from temptations from the outside, it turned away excellent souls from the ministry of the Word and from apostolic tasks. By restoring exclusive orientation toward prayer and contemplation, the reforms of Cluny and Cîteaux were diverting from monastic life souls attracted by apostolic work. Many were seeking a new spiritual family which would combine concern for personal perfection and the desire of the apostolic life. Religious communities were born which adopted the Rule of St. Augustine used among the canons. The latter had chosen this rule as an aid to their priestly life. This time, religious were being aided by the same rule in expanding their spiritual life into the ministry. These canons regular received numerous candidates. Their most famous center, the Abbey of St. Victor in Paris, became one of the great intellectual and spiritual centers of the twelfth century.

The Premonstratensians

The Benedictine ascendancy fitted in perfectly with the reform of the Church undertaken by Gregory VII and his successors. These monasteries devoted to prayer and penance were the crowning glory of this theocratical society in which the religious ideal was deeply integrated with daily life. However, the evolution of the medieval world created new deeds and the dawn of a new world could already be discerned. Religious unrest demanded a bold transformation of Christian institutions, including great monastic orders. In spite of their success, the main themes of Cluny and Cîteaux, were, in spirit and in their concrete expression, a survival of past ages. Evidence of this was the unfortunate conflict that set St. Bernard against Abelard.

A gifted man, St. Norbert, had an intuition as to the solution. Rediscovering an idea that had been dear to St. John Chrysostom, whose writings he had probably not read, he thought that the monk should not be confined in solitude, but on the contrary should contribute to the Christian community the spiritual riches acquired by the practice of virtue and various exercises of mortification. Thus, about 1120, after a number of mishaps, Norbert founded the Order of Premonstratensians (from the name of the abbey located in the Laon region) to prepare monks for the apostolate and preaching. Unfortunately, Norbert suffered the fate of all forerunners. His work was not understood. It was thought more suitable to name him archbishop of Magdeburg, and his disciples modified the structure of his order, in which Cistercian asceticism was combined with the rule of the Canons of St. Augustine. Nevertheless, the Premonstratensians maintained some pastoral activity and insured the Christianization of country places in many regions. The order thus played an important role in Christendom. Its foundations increased especially in central Europe and included hundreds by the end of the thirteenth century. In spite of the partial defeat of his plans, Norbert marked out the path which a century later was to open wide to the mendicant orders.

Dominic and Francis

The transformation of society begun in the course of the twelfth century developed in every domain—intellectual, economic, social, and political—and deeply affected the spiritual life of the Church. The authorities, and particu-

larly the pope, attempted to control the intellectual effervescence that was appearing everywhere. Moreover, in a
society eager for wealth, the Church seemed to be in
league with the spirit of mammon. The abbeys displayed
their wealth everywhere even though, as was often the
case, the monks themselves retained a great spirit of
personal poverty.

So the new stirrings in the Church sometimes assumed
disturbing appearances. Catharist and Waldensian heretics were especially rampant in the south of France and in
northern Italy and provoked a terrible suppression of the
Albigensians and the birth of the Inquisition. But this was
merely the erratic manifestation of a general unrest of
pious souls seeking a life more in conformity with the
Gospel. On every side, confraternities arose which aspired
to a renewed Christianity, without repudiating the established Church: the Humiliati of Lombardy, and the Poor
Catholics of Lyons, for example; and, of course, there was
the amazing Arnold of Brescia. An austere man and a zealous preacher of poverty, he sowed discord everywhere he
went through the very excess of his diatribes, and he
ended on the scaffold after having assumed the leadership
of the commune in Rome. We should also mention Joachim
of Flora, a pious Cistercian religious whose apocalyptic
ideas had some influence, mainly unfortunate, in the next
century, especially among the Franciscans. In this seething ferment of Christendom, stirred by numerous movements that were more or less orthodox and reformative,
concerned with poverty and return to the evangelical
spirit, Providence raised up, a few years apart, Dominic
of Guzman and Francis of Assisi.

The simultaneous appearance of these two founders of
orders, different in temperament, life, and work, perfectly
illustrates the wealth of the Church, which can provide
two widely different answers, based on the same ideal, for
the same problem.

Dominic was the churchman par excellence. This canon of the Cathedral of Osma in Spain came, together with his bishop Didacus, to ask Pope Innocent III for permission to go and evangelize the Cumans, barbarian tribes on the Russian border. The pope suggested to them that they would be giving more service to the Church if they applied their zeal to the conversion of the Albigensians. The decision was a fortunate one, for Didacus and Dominic had already worked successfully for the reconciliation of the Poor Men of Lyons by following simple but revolutionary principles. Abandoning the privileges generally conceded to ecclesiastics, the preachers went about on foot, without gold or silver, living exactly as the Apostles did and according to the recommendations of the Gospel. Dominic and his companions traveled across the south of France in this way, preaching the Gospel by word and example. He founded the Abbey of Our Lady of Prouilles, for converted heretics who wished to continue in the religious life, and then a congregation for his companions and disciples.

Dominic set forth a rule, based in its precepts on regulations in use among the Canons of St. Augustine and especially among the Premonstratensian monks. But its spirit, under these traditional appearances, was revolutionary: it established the primacy of the apostolic function and of absolute poverty.

Preaching, which was then a preserve of the secular clergy and an occasional function of the monks, became an integral part of the vocation of the Dominicans, or Order of Preachers. Everything was subordinated to this task, intellectual work replacing manual work, which had been a traditional element of asceticism since the foundation of monasteries. On the other hand, Dominic, who appreciated the value of monastic observances, demanded of his disciples the singing of the Office, rigorous asceticism, and obligatory cloister enclosure. But this discipline, encouraging the fervor of the monks and their activity, was not to interrupt their ministry. So, Dominic introduced into his rule the principle of dispensation, which permits the temporary suppression of one or another of the monastic obligations for the purposes of the apostolate.

As for poverty, Dominic saw it as Francis did—as total and absolute; but for him, it stemmed more from the evangelical idea that the Lord's disciples must not be concerned with their material needs, than it did from that passionate quest for destitution characteristic of the poor man of Assisi.

Francis of Assisi had nothing in common with Dominic unless it was that passionate and apostolic love of Christ and poverty. Institutional life had no attraction for Francis. He was a prophet, a man of God, charged with a mission of disturbing men's consciences, not able to foresee too clearly the consequences of his intervention. Behind his smile and his simplicity was dissimulated the greatest effort a man ever made to identify himself with the total destitution of Christ on the cross. Formerly, in attempting such a thing, the hermits fled into the desert. Francis, on the contrary, motivated by apostolic ardor, paraded his poverty in the heart of the city, in the public square, and upset all prejudices by his example, becoming an object of scandal and derision for some and a sublime example for the others who followed him in crowds. This flood of disciples did not dismay Francis, though he had not thought of creating an order. He accepted them and taught them to imitate the suffering Christ. For the rest, he trusted to the inspiration of the Spirit.

The very success of Francis' preaching brought him a number of troubles. The expansion of his movement led to the intervention of the Church, something that he himself desired, indeed, for Francis always manifested, even in his most difficult hours, a filial love for the Church and its representatives.

But to obtain official recognition, a rule was needed that would establish the disciples of Francis as a regular religious institution. With death close upon him, Francis wrote one: three verses of the Gospel! Subsequently, an actual rule was issued, a rule extorted from Francis, who died discouraged by the limitations which had been imposed on his ideal, though it gave rise to one of the greatest spiritual movements in the Church.

Dominicans and Franciscans corresponded perfectly to the religious ideal of Christendom. They literally drained the spiritual and intellectual elite of their epoch.

The Dominicans were above all learned men; their theology remained rather abstract and their spiritual doctrine itself retained a certain intellectual rigidity. Among a constellation of famous thinkers in the Order of Preachers were St. Raymond of Peñafort, St. Albert the Great, St. Vincent Ferrer, and, above all, St. Thomas Aquinas, the unquestioned master of Catholic thought. Not that the Dominicans confined themselves to speculative abstractions. Their spirituality retained an evangelical simplicity and freshness, and St. Dominic remains as one of the great shapers of Marian devotion. Jacopo de Voragine, the author of the *Golden Legend*, and the painter Fra Angelico expressed in their own way, but in a manner that was quite as authentic as that of the great theologians, the ideal of St. Dominic.

On the other hand, the fruitful teaching of the Poverello, directly inspired by evangelical simplicity, led souls in the most varied paths and also inspired a lofty theological doctrine. Brother Juniper proved a replica of St. Francis and likewise St. Bernardine of Siena, the "pedlar of the Lord," who excelled in stagecraft and kept his audiences breathless for hours on end. But Franciscan spirituality also produced the preacher St. Anthony of Padua and the theologians St. Bonaventure and Duns Scotus. In spite of notable differences in their theological conceptions, the two

masters of Franciscan thought were united in the fundamental idea of St. Francis: Christ is the supreme grace
offered by God to His creatures. Therefore, the spiritual
life no longer consisted in a conquest by man of abstract
virtues, but in a continuing effort to reproduce, as much
as this can be done, the very life of Christ, so that renunciation thus becomes a fullness of joy and love.

Success of Spiritual Life in the Church

In spite of the striking contrast between the old Benedictine stock and the new mendicant orders, we can nonetheless discern certain basic lines which govern religious
evolution and give a distinctive appearance to religious
thought in the Middle Ages.

First of all appears the crucial problem of the temporal
existence of the Church—its incarnation in the world. The
Benedictine renaissance and the expansion of the mendi-
cants were largely affected by an interest in reform, a difficult work by men who were anxious to restore the true
face of the Church, which had become too involved in
temporal realities. The return to evangelical fervor was
accompanied by an anarchical or revolutionary tendency
which threatened to affect the Church basically. So, the
ecclesiastical hierarchy was closely following the evolution
of the spiritual movements and attempted to orient and
channel them through disciplinary measures. For example,
the difficulties encountered by Dominic and Francis in obtaining official recognition for their orders are not explained simply by the clergy's lack of comprehension—
Pope Innocent III seemed very favorable to their undertakings—but also by its legitimate concern for confining
this spiritual drive within an institutional framework. It is
interesting to note that among all the movements espous-
ing poverty at this time, only those that submitted to the
requirements of the Church exercised a lasting and fruitful

influence. All the others failed or degenerated into anarchy
and eccentricity.

Another consequence of reformative discipline was seen
in the increasing effort to inculcate in the secular clergy
a monastic ideal, especially with regard to the rigorous
practice of celibacy.

In itself, the priestly ideal is independent of monastic
life. The priest's mission requires different aptitudes from
those of the monk: learning, apostolic zeal, knowledge of
the world—these qualities seem to be as indispensable for
this ministry as piety and holiness of life. However, the
community instinctively selects its guides from among the
faithful who are remarkable for a more strict practice of
the evangelical counsels. So, from the most ancient times,
bishops and priests were most often recruited from among
the ascetics. In the East, the Church has remained faithful
to this ancient tradition: priesthood does not necessarily
imply the monastic ideal and celibacy, except for bishops.

In the West, on the contrary, the tradition was soon established of demanding of the clergy a way of life identical
with that of monks. The controversies raised by the problem of sanctity in the fourth century were caused in part
by the hardening of an already well-implanted tradition.
The deviations of a Jovinian, counterattacked by Jerome
and Ambrose, while they set up an alternative between the
two states of life, could only lead to the obligation of
priestly celibacy. Indeed, this was an ideal that was popular at the time of the Fathers of the Church, but which was
subjected to terrible distortions during the Middle Ages,
especially in the feudal period. So, the inevitable reform
of the clergy necessarily required the return to the strict
obligation of ecclesiastical celibacy.

The two great wounds of the Church in those days have
been mentioned: simony and clerical licentiousness. Consequently, ecclesiastical celibacy was considered primarily
under its disciplinary aspect, to the great detriment of the

spiritual ideal it represents. Indeed, the historical arguments, whether juridical or pastoral, advanced to justify the strict maintenance of ecclesiastical celibacy could always provoke objections. But they have nothing in common with the ascetical and mystical ideal, of which celibacy is an element that the community can demand of its pastors. The mistake, the consequences of which were subsequently very troublesome, does not stem from the fact that the Church has fiercely defended the principle of ecclesiastical celibacy, but that, as a result of circumstances, it stressed particularly the disciplinary aspects of this ascetical practice instead of developing the spiritual values of the priesthood, which naturally implies the virtues of chastity, poverty, and obedience, fundamental elements of all Christian perfection.

Moreover, beginning with the twelfth century, the appearance of the great spiritual families produced distinctive trends in spirituality which developed in a regular manner. Thus, we may speak of a Benedictine, Franciscan, and Dominican tradition, each of which has its distinctive character and still retains the more general aspirations of the age that produced it. The liturgical interest of the Benedictines, the mystical doctrine of the Canons of St. Victor, the more rational piety of the Dominicans, and the more sentimental devotion of the Franciscans, combined and expressed under the most varied aspects the religious needs and aspirations of Christendom.

The mystery of the Incarnation of Christ was the center of devotion for the faithful, whether they were nurtured by the liturgical cycle tracing the various stages in the life of the Lord or by meditation on the Gospel. St. Bernard had the monks and the faithful meditate on the principal events in the life of Christ, the Word made flesh, while St. Thomas devoted an important part of the *Summa Theologica* to analyzing the parts of this life of Christ. In the next century, the fourteenth, Ludolph the Carthusian published a *Vita Christi*, the first "life" of Christ, which had an enormous success.

This modification of perspective also influenced the very principles of asceticism. It is true that Christians were still cultivating the same virtues, but for the purpose of imitating the life of Christ as much as possible. Francis of Assisi, in his total renunciation, was aiming at nothing else and he was followed by his disciple St. Bonaventure, who made the imitation of Christ the center of his spiritual doctrine. The book that, for centuries, was to serve as a guide to perfection, the *Imitation of Christ*, was likewise composed just at the end of the Middle Ages.

Center of the spiritual life and the goal of perfection, Christ's person likewise became the center of devotion and liturgy. In this period devotion to the Blessed Sacrament was developed. St. Thomas Aquinas composed the Office for the feast of Corpus Christi. St. Gertrude recommended devotion to the heart of Jesus. Subsequently, the devotion itself was humanized and lost a little of the majestic grandeur of traditional liturgy. Rather neglectful of the Father, piety was more interested in the Lord and those around Him, with whom simple and more affective relations could be established. St. Francis of Assisi spread the custom of the Christmas crib and the love of the Infant Jesus. Mary was especially venerated in very touching ways, both by St. Bernard and by St. Dominic and the Franciscan Jacopone de Todi, to whom we owe the verses of the *Stabat Mater*. In this period there also developed devotion to St. Joseph, notably by St. Bernard and Jean Gerson, as well as devotion to the faithful departed.

This was a time when the theology of the Mystical Body was no longer so prominent in the thought of spiritual writers, who in their mystical works followed in the footsteps of the pseudo-Dionysius and strove to determine the relations of the soul with God and to specify the various stages of the contemplative life. St. Bonaventure expounded clearly for the first time the three ways of the spiritual life: the purgative way, that is, the period in the course of which the soul is purified of its faults; the illuminative way, in the course of which the soul is enlightened by meditation upon Christ; and the unitive way, in which the soul is united with God through charity. In each stage the soul is assisted by meditation, prayer, and contemplation.

However, while the Mystical Body no longer occupied an important place in the meditations of Christians, the traditional functions of the Church, in particular its missionary duty, remained active. The Premonstratentions became the great experts on the conversion of central Europe, the Dominicans set up missions as far away as Turkestan, the Franciscans, following in the footsteps of their founder, who, with the perfect nonchalance of the saints, went to preach the word of Christ to the Sultan of Egypt, preached the evangelical message in Mongolia and created the first Church in China. The Hospitallers, the Brothers of the Holy Spirit, the Brothers of Saint-Lazare, and the Canons of Lucques de Haut-Pas devoted themselves to the care of travelers and the sick. Other, more typically medieval institutions were born. The Crusades produced military orders: the Hospitallers of Saint John of Jerusalem (Knights of Malta), the Templars, the Teutonic Knights. Some religious specialized in the redemption of captives: the Trinitarians, and the Order of Our Lady of Ransom (Mercedarians). The Order of the Bridge Builders of Avignon, the first public works project, was certainly not the least original of the monastic achievements inspired by the practical pioneers of Christendom.

Finally, it is opportune to stress the appearance of women in mystical literature at this time. Many women had already made themselves famous in the history of the Church, but in the twelfth century the period of the great female mystics opened, the age of those women who brought to the Church a spiritual message with great influence on the life of Christians.

The first of these mystic saints, Hildegarde, abbess of a monastery in the vicinity of Mainz, died in 1136. A talented administrator, gifted with a clear mind and a strong character, she maintained abundant correspondence with the popes, bishops, and the abbots of her age. Her friend, Elizabeth, Abbess of Schönau, endured physical and moral suffering and was favored by extraordinary gifts. St. Gertrude lived at Hefta at the end of the thirteenth century. She was little known in her own age, and her book the *Herald of Divine Love,* passed unnoticed. Gertrude's message, which promoted love of the Sacred Heart, was not fully welcomed by the Church until the seventeenth century. Since then, her books, especially the *Exercises,* have had a sanctifying influence upon many Christians. Her sister, St. Mathilda, a nun in the same convent, also promoted devotion to the Sacred Heart.

3. Modern Times

Women

It was not long before the great spiritual edifice of the thirteenth century began to break up. Avignon, the Great Schism, the depravity of the Roman court, and internal rivalry in the various monastic orders was soon sapping the fervor of the religious. However, two religious phenomena of capital importance marked the fourteenth century.

First of all, some great women, with extraordinary influence, true prophets of the Lord in that troubled period, powerfully intervened in the life of the Church. St. Bridget of Sweden, mother of eight children, became the confidant of the Lord and founded a religious order in the Cistercian tradition. Her *Revelations*, written in highly poetic language, include violent invectives in the style of the prophets of the Old Testament. In particular, she threatened the Avignon pope with the worst punishments if he did not return to the Eternal City as soon as possible. In the same period a similar mission was given to St. Catherine of Siena. Her *Letters and Dialogues*, likewise visionary, alternate the sharpest criticism of the clergy with outbursts of ardent love for the Church. In comparison with the other mystics we have already encountered, imbued with Benedictine liturgical life, the thought of St. Catherine was highly theological and reflected the teaching of St. Thomas, for whom she professed a great admiration.

The role of these women advisors was indeed considerably debated at the time. Men such as Jean Gerson deplored the fact that the popes allowed their decisions to be influenced by these women's visions. Actually, it is often difficult, in the writings of these women, to distinguish what is due to authentic inspiration and what to their own imagination. The Church has acknowledged the unquestionable orthodoxy of the teaching of these extraordinary mystics and the sublimity of their spiritual message. On the other hand, it has always refused, and justly, to pronounce on the value of their messages and prophecies.

Other attractive figures can be pointed out: St. Angela of Foligno, who was also a mother of a family, and of St. Catherine, abbess of a convent at Bologna; the former beautifully described the feeling of the presence of God in the soul, the second pictured the spiritual combat which a Christian must undergo. St. Frances of Rome, who was also favored with extraordinary mystic graces, remains a model of a wife and mother. On the other hand, St. Catherine of Genoa, the contemporary of St. Frances and another great mystic, was unfortunate in her family life, but nevertheless was able to attain to the highest virtues.

The Mystic Drive

This period had a flowering of mystical life, resulting from various causes. On the religious level, the influence of the writings of the pseudo-Dionysius were important because of the place they gave to contemplation in the search for perfection. The affective piety of the Middle Ages, centering on the person of the Incarnate Word, likewise encouraged the development of mystical fervor. Finally, the separation of doctrinal from pastoral instruction and the ascetic life made possible the existence of a literature that was exclusively devoted to the study of perfection and the means of attaining it. Thus, the convergence of teaching, devotion, and the spiritual life facilitated and even compelled the development of mystical theology.

From a certain point of view, St. Thomas Aquinas and St. Bonaventure can already be regarded as masters of mysticism. In their didactic instruction, they expounded its various elements. However, they integrated these elements in their theological syntheses. On the other hand, St. Anselm and St. Bernard thought and wrote as mystics at least as much as they did as theologians and philosophers. Similarly, the masters of the School of St. Victor prepared the way for the science of perfection.

This science developed especially in the Rhineland, where a number of preachers, mainly Dominicans, promoted it. The Rhenish religious centers of the fourteenth century were agitated by a religious and mystic fervor which was evident, in particular, in the formation of the "Friends of God." This association of ecclesiastics and laymen practiced a severe asceticism, sought for perfection, and fought against the disorders of the clergy. Meister Eckhart, a preaching brother who befriended them, can be considered as the inspirer of the mystical trend that developed in these regions. His disciples, John Tauler and Blessed Henry Suso, exemplify this mystical school, intellectual in tendency, exceptionally influential, and one whose orthodoxy has always been furiously disputed.

Another mystical trend, less speculative and more practical, developed about the same period in Holland with the Confraternity of the Brothers of the Common Life. Its doctrine was expounded in the *Imitation of Christ*, which became the favorite book of countless generations of Catholics. This mystical outburst, which spread through the entire Church, was one of the determining elements of the Catholic reformation. Through it, interior asceticism acquired a dominant position in the search for perfection.

However, many dangers were awaiting mysticism—the danger of foundering in illuminism, as in Spain, or straying dangerously in the direction of the Protestant reformers. It appeared necessary, therefore, to discipline it and to study the technique of exercises favoring the harmonious development of the interior life—in particular, that of meditation, the key discipline. These studies made spiritual progress possible for a greater number of Christians and limited its dangers. Of course, this organization of the interior life did not take place overnight and was not accomplished by one man alone. It was the work of an entire era, and was done by such figures as St. Teresa of Avila, St. John of the Cross, St. Ignatius Loyola, and the masters of French spirituality.

The first methodical approach to prayer, properly speaking, was developed in the Low Countries, among the Brethren of the Common Life. These laymen and secular canons experienced the greatest difficulty in meditating, so one of them conceived a progressive method and plan of meditation which were intended to guide the prayers of members of the brotherhood. The method today seems remarkably complicated, but the principles opened the road to research that subsequently proved particularly fruitful.

Methodical meditation won success in France, and then in Italy, where the venerable Louis Barbo introduced it among the Benedictines, and then in Spain, where is was promoted by Don García Ximenes de Cisneros, Abbot of Montserrat, who published the Spiritual Exercises. The influence of these writings was basic for the future of spirituality.

At this time a mystical crisis was taking place in Spain. In particular, an unreliable kind of mysticism, practiced by the *Allumbrados* or *Illuminati*, tainted with superstitions of Islamic or Jewish origins, and suspected of relations with the Protestant movements, attracted the wrath of the

Inquisition. However, an authentic mysticism, exemplified by Francis Ossuna, St. Peter of Alcantara, Blessed Louis of Granada, and Blessed John of Avila, enabled the spiritual life to survive in spite of the difficulties created by the pseudo-mystics and the inquisitorial reaction.

St. Teresa of Avila

Among the distinguished spiritual guides of this time, St. Teresa of Avila and St. John of the Cross occupy an eminent place. The Church has not had any more important mystical writers than these.

St. Teresa was born in Avila in 1515. She renewed contact, across the centuries, with the great tradition of the Fathers of the Church, with whom she felt an affinity through a temperament combining practical sense and extreme sensitivity. Indeed, Teresa seemed like a remote disciple of St. Jerome. Reading the letters of the recluse of Bethlehem, Teresa understood that she belonged to the family of Paula, the Marcellas, and the Eustochiums, and she embraced the monastic life. A true spiritual daughter of St. Jerome, she had, like him, a fierce love of life; like him, she loved solitude and had a devouring need for activity; like him, she carried on a heroic struggle to free herself from the pleasures of life; and like him, too, finally, her ardent soul knew no limits. The pursuit of perfection that she carried on could only end on the highest summits of the mystical life.

In that pursuit of sanctity, involving the dramatic events of an ardent life, almost daily miracles, and the most extraordinary mystical phenomena, Teresa, whose practical good sense remained perfectly serene in this orgy of the supernatural, wore down spiritual directors at an alarming rate. Unable to follow the dizzy pace of this athlete of Christ, they served to mark off, one after the other, the progress of this remarkable soul. However, far from being mediocre themselves—the ardor of St. Teresa was inevitably reflected in them—they all left a name in the history of mysticism. However, she exhausted all of them, from whatever spiritual family they came.

In earlier religious authors she found a source capable of feeding her religious ardor. While she was favored by the Spirit with the most extraordinary gifts, she was not "illuminated" and never made this a pretext for following an eccentric road to contemplation. The further she progressed in the love of God, the more concerned she was in deepening her spiritual knowledge and the more anxious she was to surround herself with the enlightened opinions of the most learned spiritual directors of her age. Thus, combining stubborn, hardheaded work and persevering effort with the exceptional qualities of her nature, St. Teresa exercised a decisive influence on the spiritual renaissance of her age and remains an inimitable source for every soul desirous of interior progress. She had the gift of penetrating into and of describing psychologically the succession of supernatural events that punctuated her life. Moreover, she could appreciate the role of prayer in the spiritual life, its difficulties and its dangers. That is why Teresa remains the unchallenged master of the science of prayer.

St. John of the Cross

At the end of her life, St. Teresa had a spiritual director whose sanctity was on the same scale as her own, St. John of the Cross, a young Carmelite who was ordained in 1567. For fifteen years Teresa and John communed with equal fervor in that love of God that had borne them to the heights of the mystical life. John continued his earthly pilgrimage alone for ten years. A delicate and sensitive soul, he received his share of physical and moral buffeting. He was spared no rebuff. The reform he undertook annoyed the Carmelites of the old observance, who did not hesitate to have him flogged until the blood flowed and to imprison him in a dungeon for seven months. But subsequently he inspired the reform movement, though he never occupied a position in the foreground. A last humiliation awaited him a few months before his death: the superior general expelled him from the movement of which he had been one of the most ardent promoters. John of the Cross died in disgrace in a convent in Andalusia in 1591.

By temperament and by vocation, he holds a very special place in the history of spirituality. His writings, which seek to describe the union with God through contemplation, are addressed to the initiated. Such a subject could not be treated in didactic form. John sings, rather than explains, the love of God.

His poems, in which he first set forth his doctrine, figure among the most beautiful in Spanish literature. Then, at the request of certain readers, he explained them in prose works: the *Ascent of Carmel, the Dark Night, the Spiritual Canticle,* still retain the lyrical inspiration of his love songs. This literary genre and the sublimity of his doctrine require a certain preparation. But the normal educational effort required to appreciate the writings of the most perfect singer of the love of God is largely compensated by the spiritual enrichment acquired through such an undertaking.

The Reform of the Orders

Far from being an exceptional phenomenon, mysticism, at its height in the sixteenth century, merely reflected in a spectacular way the rebirth of interior life in the Church. Moreover, it was to be one of the strongest elements in the Catholic reformation undertaken after the crisis of the Renaissance. The disorders that had entered into the vari-

ous ecclesiastical institutions had also led to the decadence
of the religious orders. The mendicant friars, who represented the moving spirit of the Middle Ages, had not escaped this decadence. The decline reached such a point
that certain reformers of the Roman Curia decided to
recommend the suppression of most of the monasteries by
forbidding all recruiting. Still, while its institutions were
endangered, the Church's spiritual capital remained intact, and once the proper impulse was supplied, the recovery of the various spiritual families took place very
rapidly. Thus, the reform of the Carmelites carried out by
St. Teresa and St. John of the Cross, gave such an impetus
to this Order that for nearly two hundred years it remained
a brilliant center of intellectual and spiritual life. One
after the other, the Camaldolese, the Augustinian hermits, the Benedictines, and the Dominicans, courageously
undertook to restore the old discipline and to return to a
monastic ideal that was more in conformity with the view
of their founders.

But the most spectacular form—and the most painful
one—took place in the order of St. Francis. The life of the
Friars Minor had been particularly disturbed during the
Middle Ages. There was violent conflict over guiding principles, resulting in numerous schisms. Most often, the
various attempts at reform only resulted in the creation
of a dissident branch, which simply increased the confusion. The crisis reached its height in 1523 when a pious
but somewhat unpolished monk, Matteo de Brescia, issued
a proposal for a literal return to the ideal of the poverty of
St. Francis. The sanctity of Matteo soon awakened a wave
of enthusiasm for his reform, and, after many difficulties
the Capuchins (from the name of their peculiar hood),
became an autonomous branch of the order of St. Francis.
The new order experienced many disappointments. Matteo, the founder, returned to the Franciscans of the Strict

Observance, his successor was expelled from the order by a papal bull, their most famous preacher and the third superior of the order apostasized and joined the Lutherans. The order prospered in spite of all these setbacks and, a century later, it included over twenty thousand religious.

The Congregations of Clerks Regular

The reform of the Church at the time of the Council of Trent was not aimed simply at a return to order. It was necessary to confront new needs created by the evolution of society itself.

The secular clergy, a pure and fervent clergy, able to lead a life of perfection while continuing in the world, was being seen more and more as the instrument of Christian restoration. This concern with the sanctification of the clergy characterized the spiritual renaissance of this period. The problem had already arisen in the fourth century and the Fathers had recommended extraordinarily simple solutions. St. Augustine lived in community with his priests, his deacons, and his other clerics, under a strict rule, dominated by chastity, poverty, and the apostolate. It is an odd thing that, over the centuries, this ideal of priestly life lost its original purpose and reappeared in the Middle Ages as the model of a rule of canons regular. As monastic life solidified in institutions along well-determined lines, the perfections that the Fathers had seen as an ideal for everyone, and especially for the clergy, became the monopoly of the monasteries. And through a reverse process, the monks confined themselves more and more in their monasteries, protecting the tranquility of their contemplative life by the barrier of the cloister. Thus, the monks had to rediscover the apostolic life, and the clergy had to consider the monastic virtues in a form compatible with their state in life. There was still a long

road to travel to attain this ideal—so long a road, that in
our day still, the priestly ideal of Augustine seems quite
revolutionary to many secular priests. The medieval contrast between contemplative and active life still finds many
supporters today.

However, even in that era, the monks had attempted to
adapt to the apostolic life. Following St. Norbert's mis-
understood experiment, came the mendicant monks. But
these latter exercised only certain functions of the apostolic life: preaching and teaching. The problem of the
priestly ministry, that is, parish ministry remained un-
solved. Indeed, it had even been complicated by the hostility between seculars and regulars and the bad repute
of some religious orders. On the other hand, except for a
rare few, the secular clergy did not appear ready to assume
their obligations. It was therefore, urgently necessary to
show priests that fidelity to the canonical rules for their
state in life could be achieved in the world.

The originality of the sixteenth century disclosed itself
in the appearance clerks regular. Theatines, Barnabites,
and Somaschi refused to be ordinary religious and wished
to be associations of priests animated by the religious
ideal. These associations accepted only the finest candidates and became veritable nurseries for bishops, who
were to carry out the decisions of the Council of Trent
in their dioceses. One of these priests, perhaps the Thea-
tine Lorenzo Scupoli, prepared a little book on spirituality,
the *Spiritual Combat*, whose success equalled that of the
Imitation. Typical of his times, the author, in his treat-
ment of Christian perfection, insisted on the predominance
of inner mortification over exterior practices. Other congregations, such as the Oratory of St. Philip Neri and the
Oblates of St. Charles Borremo, were inspired by the same
spirit. This blossoming of the clerks regular filled a need
and led the way to a prodigious spiritual renewal, created
by St. Ignatius and the French school of spirituality.

The Society of Jesus

Ignatius of Loyola, born in 1491, an officer of the Spanish army, became, as the result of a war wound, one of the most prominent masters of Catholic spirituality. To while away the dreary hours of his convalescence, he had only the *Life of Jesus* of Ludolph the Carthusian, and the *Golden Legend* of Jacopo de Voragine. Six months later, Ignatius was at the monastery of Montserrat and then withdrew to Manresa, where he practiced severe austerities. The experiment was a definitive one. In a few months, under an exhausting regimen, Ignatius learned to his cost (he almost died of it) that one must beware of searching too impetuously for sanctity by bodily mortification. A thousand years earlier, John Chrysostom had had a similar misadventure. On the other hand, during his retreat Ignatius had the opportunity to develop his *Spiritual Exercises*, a systemization of the effort pursued by the Brethren of the Common Life, the aim of which was to present a method of prayer and spiritual asceticism that could be used by everyone.

Conversion did not dull the personality of Ignatius. The soldier breathes forth from every page of the *Exercises*, a fighter's manual intended to transform a reader into an apostle in the school of Christ. He himself did not delay in putting into practice the ideal he proposed. As Francis of Assisi had done, Ignatius departed for the Holy Land, with the firm intention of preaching the doctrine of Christ to the infidels. The superior of the Franciscan monastery in Jerusalem, which was maintained by special privilege of the Sultan, was frightened by the evangelical boldness of this trouble-maker and at once put him on board a ship for his native Spain.

Ignatius then decided to become a priest, and began his studies at the University of Alcalà. But he made the mistake of having his *Exercises* distributed, which earned him a stay in the sinister dungeons of the Inquisition. When he was liberated, he thought it best to depart and went to finish his studies in Paris. His famous *Exercises* again led to some rebuffs from the university, but these were of a milder nature than the prison of the Inquisition.

Finally, Ignatius became a priest, and not before he had won over some companions to his ideal, among whom was St. Francis Xavier. Meeting in the Montmartre chapel on August 15, 1534, they made the vow to spread the faith of Christ among the infidels. This project having miscarried once again, Ignatius and his companions understood that the missionary vocation was not simply an evangelization of the infidels; that it was a permanent call within the Church, inherent in its nature, and capable of being exercised at all times and in all places. They then decided to found a congregation of missionaries completely and unreservedly at the disposal of the pope. Thus was born the Society of Jesus.

Ignatius organized the society according to the most advanced ideas of the age. It took its inspiration from the spirit of various congregations of clerks regular, that is, a religious life that was as close as possible to that of secular clergy, but differing from it in its missionary spirit —its basic distinction—and in the military organization that its founder gave it. The long probation required of future Jesuits—often more than ten years—and the strict discipline that prevails in the order, have often been criticized. But these things were indispensable conditions for the efficacy of an institution that aimed less at the sanctification of its members than at the salvation and spiritual good of others. Ignatius had understood that the missionary objective required a strong development and a great solidarity. The history of the Jesuits seems to have proved he was right. In less than seventy years the congregation extended its influence throughout the world and included more than thirteen thousand members. Since that time it has always been in the advance guard in the evolution of the Church.

St. Francis de Sales

The spiritual awakening that developed in Spain and Italy soon found its destined field in France.

The charming Bishop of Geneva, St. Francis de Sales, is with St. Teresa and St. John of the Cross, the great teacher of the spiritual life. Master of spirituality for the layman and for all those who seek the evangelical ideal without leaving daily life, he continued the great tradition of the Fathers of the Church. It was not by chance that this humanist bishop drew the essence of his teaching from the writings of St. Augustine, St. Gregory the Great, St. Jerome, and St. Bernard. Imbued with the thought of St. John of the Cross, St. Teresa, and Italian spiritual writers, he long used the *Spiritual Combat* as bedside reading.

Francis de Sales founded no spiritual family, and the reformers of the French School, while they admired him, found little inspiration in his writings. There is no reason for surprise in this. His mission was in a different direction. He did not seek to reform the clergy, but to bring Christianity into everyday life. The thousands of Christians who have found their ideal in his writings constitute the spiritual family of St. Francis de Sales. The Bishop of Geneva, an apostle of unlimited activity, had an understanding of the demands of modern life on Christians. Very advanced for his age, he even established a congregation of uncloistered religious, who were to care for the sick. But such an innovation created a scandal, and the Archbishop of Lyons soon ordered the Daughters of the Visitation to restore the cloister.

St. Francis de Sales exerted no direct action, therefore, on the evolution of the religious orders. On the other hand, he had a keen understanding of the fact that "Christendom" belonged to the past, and that a new world was developing. It seemed to him that Christian life should be no different in his time than it was in the early centuries. His aim was to put religion into daily life and to make devotion the flowering of goodness. As is usual in such cases, far from being exceptional, the attitude of the Bishop of Geneva fitted into the attempt at interior renovation planned by the Council of Trent. The Protestant controversies, which challenged, not simply a particular point of doctrine, but the very essence of Catholicism, had shaken Christendom out of its inertia, and posed the religious problem for every conscience. So the Catholic reformers did not limit their efforts to the secular or regular clergy but worked to awaken the Christian leadership. Unfortunately, the spiritual writers of the Middle Ages, writing to increase the fervor of the religious and laity, had produced only insipid, uninspired works. Christian perfection, in these works, seemed to be attainable only in cloisters, and the layman appeared to be condemned to a sterile repetition of formulas, gestures, and rites. St. Francis de Sales published works of spirituality in which the style was perfectly adapted to the tastes and needs of his age but which in no way softened the ideal of Christian perfection. With his *Introduction to the Devout Life* and *Treatise on the Love of God*, Christians possessed a sure, available, and attractive guide for advancement on the road to virtue.

The French School

While St. Francis de Sales was offering the laity substantial modern works on spirituality, the French clergy was undergoing a profound transformation that had, subsequently, an important effect on all of the Catholic clergy.

Cardinal de Bérulle, a member of the salon of Madame Acarie, introduced into France the spiritual doctrine of the Carmelites. Bérulle had set himself a two-fold goal: to establish in France the Carmel of Teresa of Avila and the Oratory of Philip Neri. This combination of Spanish mysticism and Italian spirituality produced a particularly fruitful synthesis. Bérulle's teaching was based on the virtue of religion, the feeling of the awareness of the greatness of God, and devotion to the Incarnate Word. But, in this last point, the imitation of Christ was to be based less on the actions of Jesus than on their interior motivation. In addition, he had a basic pessimism concerning human nature. While he did not go as far as the Jansenists, he gave birth to that austere spirituality that was forced upon the French clergy and which is so different from the optimistic attitude of St. Francis de Sales.

In imitation of St. Philip Neri, Cardinal de Bérulle had intended the reform of the clergy. As a matter of fact, his Oratory, though different from the Italian Oratory, did not develop entirely as planned. Nevertheless, through his followers, Bérulle remains the master of spirituality for the clergy.

Indeed, one of his followers, St. John Eudes, established a society intended for seminarians, but which is especially important for having spread devotion to the hearts of Jesus and Mary in Brittany and Normandy. Another of Bérulle's disciples, John Olier, established the Society of Priests of Saint Sulpice, which thereafter trained the majority of the clergy for France and North America during this period.

Finally, Bérulle was to point out to St. Vincent de Paul his missionary vocation. Not that he was Vincent's teacher, since St. Vincent de Paul was not anyone's follower. The son of poor peasants, he preached at nineteen, lived at the Roman court, and then at the court of the King of France. When, on returning to his homeland, he encountered Bérulle, he discovered his own mission: the evangelization of the people. Like St. Thomas Aquinas, he understood that a minimum of well-being is indispensable for the practice of virtue. Therefore, he devoted all of his apostolate to loving men as brothers and to helping them in their material and spiritual poverty. For this purpose he founded the Congregation of the Mission, bringing together priests charged with preaching the Good News in the countryside. He organized charity for the poor and sick in his Brotherhood of Charity, which utilized the Christian elite. Finally, his tenacity succeeded in producing an establishment dear to his heart and one which realized the desire of St. Francis de Sales: a congregation of uncloistered religious, exclusively in the service of the poor and sick, the Daughters of Charity, the well-known sisters of St. Vincent de Paul.

Spiritual Asphyxiation

The exuberant vitality of the Church in France was expressed again in the seventeenth century in the eloquence of the preachers who have already been mentioned.

The zeal of all these apostles awakened in the faithful a spirit of emulation which has not always been appreciated: the Society of the Blessed Sacrament, the Brotherhoods of Charity, enabled the laity to develop their spiritual life and to exercise their devotion in a practical way. Port-Royal, later stained with Jansenism, in its early years displayed a great spiritual elevation and a profound faith. The Arnauld family, Lemaistre de Sacy, and especially Pascal manifested the remarkable faith of this spiritual center.

The ordinary concerns of spirituality and the Church's own activities could not escape this renovation. The famous Abbey of St. Maur enabled the Benedictines to recover their former glory, while the extraordinary Abbot de Rancé, after a spectacular conversion, hurled an anathema against the laxity of his brethren in religion and reformed the Abbey of La Trappe. The Franciscans and Capuchins achieved splendid progress. St. John Baptist de La Salle founded the institute of the Brothers of the Christian Schools; St. Grignion de Montfort, emulating St. Vincent de Paul, started the Company of Mary and the Congregation of the Daughters of Wisdom. The Jesuits, too, had their great spiritual masters and the missions were at the height of their expansion.

Thus, the Church's vitality can be compared in every respect with that of its peak periods. There was sanctity here, too, but of a very different kind. Devotion to the Word Incarnate developed, but it was more sentimental and less sensitive than in the Middle Ages. Mysticism emphasized the quest for the love of God, and gave priority to interior asceticism as compared with bodily mortification. Finally, the controversies on the subject of justification and grace stressed the problem of salvation and redemption. Mystical and ascetical theology—the science of sanctity and the means of attaining it—took the lead over more speculative research.

For all this, it should not be supposed that seventeenth century Christendom was imbued with bourgeois individualism. While the accent was on man, spiritual life continued to be essentially missionary. All the reformers of this age were animated with a devouring apostolic zeal and the ideas of all these spiritual teachers seem bold and, often, even revolutionary. The Church has lived since that time on the spiritual capital that they built up. Their institutions have continued down to our own time and it has often been through contact with their thought, restored to its original context, that the secular and regular clergy of the twentieth century have obtained the elements of the present-day revival.

Unfortunately, this generation of famous men had no successors. The eighteenth century began a period of stagnation and decline, with a mediocrity as dangerous for the Church as the ills of feudalism and the Renaissance. It is true that the magnificent structure produced by the Council of Trent and the teachers of that period still existed, but it was gradually depleted and lost its flexibility, and at the time of the revival, its various elements were deprived of their spirit and seemed more like hindrances than efficacious means.

I have stressed in the preceding chapters some of the many causes of this asphyxiation of the Church after the Council of Trent, which at the outset had been so full of promise. In particular, the doctrinal revival did not experience the same broad development as the spiritual one and could not be adapted to the modern world. The interminable Jansenist dispute, a catastrophe of incalculable extent, dried up souls by taking them too far away from God, and killed off mysticism. The Byzantine disputes, in which sophistry ruled, scandalized the masses and prejudiced Christians against a theology that could occasion such trivial debates.

The controversy on Quietism, in which Bossuet and Fénelon were engaged and whose development was greatly reinforced with court gossip, was the final factor in weakening the faith. Fénelon's condemnation led to a middle-class piety which was limited to the most insipid commonplaces and the most conventional formulas.

The blows of Jansenism and Quietism cut short the powerful spiritual movement of the seventeenth century. The founders would certainly not have recognized their institutions, in which the high missionary spirit of the early years had given way to lifeless, conventional moralism which neutralized any mystical or apostolic impulse.

A single man stood apart at the end of this era, St. Alphonsus de Liguori, whose masterpiece was his work on moral theology. The apostolic zeal of his predecessors inspired him, but his work still reflects this unhappy age.

He fought endlessly against Jansenism and Quietism. A great saint, but not the leader that was needed for a real renaissance in Christian life, he nevertheless limited the extent of the decline. And this was already a step in the right direction.

The Nineteenth Century

The revolutionary crisis could have aroused this languorous Christianity. Unfortunately, the throne and the altar, linked by the same previous misfortunes, joined in attempting the restoration of a precarious past. The Christian leadership spent its efforts on struggles aimed more at restoring the political prestige of the Church than at restoring its religious ideal. Prudence and moderation replaced the boldness and apostolic zeal that are indispensable for any religious drive. Virtuous but lacking initiative, helpless on the intellectual level because of the mediocrity of its philosophical and theological education, helpless on the spiritual level through its formalistic and undynamic training, helpless on the material level through a concordat provision that placed its daily subsistence at the mercy of the prince, the clergy limited its activity to "right thinking" and transformed the Christian community into a spiritual ghetto, carefully protected from the harmful atmosphere of the world.

Still, the extraordinary case of the Curé of Ars shows how sanctity can, even in the worst conditions, exercise a considerable influence on the age. The radiant influence of John Marie Vianney stemmed essentially from his apostolic zeal, his profound inner life, and extraordinary graces received from God. Unfortunately, his eminent qualities were too often used to justify a priestly ideal that put on the same level (and sometimes even accorded a certain preponderance to) contingent elements that actually hindered the saintly Curé, such as the moral rigorism inherited from his ecclesiastical training. Moreover, people have overly exaggerated his intellectual poverty, forgetting the great works he accomplished.

Nevertheless, there were some foretokens that the Spirit was preparing to breathe forth again and to awaken in His Church a spiritual and apostolic revival.

The Oxford Movement, the schools at Tubingen and Munich initiated the intellectual restoration, while pioneers in France were scattering the seeds of social Catholicism. The religious orders were gradually reestablished in their original fervor. In certain cases one can even speak of a renaissance or resurrection: for example with regard to the Benedictines at Solesmes with Dom Guéranger, the Dominicans with Father Lacordaire, and the Jesuits with Father de Ravignan.

Missionary efforts enjoyed an unprecedented success. The great established orders—Jesuits, Franciscans, and Dominicans—were implemented by a host of new foundations, among which were the Holy Ghost Fathers and the Marists, to mention only two. St. John Bosco, in the spirit of St. Francis de Sales, exhibited an intense apostolic activity among youth and founded the Salesian Fathers and the Daughters of Our Lady (Salesian Sisters).

All these efforts were leading to a new advance of the Church, the elements of which were to materialize following three events of the last ten years of the nineteenth century: the intense resumption of scientific studies in the various religious disciplines, the appearance of Catholic action and the development of social Christianity, and finally the message of St. Thérèse of the Child Jesus.

Indeed, these last years of the nineteenth century marked the decisive turning point in the history of the Church. Life was changing everywhere. The intellectual renaissance was accompanied by a spiritual revival reflected in all the religious orders by a return to original zeal together with a considerable attempt at adaptation to modern life. New foundations rose up with missionary and apostolic goals adapted to the times. The liturgy itself was renewed through a more searching investigation of its origins and its educational value. Finally, the discovery of the non-Christianization of the working world forced Christians to a serious examination of conscience.

All these efforts produced a profound shakeup in the spiritual conceptions of Catholicism. Christians finally emerged from the deadly lethargy of the nineteenth century. As in the early centuries, the Church became the first preoccupation of Catholics. This development did not stem simply from a turning backward, for it benefited from the resources that had accumulated in the course of the centuries. The spirituality of the Mystical Body excluded neither imitation of the life of Christ, nor meditation on the Word Incarnate, nor reflection on our salvation; and this necessarily, since it could not dismiss the conquests of ascetical and mystical theology. On the contrary, the interest in spiritual growth shown by a laity conscious of its responsibilities and duties has led Catholics to seek among the great masters of thought and spirituality for a solid nourishment, able to sustain their apostolic zeal.

But the spirit, always attentive to the Church's progress, as Christ promised, raised up a guide to direct the spiritual thinking of Christians.

St. Thérèse of the Child Jesus

It was to be granted to a humble disciple of St. Teresa of Avila and St. John of the Cross to make a significant impression on modern spirituality.

At the moment when Catholics felt themselves torn between apostolic zeal and no less intense aspirations to a fervent contemplative life, Thérèse pointed out a road in which love's sublimity dissolves all antagonisms, and, on the spiritual heights, combines action and contemplation.

For this was the basic lesson of her "little way" of spiritual childhood.

To an age eager for achievements and records, Thérèse offers the most total abnegation a saint has ever presented as a model. Where could one find so complete a poverty as in this short life in which no event worth relating stands out. The life of St. Thérèse is the disturbingly ordinary story of a little middle-class girl who entered the Carmelites at the age of fifteen and died at twenty-two, after having scrupulously fulfilled the petty and sometimes mean provisions of the convent regulations. She exerted no temporal influence; she did not even experience what we call exceptional graces: visions, stigmata, supernatural phenomena. Her life thus resembles the hidden life of Jesus, summed up in a few words by St. Luke, and so has the rare and impressive distinction of representing sanctity in its pure state. In fact, Thérèse proceeded directly to the sublime heights of mystical life described by St. John of the Cross, to that stage of heroic sanctity at which the power of love transfigures humble, daily occupations, and where the most commonplace mortifications—Thérèse never practiced any others—acquire a redemptive value of the same extent as Christ's love.

The fullness of monastic life does not consist, as we have seen, in the various ascetical or mystical exercises which implement it but in the exaltation of the ideal of Christians at a given moment in history. At the time when the Church was going to associate laymen in an apostolic effort unprecedented in its history, the Spirit gave this humble Carmelite the privilege of exalting the everyday virtues and thus pointing out the road to perfection to all those who would have to combine the interior life with missionary zeal.

Beyond the traditional virtues of poverty, chastity, and obedience, through her life and message Thérèse showed the indispensable virtues for active, dedicated Christians:

complete abnegation, since all that counts is the intense love of the divine paternity; utter subjection to Providence; and, above all, hope founded on the unconditional love of God.

This way outlined by Thérèse, profoundly evangelical through a renunciation of all but the essential, gives a fundamental answer by the Spirit to our utilitarian age. In the age of efficiency, Thérèse reminds Christians that God alone guarantees efficiency and that in our humble daily task all that is asked of us is loyalty and love.

Springs and Autumns
of the Church

Such is the Church of Christ historically. Not yet the radiant image of the heavenly Jerusalem, it remains human in the defeats, weaknesses, and mistakes of its members. But observing the development of its doctrine and its spirituality, we sense that at every instant it is stirred by the breath of the Spirit and animated by the presence of Christ.

Undoubtedly, the association of its divine ideal with man's limitations and the inertia of institutions have given it this uneven pace in which periods of fulfillment alternate with difficult times of mediocrity, sterility, and treason. Thus, the Church has had its instants of climax and moments of decline. But would it not be better to speak of its autumns and its springs, for, in this cycle, we note above all the Spirit pulsating in rhythm with the world. The Church must first encounter the civilizations that it is to absorb.

Sin has never been absent from this history and it could not be otherwise, for the Church has been given responsibility for humanity. Schisms, the result of sin, open the way to the redemption which only at the end of time will establish Christ's decisive victory over sin and death. Besides, what is the perversion of a Borgia compared with the sanctity of a Catherine of Siena or an Ignatius of Loyola, or what are the errors of the Inquisition compared with the order of St. Francis?

But the great lesson of history is the concrete revelation of the Church's basic unity. In spite of the organic diversity of its functions, it remains indivisible and one cannot accept one aspect of it and reject others. For example, some people would like to contrast prophetism with the established Church. But in reality this contradiction is not justified. It is true that illuminism proves incompatible with clericalism, but this is a matter of two unwholesome excesses, the presence of which always constitutes a mortal danger for the Church. On the other hand, while there is a certain beneficial tension between the prophetism that inspires daring undertakings and the hierarchy responsible for the organization and life of the community, these two functions appear to be absolutely inseparable, since they are complementary. Francis and Dominic cannot be dissociated from the reform of Innocent III, just as Ignatius, John of the Cross, or Francis de Sales cannot be understood as being of marginal importance, or in opposition, to the reforms of the Council of Trent.

Indeed, there is always interpenetration of spirit and institutions. And this conjunction has insured the fruitfulness of the great spiritual trends and is not motivated simply by the duty of obedience and the primacy of the hierarchy. It appears as the necessary consequence of the Church's organic unity. The masters of the thought and life of the Church have not been prodigies who arose by chance or through a miracle to save Christendom. They generally came at the conclusion of a long attempt at contemplation and purification by the Church, which mobilized all its available forces, institutional as well as spiritual. Thus, institutions do not seem to be the result of an incarnation of the Spirit which hardens under the pressure of power. The development and reform of institutions has always accompanied and sometimes preceded the appearance of the great movements of spiritual reform. They are the fruit of the Church's efforts and at the same time the reason for its animation.

The same organic bond unites the contemplative life and the active life, which some have sought to contrast. Vocations can undoubtedly differ, but the two functions remain complementary and are never mutually exclusive. It is only necessary to recall the apostolic activity of the great mystics, such as St. Bernard, St. Teresa, or St. John of the Cross, and the profound interior life of St. Dominic, of St. Thomas Aquinas, of St. Ignatius. Prayer and the apostolate are equally important for Christians and cannot be dissociated. Climactic periods have always been marked by a deep faith and missionary progress.

Finally, history shows us that the spread of the Church cannot come about through a few men, but through the work of the entire body of the Church. Far from contrasting leaders and masses, we must see the intimate relationship of the leaven and the dough. An impure leaven cannot make the dough rise, but a good leaven will remain ineffective if it is not mixed in with the mass. This has been the case in the Church's great successes. The message of the great apostles could be expressed only under certain historical circumstances, preceded by a long period of incubation in which the entire community was associated. The continued existence of the Church in a given society is won and protected in the same way. Periods of expansion have often been followed by a rapid decline, as a result of the laxity of Christians, who were more concerned with preserving the positions that had been attained than in keeping in touch with the spirit and the world.

Thus, evangelization depends upon the entire Church, and while there is a hierarchy of duties there is equality of responsibilities. The world's salvation has been entrusted not to an elite but to the entire Church, to that temporal Church, made up of good and wicked, of generous souls and mediocre spirits, according to the doctrine expressed in this admirable prayer of Holy Saturday:

"O God, immutable force and eternal light, look kindly upon the development of the marvelous mystery of your Church, and may your serene power lead the salvation of humanity to its fulfillment according to your eternal plans; so that the entire world may experience and see the raising

of all ruins, the renewing of all that is old, and the attain-
ment of all things to perfection, through the One from
whom they take their origin, Our Lord Jesus Christ, your
Son. Amen.

Texts

THE CHURCH

Next comes the Holy Catholic Church, your mother:
This is the heavenly Jerusalem, the holy city of God,
worthy object of your veneration, your love, your praise.
This Church, made fertile by faith, bears fruit and spreads
throughout the entire world; this is the Church of the
living God, the pillar and foundation of truth, who here
tolerates communion of the wicked in the sacraments, the
wicked who will be separated from her bosom at the end
of the world and from whom she is separated even during
this life by the contrast of their morals. It is to save the
good seed, which now suffers from its being mixed with
the straw and all of which will be separated by the final
work of the celestial gleaner and gathered into the eternal
storehouse, that she has received the keys of the kingdom
of heaven, in order to forgive sins in her midst through
the blood of Jesus Christ and the operation of the Holy
Spirit. It is in this Church that the soul takes on a new life,
to rise again with Jesus Christ, through whose grace we
have been saved.

ST. AUGUSTINE
Sermon 214

PRAYER

Creator and ruler of every spirit,
Thou who dost multiply the peoples of the earth,
And who hast chosen from amongst them those who
    love thee,
Through Jesus Christ, thy well-beloved child,
Through whom thou hast instructed, sanctified, and
    blessed us.
We beg thee, O Master,
Be for us a protection and support. . . .
So that all men may know
That thou art the only God,
That Jesus Christ is thy child,
That we are thy people and the sheep of thy flock.
Give harmony and peace
To us and to all the inhabitants of the earth,
As thou gavest it to our fathers,
When in sanctity they bore witness to faith and truth.

                ST. CLEMENT
                Epistle LIX, 3, 4.

THE CREATION OF THE CHURCH

Seven weeks after the resurrection, on the fiftieth day, the disciples being gathered together with the women and with Mary, the Mother of Jesus, suddenly a sound came from heaven, like the sound of a strong wind. The Spirit then came down upon that group of one hundred and twenty persons and appeared in the form of tongues of fire, because it was going to give speech to their mouth, light to their intelligence, and ardor to their love. All were filled with the Holy Spirit, and began to speak various languages according to the inspiration of this same Holy Spirit. He taught them all truth, inflamed them with perfect love, and strengthened them in every virtue. So, aided by His grace, enlightened by His teaching, strengthened by His power, although few in number, and simple people, at the cost of their life's blood they planted the Church throughout the world, through inspired discourses, perfect examples, and prodigious miracles.

This Church, purified, enlightened, and led to perfection by the power of this same Holy Spirit, made herself pleasing to her Spouse and His attendants, so that she appeared completely beautiful and wonderfully adorned, but to Satan and his angels as terrible as an army arrayed for battle.

Over this holy Church, variegated in many ways, but grouped into a single body through the admirable work of the Holy Spirit, presides a pontiff, Christ, the supreme head. Following an excellent plan and according to the design of the heavenly city, He distributes the duties of the offices as He dispenses the gifts of His graces. He establishes some as apostles, some as prophets, some as evangelists, others as pastors and teachers, in order to insure the perfection of the saints and to build up the Body of Christ.

He has also instituted, according to the seven-fold grace of the Holy Spirit, the seven sacraments, like seven remedies for our ailments. The administration of the sacraments confers sanctifying grace and forgives sins, never to be forgiven without faith and union with this same holy Church, our Mother.

But since the fire of tribulation purifies from sin, just as God submitted Christ, the head of the Church, to a flood of suffering, likewise He permits that His body, that is to say His Church, be tried and purified by tribulation until the end of time. That is why the Patriarchs and Prophets, the Apostles, the Martyrs, the Confessors and Virgins, as all those who please God, faithfully undergo numerous tribulations. And that, finally, is why all its members chosen by Christ, until the day of judgment, will have to bear them.

ST. BONAVENTURE,
The Tree of Life, 39, 40

THE UNIVERSAL CHURCH

The Church, although it has spread throughout the universe unto the ends of the earth, received from the Apostles and their disciples faith in one God, Father Almighty, who made heaven and earth and the seas and all that is found therein, and in one Jesus Christ, the Son of God, who became flesh for our salvation, and in one Holy Spirit. . . .

It is this preaching, this faith that the Church has received, as we have said, and although the Church has spread throughout the entire world, it guards this faith carefully, as if it dwelt within one house, and it believes in this teaching unanimously, as if it had but one soul and one heart. With perfect harmony, she preaches and teaches this faith, and transmits it as if she had but one mouth. Undoubtedly, languages throughout the world are different, but the force of tradition is one and the same. The Churches founded in the Germanies do not have another faith nor another tradition, nor the Churches founded among the Iberians, nor among the Celts, nor in the Orient, nor in Egypt, nor in Libya, nor in the center of the world; but just as the sun, that creature of God, is one and the same throughout the whole world, so the preaching of the truth shines everywhere and enlightens all men who wish to attain to knowledge of the truth. And the most skilled in words among the leaders of the Church will teach no other doctrine—for no one is above the Master—nor shall the least skilled in words in any way diminish this tradition. But the faith being one and the same, it is neither enriched by him who can speak abundantly nor impoverished by him who can speak but little.

ST. IRENAEUS
Adversus Haereses, III, x, 2

THE UNITY OF THE CHURCH
FOUNDED ON PETER

To subvert faith, to corrupt truth, to destroy unity, the old enemy has invented schisms. Those whom he cannot hold back in the blindness of the old way, he circumvents, deceives, and shows them a new way that is as bad. He snatches men from the very bosom of the Church; while they suppose they are approaching the light and escaping the dark night of their age, he plunges them all unwitting into new darkness. And those men who are no longer in agreement with the Gospels of Christ, His precepts and His laws, still call themselves Christians; walking in the shadow, they believe themselves to be in the light, and this through the trickery and deception of the Adversary who, according to the Apostle, transforms himself into an angel of light, and presents as ministers of justice his own ministers, who bring darkness instead of light, death instead of salvation, despair under the pretext of hope, falsehood in the name of good faith, the Antichrist under the name of Christ. Lying artfully, they conceal the truth with their quibbling.

And all this happens, my dearly beloved brethren, because we do not know how to go back to the source of truth, because we do not try to find the head of it, because we do not keep the teaching of the heavenly Master. If we took the trouble to reflect, to examine, there would be no need for a long treatise, nor laborious argumentation. The proof that leads to faith is easy, for truth is not complicated. The Lord speaks to Peter: "And I say to thee, thou art Peter, and upon this rock I will build My Church, and the gates of Hell shall not prevail against it. And I will give thee the keys of the kingdom; and whatever thou shalt bind on earth shall be bound in heaven, and whatever thou shalt loose on earth shall be loosed in heaven." And again, He said to him after the resurrection: "Feed My sheep." It is therefore upon him alone that he built His Church; it is to him that He entrusts the task of feeding His sheep. And after His resurrection, He gave a like power to all His Apostles, saying: "As the Father has sent Me, I also send you . . . receive the Holy Spirit, whose sins you shall forgive, they are forgiven them; and whose sins you shall retain, they are retained." Nevertheless, in order to emphasize its unity, He instituted but one episcopal throne, and decreed by His sovereign authority that a single one of the Apostles would be a source of unity. Indeed, the other Apostles were what Peter was, shared the same honors and the same power; but the origin of the Church is in unity, and the primacy was given to Peter, so that it would be quite clear that there is but one Church and one Chair. All the Apostles are shepherds, but there is but one flock, which must be led by all the Apostles together. Does one who does not remain in unity with Peter believe that he is still in the faith? Can anyone who abandons the Chair of Peter, upon whom the Church was founded, claim to be in the Church?

Does not the blessed Apostle Paul teach the same thing, does he not reveal the mystery of unity when he says: "One body and one spirit, even as you were called in one hope of your calling, one Lord, one faith, one baptism; one God and Father of all"? Such is the unity which we must firmly keep and defend, especially we bishops, who preside in the Church, in order to show that the episcopacy is one and indivisible. Let no one disturb you with his lies, dear brethren, let no one corrupt the truth of faith with perfidious prevarication. There is but one episcopacy, of which each of us possesses a part. And there is also but one Church, which through the increase of its fruitfulness is extending more and more. The sun has a host of rays and but one light, the tree has a multitude of branches, but there is but one source for its strength, in a single root; a spring expands into several brooks, but while the abundance of its waters seems to flow off into several channels, its waters still have but a single source. Separate out a ray of light, the light's unity does not suffer any division; break off from the tree a branch and this branch can no longer bear. Separate the brook from its spring, and it dries up at once. Likewise, the Lord's Church spreads the rays of its light throughout the world; but its unity is not divided thereby. A fruitful tree, the Church extends its branches into all the world; an inexhaustible spring, it pours forth its waters afar. And nevertheless, there is but a single head, a single origin, a single Mother, rich in her fruitfulness.

It is she who gives birth to us, feeds us with her milk, who enlivens us with her spirit. The Spouse of Christ, she knows no adultery, she is chaste, she is modest. She has but one abode, she guards with holy modesty the chastity of her nuptial couch. She preserves us for God; she marks out for her celestial kingdom the sons whom she has borne. Whoever separates from the Church to take part in adultery, cuts himself off from the Church's promises. He who abandons the Church of Christ will never attain to the reward of Christ: he is a stranger, he is profane, he is an enemy. He cannot have God for a Father who has not the Church for his Mother.

ST. CYPRIAN,
De Unitate Ecclesiae

OBEDIENCE

Whoever says he is inspired, and refuses to obey his superiors and to follow their advice is an imposter. All the prophets and preachers who have been inspired by God have always loved the Church, always adhered to her teachings, and have always been approved by her, and have never preached anything as vigorously as this truth, that the lips of the priest hold knowledge and that one must seek the law from his mouth. Thus, extraordinary missions are diabolical illusions and not heavenly inspirations, if they are not recognized and approved by the pastors who have the ordinary mission, for so it is in Moses and the prophets. St. Francis and St. Dominic and the other Fathers of religious orders came to serve souls through an extraordinary inspiration, but they submitted all the more humbly and readily to the Church's sacred hierarchy. To sum up, the three best and most certain marks of legitimate inspiration are perseverance, as compared with inconstancy and flightiness, peace and mildness of heart, as compared with restlessness and impetuosity, and humble obedience as against stubbornness and resentment.

ST. FRANCIS DE SALES
Treatise on the Love of God,
Book VIII, c. 13

SUFFERING FOR THE CHURCH

Divine Providence often permits even the just to be driven from the Christian community by the violence of earthly men. If the victims of such unjust affronts endure them in complete patience for the sake of the Church, without fomenting either schismatic or heretical movements, they give all men an example of the righteousness of feelings and of pure charity which must be brought to the service of God. It is the intention of these men to return to port, once the squalls are over; but if they cannot, whether because the squall is prolonged or because they are afraid they will awaken another or more serious storm through their return, they keep the intention of helping toward salvation even those whose seditious meddling has forced them to depart, and they never isolate themselves or form little groups. They defend to the death and serve through their witness the faith which they know the Catholic Church preaches. Their crown they receive secretly from the Father, who watches in secret. These cases are rare, but they do exist. They are even more frequent than one might believe.

ST. AUGUSTINE,
De vera Religione

THE EUCHARIST, PRINCIPLE OF UNITY

To bring us together in union with God and among ourselves, although we each have a distinct personality, the only begotten Son has devised a marvelous means: through one body, His own, He sanctifies His faithful in mystic communion, making of them one body with Him and with themselves. No division can subsist within Christ. If we are all united to the one Christ through His own body, and if we are all receiving Him, one and indivisible in our own bodies, we are members of this one body, and it is for us the bond of unity.

We are all of us, by nature, enclosed in our own personalities. But, in another way, all of us together, we are united. Divided in one sense into quite distinct personalities, so that one man is Peter, or John or Thomas or Matthew, we are, as it were, fused into one body in Christ, and are fed by one flesh. One Spirit is the sign of our unity, and as Christ is one and indivisible, we are all of us but one in Him. So He said to His heavenly Father: Let them be one as We are one.

ST. CYRIL

COEXISTENCE OF THE TWO CITIES

A family of men who do not live according to the faith seek earthly peace in the goods and commodities of this temporal life. A family of men who live according to the faith, hope for the eternal goods promised later and use earthly and temporal goods as incidental things, not as lures to distract them from the way to God, but to make more endurable and aggravate as little as possible the corruptible body that weighs down the soul. That is why both sorts of men and both families commonly use the things needed for this mortal life. But in this usage, each has his own purpose, very different from that of the other. Likewise, the earthly city, which does not live according to the faith, seeks earthly peace and it makes the peace of its citizens, both inferiors and superiors, consist simply in this, that they are in agreement on the goods that affect mortal life. The heavenly city, or rather that part of it which, journeys from this mortality and which lives according to the faith, must also make use of this peace, until this mortality that needs such peace has ended. Hence it happens that, as long as it lives with the earthly city, as a captive and in pilgrimage, though having received the promise of deliverance and the pledge of the Spirit's gift, it does not hesitate to obey the laws of the earthly city, which regulate the use of goods proper for sustaining mortal life; so that the two cities, having these mortal conditions in common, are in agreement with each other on everything which concerns it. . . .

While its pilgrimage on earth is continuing, this heavenly city calls out to the citizens of all nations; it assembles a company of all languages for this pilgrimage; it does not look upon differences in customs, laws, institutions which serve to secure or maintain earthly peace; it does not cut off or destroy anything; on the contrary, it conforms and submits; and it ordains all the differences of the various nations to the same and sole end of earthly peace, provided that nothing is contrary to the religion which teaches the worship of the one true and supreme God. Thus, the heavenly city makes use of earthly peace during its pilgrimage; it protects and it seeks, to the extent that this can be done without harm to religion and piety, agreement in human wills in everything concerning the mortal condition of men and it relates this earthly peace to the peace of heaven.

ST. AUGUSTINE,
City of God, XIX, c. 17

THE CHURCH AND POLITICS

Among the different political systems linked to the periods on which they depend, the Church cannot be asked to adopt one rather than another. Within the limits of divine law, which is valid for all and whose authority obliges not only individuals but peoples, there is a large field and freedom of exercise for the most varied forms of political concepts. The practical application of a political system often depends to a decided extent on circumstances and causes which, considered in themselves, are foreign to the Church's purpose and activities. The Church is the guardian and mistress of the principles of faith and morality, and its sole interest and its sole desire is to transmit to all people, without exception, with its educational and religious means, the clear spring of the heritage and values of Christian living, so that every nation, to the extent proper for its special needs, may use the teachings and ethico-religious themes of Christianity to establish a worthy human society, spiritually elevated and a source of true well-being.

PIUS XII,
Christmas Message, 1940

THE CHURCH TODAY

As in the times of the most violent storms in the history of the Church, the basic remedy today, consists in a sincere renewal of private and public life, according to the principles of the Gospel, among all those who glory in belonging to Christ, so that they may be truly the salt of the earth and preserve human society from total corruption.

With a profound sense of gratitude to the Father of Lights, from whom comes every excellent gift and every perfect grace, we see on all sides encouraging signs of this spiritual renewal, not only in the specially chosen souls who in our era have reached the summits of sublime sanctity and in the ever-increasing number of souls who generously strive toward these heights of light, but also in a rebirth of piety sensed and realized in all social classes, even the most cultured, as we recently recalled in our *motu proprio, In Multi Solaciis*, of last October 28, on the occasion of the reorganization of the Pontifical Academy of Sciences.

However, it must be confessed that, in this work of spiritual renewal, there is still much to be done. Even in Catholic countries, a large number of people are, so to speak, Catholics in name only. While observing more or less faithfully the essential practices of the religion they claim to profess, too large a number are not interested in perfecting their religious knowledge and acquiring more profound inner convictions; still less do they seek to live in such a way that the external appearance really corresponds to the inner beauty of a correct and pure conscience, understanding and accomplishing all their duties in the eyes of God. This superficial religion, a vain and deceptive show, is supremely displeasing to the Divine Savior, for He wishes that all should adore the Father in spirit and in truth. He who does not truly and sincerely live the faith he professes, could not long resist the wind of persecution and the violent storm that is blowing up today; he will be miserably swept away by the new deluge that is threatening the world and in losing himself he will make the word "Christian" an object of derision.

PIUS XI,
Divini Redemptoris, March 19, 1937

THE PRIEST

The soul of the priest must shine like a torch enlightening the universe. . . . The priest is the salt of the earth. . . . To receive these sublime functions, it is not enough to be pure; prudence and various kinds of knowledge are no less necessary. The priest must even be versed in the affairs of the world, and in this respect he must not be inferior to those whose life is taken up with these matters; but, nevertheless, he must remain apart from the world, like the lonely men who live upon the mountains. Talking with men taken up with the bonds of marriage, who have children to raise, servants to train, extensive possessions to manage, sometimes including government and the administration of public affairs, he must be a master of tact and politeness. Certainly, I do not mean by this that he should be a two-faced person, a flatterer, a hypocrite; what I mean is that he should always act with entire confidence and complete freedom, that he should prudently adjust to circumstances so that he will aways succeed in doing good, that he should be at once entirely gentle and serious. It is impossible, indeed, to treat all men in the same way; doctors do not apply the same remedies to all diseases. The pilot does not battle against all winds with the same maneuvering of his ship; the vessel the hand of the priest is guiding is likewise driven by endless storms; and these storms do not come only from without, the roaring comes from the very depths of the ship. What extraordinary moderation and what strength must then be employed! Now, all these things, though quite different, tend toward a single end, the glory of God and the building up of the Church.

ST. JOHN CHRYSOSTOM,
De Sacerdotio, VI, 5

THE UNITY OF THE MYSTICAL BODY

The Church is also made up of a large number of varied members, some very worthy, and others less so; there are the choir of virgins and the ranks of the widows, as there are the assemblies of those distinguished by the claim of a virtuous marriage; quite numerous are the degrees of virtue. There are also degrees in almsgiving: some give all that they have, others keep only what they need and reject all the rest, and still others take only from the surplus for their gifts; but all of them share a mutual distinction, and, if the most highly placed should come to despise the humblest, it is mainly himself that he would be injuring. Let a virgin despise a married woman, and she loses much of her own merit. Let him who has given everything conduct himself meanly toward him who has not gone so far, and he will likewise diminish the value of his sacrifice. . . . If it is the duty of each person to work for his neighbor's salvation, do not talk to me about more or less; there is no more or less here. As long as the body exists, some differences can be perceived; if it happens to perish, there are no more differences; now, it perishes when the lesser members do. Therefore, as long as the preservation of the major parts depends on that of the lesser, the former must take as much care of the smaller members as they do of themselves; the destruction of the one group means the destruction of the rest. It would matter not how many times you said: Such a member is of small account, it is without dignity. If you do not have it in your heart to protect him as yourself, if you neglect him under the pretext that he is inferior to you, you are only hurting yourself. Hence, Paul does not simply demand mutual solicitude; he wants it to be equal for both and in the common interest, that is, that the same vigilance be shown with regard to lesser and greater members. Avoid saying: This is only an insignificant member. Rather remember that he is a member of this body to which we all belong; he is as essential as the eye for making our body what it is. In this marvelous structure, no one has any more than his neighbor. What constitutes the body is not one member being worthy and another less so, but that they are numerous and diverse. Just as you are of use to the whole organism because you are larger, he serves it because he is smaller. His littleness is thus no less worthwhile than your largeness, contributes no less to the total result, and in no way overshadowed by you in this magnificent whole.

SAINT JOHN CHRYSOSTOM
Commentary on I Cor.,
Hom. XXX and XXXI, 120, 1.

UNION WITH GOD

If, therefore, on the village common
From this day forth I am no longer seen nor encountered,
They can say I have been lost,
That advancing in joy and love,
I have willingly been lost, and I have been found!

The spirit of the world, even without speaking, secretly blames persons who give themselves entirely to God. In this stanza the soul refutes such objections. First there is the charge of exaggeration, oddness, isolation, which the behavior of these souls seems to deserve. Thus it comes about that they are treated as useless in the struggle for advancement, and this because thy scorn what the world approves and admires. There is no reply to the soul's loving answer to these accusations. Boldly and decisively, it faces the demands of the world, the only objections that can be made to it. Since it possesses a keen love of God, what does the rest matter? It is happy to have an opportunity to defend its life; it takes pride in the excesses that it is accused of; it acknowledges that it is pleased to be lost to the world and to itself in order to belong to its beloved. And addressing itself to those who blame it, it says to them: If you no longer see me among my former acquaintances, taking part in the distractions of the world, nothing should keep you from believing and saying that I freely departed from these misfortunes and that I no longer wish to share in them. I now know but one good and I value but one prize, and I have chosen to be lost myself in order to discover whom I love with all my heart!

The soul thus shows the world the profit it has gained from what is regarded as a loss and, lest it be taxed with

madness or illusion, it proves that all its happiness proceeds from this supposed misfortune and that it was wise
in purposely losing itself.

If, therefore, on the village common
From this day forth I am no longer seen nor
  encountered. . . .

The common is the land on which the villagers custom-
arily meet to relax and amuse themselves; it is there, too,
that the shepherds pasture their flocks together. For the
soul, this is a symbol of the world with its relations and
diversions, where the flock of worldly appetites never
lacks for pasturage. If the soul does not take part in these
meetings, if it is no longer seen there, as it was in the
days when it did not belong entirely to God, the men of
the world are right to regard it as lost for this kind of life.
But it is even pleased that they should proclaim this, nothing is more agreeable to it, for such a reputation is the
very expression of its happiness!

They can say I have been lost!

When one loves God, and is not ashamed of this in the
face of the world, and one is proud of what one has done
for Him. Any dissimulation would be shameful, and it
would be wrong to conceal one's love out of fear of blame.
If anyone blushes to confess, through his works, the Son
of God before men, He himself, according to St. Matthew,
will deny that man before His Father. That is why the soul,
made courageous through love, holds it an honor to proclaim what it has done to glorify its beloved; let it be
known, then, it has left the world voluntarily and has
chosen to be lost out of love for Him.

But such perfect courage, such a clear-cut decision in
the direction of their life, is rarely found among the
spiritual-minded. Undoubtedly there are many who believe they are following such a line of conduct—those who,

in good faith, believe they have broken with the world; but this break is still incomplete. In certain respects their attachments persist, whether they be attachments to the world or to themselves, and they never succeed in breaking them. Although they act out of love for Christ, their works lack the complete detachment which alone can make them perfect. They cannot say from their soul that "I have been lost." Indeed, they are seen concerning themselves with "what will people say," and fearing the judgment of others; they are careful *not* to be lost, for attached to themselves and dominated by human respect in their works, they are ashamed to confess Christ before men and, through this weakness, they do not really live in Him.

Advancing in joy and love,

That is, progressing, on fire with Divine Love, in the practice of all virtues,

I willingly have been lost, and I have been found!

There is in the Gospel a word of the Bridegroom which the soul particularly remembers: "No one can serve two masters," for he will have to be unfaithful to one or to the other. Now, in order not to be faithless to the Bridegroom, the soul has left everything which is not His, that is, the world and itself, so that it shall live only through His love. The heart where true love reigns at once empties itself of all other affections, in order to offer itself completely to that which it loves. This truth is applied to the soul when it declares that it has freely lost itself, or has become lost of its own free will. This is done in two ways.

At first it is lost in respect to itself. In giving itself to the Bridegroom, it has made a free sacrifice of all personal interest, and it may be said that it is lost because it seeks no satisfaction.

In the second place, it is also lost through a complete renunciation, becoming a stranger to all which is not the service of God, and in retaining no other desire than that of being found. And this again is a way of being lost. Thus the soul acts; seized with Divine Love, it is indifferent to gain and reward, it has but one will: to lose all and to be lost itself in order to belong to God, the only gain to which it aspires.

This is the meaning of the saying of St. Paul: "To die is a gain for me." To die spiritually for Jesus Christ, to everything and to myself, this is my profit. The soul is therefore right in saying: "I have been found." He who does not know how to lose himself can not be found. On the contrary, he is really lost according to that judgment pronounced by our Lord in the Gospel: "He who would save his life will lose it; but he who loses his life for My sake, will find it."

ST. JOHN OF THE CROSS,
The Spiritual Canticle,
Part 3, Stanza XXIX.

VIRGINITY

We do not exalt virgins from the mere fact of their virginity, but because they are consecrated to God through a truly loving filial continence.

ST. AUGUSTINE,
De Sancta Virginitate, XI, 11.

PRAYER OF ST. FRANCIS OF ASSISI

Almighty, eternal, just, and merciful God, grant us, wretches that we are, for Thy sake to do what we know Thou dost wish and to always do that which pleases Thee; so that purified without, enlightened within, and filled with the fire of the Holy Spirit, we can follow in the footsteps of Thy Son, our Lord Jesus Christ, and through Thy grace, attain to Thee, O most High, who in perfect trinity, and most simple unity, livest and reignest and gloriest, God Almighty, for ever and ever. Amen.

ST. FRANCIS OF ASSISI,
Letter (1226)

ACTION AND CONTEMPLATION

The entire theory of perfection comes down to the problem of action and contemplation; the latter being more sublime, but also more dangerous, and the former being a more humble way but also more profitable. With us Christians, each of the two ways is enriched by the contribution of the other; we make contemplation our companion in traveling toward the beyond and we make action our guide toward contemplation. It is impossible to see, moreover, how those who do not live wisely could participate in wisdom.

ST. GREGORY OF NAZIANZEN,
Or., IV, 113.

CHURCH AND POLITICS

The divine Redeemer founded the Church for the purpose of communicating His truth and grace to humanity through it until the end of time. The Church is His Mystical Body. It is entirely of Christ and Christ is of God. Political persons and sometimes even men of the Church, who wish to make the Spouse of Christ their confederate or the instrument of their national or international political schemes, attack the very essence of the Church and threaten its life, reducing it to the level on which conflicts of temporal interests are waged. And this is and remains true, even when the interests in question are legitimate in themselves.

PIUS XII,
Christmas Message, 1951